U.S. Trust and Estate Planning
美國信託規劃實務

作者 呂旭明（**Peter Lu**）
　　　呂嘉昕（**Max Lu**）

Preface

In recent past, Asian immigrants have spread out all over the world, with the United States becoming an increasingly popular destination. As Asian immigrants settle and grow in the U.S., the wealth they accumulate have become increasingly diversified. For cross-border families, especially those with substantial wealth, transitioning wealth to the next generation has become increasingly arduous.

In the past 30 years, I have advised my predominantly Asian clients on their wealth succession strategies and observed commonalities between them. Challenges often stem from differences between generations.

The "first generation" wealth creator is typically defined as the first generation to accumulate substantial wealth. Often having modest beginnings, the first generation typically share certain characteristics, such as being dedicated, hardworking, and adamant in their beliefs. Their often strict values and approach to business may create obstacles to communicating to their descendants, particularly their children (generally referred to as the "second generation").

This lack of clear communication can potentially result in an ineffective transition of the family business (if one were created), wealth, and familial values. The divide can be further exacerbated by their differing views on legal and tax matters.

To this day, many first-generation Asian wealth creators believe that they are not subject to U.S. tax or disclosure requirements, even as many of them (or their descendants) immigrate to the U.S. or invest in the U.S. Despite efforts to persuade them otherwise, many remain obstinate. Over the years, I have spent considerable effort on correcting these misconceptions. The end goal is to have wealth creators acknowledge and understand their (and their descendants') U.S. tax and legal obligations.

The second generation, especially those residing in the U.S., may also face considerable obstacles when consolidating family assets. Those who are

作者序

家族事業與財富的永續傳承

　　亞洲華人移民現今已經遍布全球，移民國家莫屬美國的人數最眾。隨著這些亞裔家族在美國落地生根並壯大，他們所創造的財富型態也越形複雜，要將這些財富有效傳承給後代，傳統模式已不再適用。

　　過去三十年間，本人參與了許多亞洲高財富個人傳承案件，觀察到他們的財富傳承的方式具有高度一致性——第一代努力工作並累積經驗，期望後代能夠過上富裕生活；然而，財富的經驗法則往往很難從第一代順利地轉移到第二代。對第二代來說，財富雖然是助力，但接棒過程中充滿危機，常源自對於財富抱持著不同的看法。

　　第一代創富者的行事風格和個性理念通常主導了企業經營和家族傳承，他們這代多是白手起家，經過重重的嚴苛考驗、付出許多心力再加上些許的運氣，才創造出今日的財富，也因如此，他們挾著個人叱吒事業場的豐富經驗、主觀意識及價值判斷，經常是以權威之姿來主導傳承大局，多年內化的主觀意識使得他們難以向第二代解釋其思維脈絡，而第二代更難以揣測上一代的心意，這會導致兩代之間在經營企業、財富管理及傳承的溝通上產生阻礙，喪失了許多創造財富的機會，無形的家族價值也在無效溝通中逐漸消失。

　　在過去本人協助處理過的許多家族紛爭中，除了上下代對立，還發現有不少的第一代抗拒交接給下一代，當中的一個原因源於跨國稅務的申報與財產揭露問題。許多擁有雙重國籍或是美國稅務身分的第一代，固執地認為美國國稅局不可能找上門，因而不申報美國稅、不揭露海外金融帳戶，任憑第二代如何勸說，他們始終冥頑不靈。

　　本人常花費大量心力引導這些高資產人士合法申報美國稅並將財

beneficiaries of their family fortunes can and often are subject to substantial taxation when they receive distributions, especially if the first generation failed to create, adopt and maintain an adequate estate plan.

A viable solution to the challenges set forth above is the dynasty trust, a vehicle that can help cross-border families hold, preserve, manage and even grow their wealth. Wealth creators who have created their wealth outside of the U.S. can effectively and safely gift assets to their descendants, whether they be based in the U.S. or elsewhere.

This book aims to bridge the generational gap and help families with planning their cross-border wealth transfers and consists of the following sections:

- Chapter 1 discusses several case studies and provides general frameworks that cross-border families may customize to fit their specific estate planning goals.

- Chapters 2 and 3 provide specific recommendations for families interested in establishing revocable and irrevocable trusts based in the U.S.

- Chapter 4 details the necessary tax and disclosure forms required by the U.S. for families with U.S. based trusts, assets or individuals.

- Chapter 5 introduces family offices and discusses their types, roles and services and discusses the role of European Union (EU) permanent residency in wealth planning.

When writing this book, I have collected numerous case studies and excerpts from laws and regulations in various jurisdictions. Over the years, various professionals have helped in the creation of this book. These include lawyers and representatives from trust companies and financial institutions based in the U.S., Switzerland, Liechtenstein, Singapore, Hong Kong, and China. Our singular focus was to create legal frameworks that would help our clients with their unique problems and considerations. Thanks in large part to the accumulated experience of current and past colleagues at KEDP, this book includes detailed explanations.

Over the past couple of years, KEDP has assisted clients with

產納入美國管轄。反觀居住在美國的第二代，雖然繼承了上一代的財富，卻也同時面臨申報美國境外稅和揭露海外資產的情況。他們的稅務難題有二：一是在境外所得與財產應繳美國稅卻未履行其納稅義務；二是上一代未妥善規劃財富傳承，造成第二代的稅務困擾。

針對上述種種問題，若能及時提供有效的傳承工具——設立美國朝代信託，將有助於財產持有、財富保全與資產管理。具體作法是將美國以外地區之繼續營運、持續為家族帶來財富的資產置入美國可撤銷信託；而將長期落地美國、在美國累積的驚人資產置入美國不可撤銷信託，家族的事業與財富即可永續傳承。

本書第一章基於本人三十餘年的執業經驗，提出具體的家庭傳承規劃架構；第二、三章詳述可撤銷信託與不可撤銷信託的具體架構、執行步驟與方法；第四章列出信託成立後的年度維持相關稅表與必要揭露表格；最後於第五章闡述家族辦公室在家族信託中的角色，以及家族成員如何取得歐洲居民、公民身分，例如保加利亞居留證或護照。期望本書能夠搭建起家族上下代間的橋樑，最終達到家族財富跨境傳承與風險分散的永續目標。

本書出版經歷了多年的努力，從案例蒐集、各國繼承法令和信託法規彙整，到美國信託實際操作說明。期間拜訪了美國、瑞士、列支敦士登、新加坡、香港和中國的上百位信託律師、稅務律師及信託受託公司主管，他們提供了各國信託的實際操作資料並探討了現行信託成立中的問題，為本書提供了最基本的材料。

此外，安致勤資（KEDP）同仁多年來在信託成立與維持方面積累的經驗，通過流程圖、比較表和執行步驟詳細說明了信託的實際操作，對此深表感謝。由於本人的直系家族成員主要是美國公民，因此早已為家族成立了美國不可撤銷信託和可撤銷信託，書中將實際成立過程穿插於細節，使其更具實務操作性。

establishing and maintaining their U.S.-based trusts. Inspiration was drawn from countless discussions both internally and with clients. These discussions featured expansive flowcharts, comparison tables and execution timelines that have further increased the depth of the discussion firm wide. I express my deep gratitude for their contributions.

Lastly, in this ever evolving landscape, we continue our time-honored tradition of welcoming open discussions with other experts and professionals. We believe that through these discussions, all professionals are able to learn more and give the clients better and more practical solutions to their most pressing problems.

Since my immediate family consists primarily of U.S. citizens, I have a deep rooted sense of responsibility for the structures I have set forth for them. In the past two decades, I have established both irrevocable and revocable U.S. trusts for my descendants. As such, this book incorporates my experience as both a client and as a well-respected advisor to other families. This book seeks to serve as relevant discussion material for both high-net-worth families and professionals in their service.

Peter L.

隨著信託專業與稅務法令的不斷更迭，本書的改版特點在於全書內容以中英文雙語對照呈現。本次改版最大的變化是內容先以英文撰寫，完整地表達美國信託成立的相關實務操作，然後再翻譯成中文。相信如此能夠拉近不同世代之間對美國信託的理解距離，進而更能妥善地利用這一傳承工具。

　　由於信託法令和實務操作的內容繁多，且需要以簡明的中英文呈現，因此難免會有疏漏之處，敬請專家先進不吝指正。

Table of Contents

Chapter 1 Introduction to Cross-Border Estate Planning

- What is Estate Planning? 18
- Shouldn't estate planning be customized? Aren't U.S. attorneys the best solution when it comes to estate planning? How do I know if the solutions this book provides really work? 18
- Case Study 1: How can Asia-based Wealth Creators utilize U.S. trusts to their advantage? 22
- Case Study 2: How should Non-U.S. Wealth Creators transfer wealth to their descendants if their descendants are primarily U.S. Persons? 26
- Case Study 3: What happens when Foreigners Purchasing U.S. Real Property? 34
- Case Study 4: What happens if an offshore trust does not adequately protect the trust's assets? What is an illusory trust? 46
- Case Study 5: Planning prior to immigrating to the U.S. 56

Chapter 2 U.S. Irrevocable Dynasty Trusts

- What is a Dynasty Trust and how is it relevant to me? 66
- Why should I establish an irrevocable trust, rather than a revocable one? Does it make a difference where I settle my U.S. trust? 66
- Why do Grantors select directed trusts 68

when passing down their wealth?	
• How does an Irrevocable Trust established in the U.S. compare with an Irrevocable Trust established outside of the U.S.?	74
• Should I still consider establishing a U.S.-based trust if I have no U.S.-based descendants?	80
• What is an ILIT (Irrevocable Life Insurance Trust)? How can an ILIT play a role in my estate planning?	118

Chapter 3 U.S. Revocable Dynasty Trusts

• What is a Revocable Trust and how is it relevant to me?	130
• What are the roles in a Foreign Grantor Trust?	132
• Which assets should I place in my Foreign Grantor Trust?	134
• Could you provide an example of a Foreign Grantor Trust structure?	136
• Are there assets I shouldn't put into my Foreign Grantor Trust?	136
• Is Foreign Grantor Trust status relevant to me if I previously settled a non-U.S. (offshore) trust?	140
• What do I do if I want to transfer assets held by my offshore trust to a U.S. trust?	142
• What happens to my Foreign Grantor Trust after I die?	148
• Is there any way to reduce income taxes after an FGT converts to a U.S. irrevocable trust?	152

Chapter 4 Relevant U.S. Tax Forms for U.S. Trusts & Individuals

- Summary — 156
1. Form 1040 — 170
2. Form 3520 — 172
3. Form 1041 (including Form 7004) — 176
4. Form 1065, 1120, and 8832 — 180
5. Form 5471 — 186
6. Form 8621 — 192
7. Form 8858 — 196
8. Form 8938 — 202
9. Form 8992 and Form 8993 (including Section 962 Election) — 208
10. Form SS-4 — 212
11. FinCEN Form 114 (FBAR) — 214
12. FinCEN Beneficial Ownership Filing (Corporate Transparency Act) — 218
13. Streamlined Procedures (Form 14653 and 14654) — 222
14. California Form 541 — 228

Chapter 5 The Rise of the Global Family Office

- What is a Family Office? How does a Family Office typically add value? — 234
- When establishing a U.S. family trust, are there additional professional staffing requirements? — 238
- How is a Family Office different from a Multi-Family Office? — 240
- What are the most important criteria — 242

- when selecting a Multi-Family Office?
- What is bookkeeping? How can it help Wealth Creators? — 248
- How do Wealth Creators pass on their relationships with their advisors to their next generation? — 264
- Should Wealth Creators Pass on Their Relationships with Advisors? — 266
- How can Wealth Creators use Offshore (BVI) Companies to their advantage? — 268
- What role does Europe play for Cross-Border Wealth Creators? — 274
- Advantages of EU Member State Status in Cross-Border Wealth Transfer Planning — 278
- Should Wealth Creators apply for Permanent Residency (PR) in the EU? As an example, would applying for a Bulgaria PR be appropriate for them? — 280
  - Advantages of Obtaining Bulgarian Citizenship — 282
  - An Overview of Bulgaria — 286
  - How to Obtain Bulgarian Citizenship & Investment Planning After Obtaining Bulgarian Citizenship — 288
  - Bulgaria Investment Immigration Program & AIF Investment Immigration Fund — 292
  - The process of immigration and obtaining Permanent Residency (PR) — 296
- How do I apply for Permanent Residency in Bulgaria through investment? — 298

目 次

第一章　何謂跨境資產規劃？

- 甚麼是傳承規劃？ 19
- 傳承規劃不應該客製化嗎？解決傳承規劃的最佳方案，不就是尋求美國律師的協助嗎？我該如何確認本書提供的解決方案實際可行？ 19
- 案例研究（一）：亞洲的創富者該如何善加利用美國信託？ 23
- 案例研究（二）：當非美國人創富者的後代主要為美國人時，該如何將財富轉移給後代？ 27
- 案例研究（三）：外國人購置美國房地產時有何影響？ 35
- 案例研究（四）：若離岸信託未能充分保護信託資產，會有甚麼後果？甚麼是偽信託？ 47
- 案例研究（五）：移民美國前的規劃 57

第二章　美國不可撤銷朝代信託

- 甚麼是朝代信託？它與我有何相關？ 67
- 為甚麼要選擇設立不可撤銷信託，而不是可撤銷信託呢？在美國哪個州設立美國信託有何差別？ 67
- 委託人如何利用指示型信託達成財富世代傳 69

承的目的？
- 美國境內設立的不可撤銷信託與美國境外設立的不可撤銷信託有何不同？ 75
- 如果我沒有美籍後代，我仍須考慮設立美國信託嗎？ 81
- 甚麼是不可撤銷人壽保險信託？不可撤銷人壽保險信託在遺產規劃上可以扮演甚麼樣的角色？ 119

第三章　美國可撤銷朝代信託

- 甚麼是可撤銷信託，它與我有何相關？ 131
- 外國委託人信託中的角色有哪些？ 133
- 哪些資產適合放入外國委託人信託（FGT）中？ 135
- 能舉一個外國委託人信託架構為例嗎？ 137
- 哪些資產不應該放入外國委託人信託中？ 137
- 如果我已經設立非美國（離岸）信託，我仍須關注外國委託人信託嗎？ 141
- 如果我想將離岸信託持有的資產轉移到一個美國信託，該如何進行？ 143
- 委託人去世後，外國委託人信託會發生甚麼變化？ 149
- 外國委託人信託轉變為美國不可撤銷信託後，有辦法減少所得稅嗎？ 153

第四章　信託與個人之相關美國稅表

- 引言　157
  1. 1040 表　171
  2. 3520 表　173
  3. 1041 表（包含 7004 表）　177
  4. 1065 表、1120 表及 8832 表　181
  5. 5471 表　187
  6. 8621 表　193
  7. 8858 表　197
  8. 8938 表　203
  9. 8992 表及 8993 表（包含 Section 962 選擇表）　209
  10. SS-4 表　213
  11. FinCEN 114 表　215
  12. FinCEN 實質受益人申報（企業透明法案）　219
  13. 簡易自首申報計畫（14653 表及 14654 表）　223
  14. 加州 541 表　229

第五章　全球家族辦公室的崛起與家族信託

- 家族辦公室是甚麼？家族辦公室如何提供加值服務？　235
- 設立美國家族信託時，家族辦公室是否需配置專業人員？　239
- 單一家族辦公室（SFO）與聯合家族辦公室（MFO）有何區別？　241
- 選擇聯合家族辦公室（MFO）時最重要的標　243

- 準是甚麼？
- 甚麼是記帳？它如何幫助創富者？ 249
- 創富者如何將他們與顧問的關係傳遞給下一代？ 265
- 創富者應該將其與顧問的關係傳承下去嗎？ 267
- 創富者如何運用離岸公司（英屬維京群島（BVI）公司）獲取優勢？ 269
- 歐洲對跨境創富者得扮演甚麼角色？ 275
- 歐盟成員國身分在跨境財富傳承規劃中的優勢 279
- 創富者是否該申請歐盟國家的永久居留權？以申請保加利亞的永久居留權為例，是合適的選項嗎？ 281
  - 取得保加利亞國籍身分的優勢有哪些？ 283
  - 保加利亞是一個甚麼樣的國家？ 287
  - 如何取得保加利亞身分及取得之後的投資規劃 289
  - 保加利亞投資移民方案 & AIF 投資移民基金 293
  - 移民程序與永久居留權取得流程 297
- 如何通過投資在保加利亞申請永久居留權？ 299

NOTE :

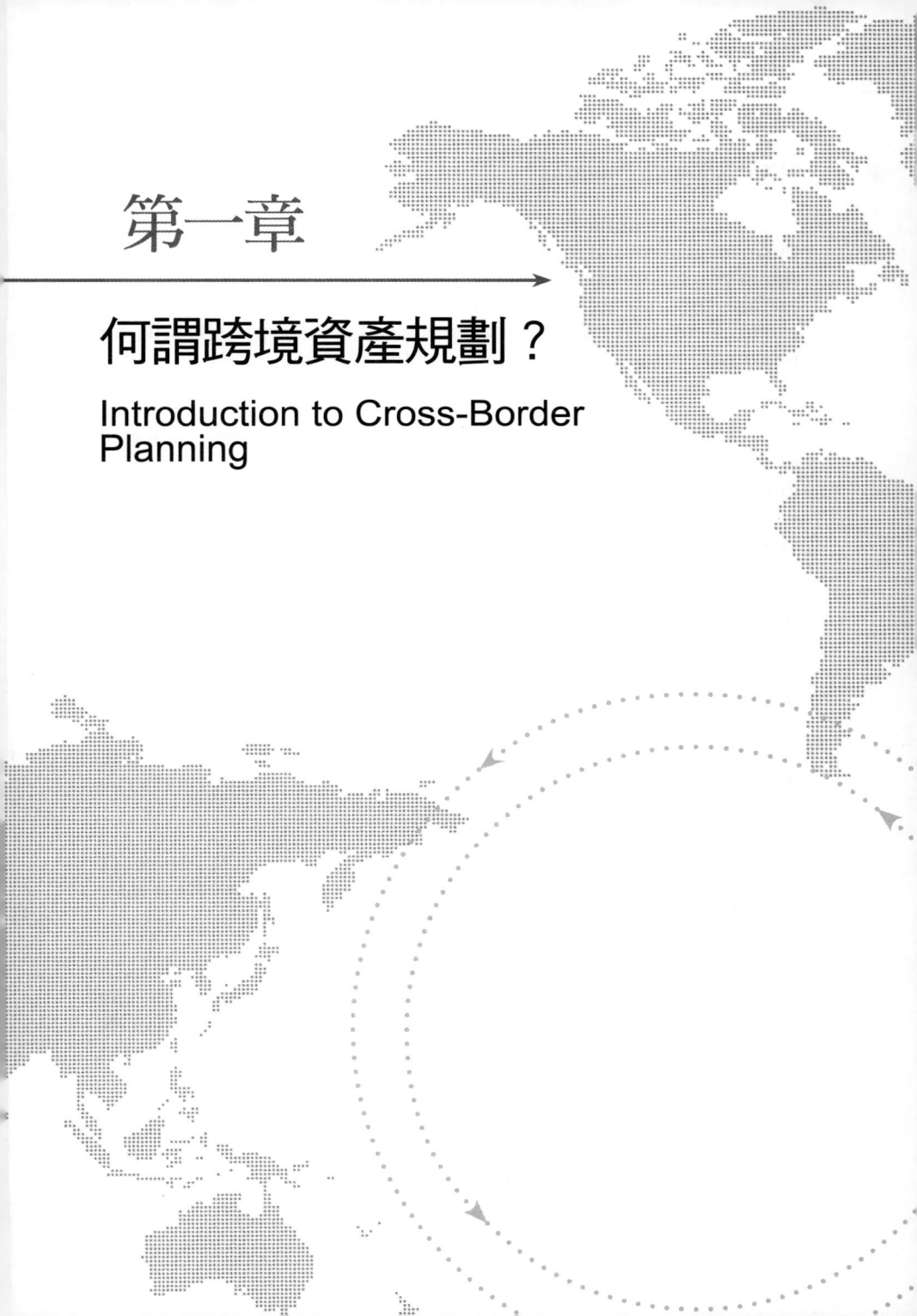

第一章

何謂跨境資產規劃？

Introduction to Cross-Border Planning

What is Estate Planning?

Estate planning is the process of anticipating and arranging for the management and disposal of a person's assets during the person's life in preparation for a person's future incapacity or death. While on its face, this may come off as simple, many individuals struggle with estate planning for a variety of reasons. This is especially true for those who have accumulated substantial wealth, referred to in this book as Wealth Creators.

For families based in multiple jurisdictions (commonly referred to as "Cross-Border Families"), estate planning may be even more arduous. This book aims to deliver workable solutions to Wealth Creators with family members and assets spread throughout several countries.

For non-U.S. persons with assets in the U.S. or descendants in the U.S. with U.S. citizenship or a U.S. green card, both the perceived cost of estate planning and the out-of-pocket legal fees and accounting expenses can be quite considerable. Moreover, depending on the Wealth Creator's circumstances, the estate planning process can be unpredictable and may change over time. While each Wealth Creator's approach to estate planning can and should be customized, we believe that knowledge of common structures used by others can serve as an important reference point.

Shouldn't estate planning be customized? Aren't U.S. attorneys the best solution when it comes to estate planning? How do I know if the solutions this book provides really work?

Estate planning can and should be customized to each individual. That is why there is an entire industry devoted to wealth and estate planning. In our experience, Asia-based families frequently struggle with the same issues and have similar concerns when it comes to estate planning.

The most common theme is that Wealth Creators who generated substantial holdings in Asia have:
1. immigrated to the U.S. themselves
2. had their spouse and / or descendants immigrate to the U.S.

甚麼是傳承規劃？

傳承規劃是指個人在世時就其資產的管理及處分進行預測及安排的過程，為其將來可能喪失行為能力或過世作準備。雖然傳承表面上看似簡單，但許多人卻因各種緣由在傳承規劃時備感艱難，對於那些已積累大量財富的人士（本書簡稱其為「**創富者**」）來說尤其如此。

對於成員位於多個司法管轄區的家族（通常稱為「**跨境家族**」），傳承規劃可能更加艱巨。本書旨在為家族成員及資產分布於多國之創富者提供可行的解決方案。

對於在美國擁有資產、或後代有美國公民身分或美國綠卡的非美國人來說，傳承規劃需考慮的各項成本及法律、會計相關費用皆相當可觀。此外，每個創富者的個別情況不同，而傳承規劃的過程亦可能隨著時間推移而改變，進而無法預測。即使每位創富者之傳承規劃方法應客製化，但我們認為，瞭解其他創富者所使用的常見架構也極具參考價值。

傳承規劃不應該客製化嗎？解決傳承規劃的最佳方案，不就是尋求美國律師的協助嗎？我該如何確認本書提供的解決方案實際可行？

傳承規劃應就每一個案的具體情況來量身訂製，這也就是為甚麼現今有整個行業專注於財富及傳承規劃。根據我們的經驗，亞洲家族在傳承規劃上經常遇到同樣的問題，也有類似的擔憂。

對在亞洲擁有大量資產的創富者來說，最常見的情境為：

1. 已移民至美國；
2. 其配偶及／或後代亦已移民到美國；或

3. invested in the U.S. by transferring all or a portion of their wealth from Asia.

When completing such a change in identity (becoming a U.S. person) or transfer in assets (moving assets into the U.S.), Wealth Creators may not fully understand the legal and tax implications. To this end, Asian Wealth Creators often attempt to resolve these issues by hiring professionals both in the U.S. and in Greater China.

Some even retain the services of the Big Four Accounting Firms or large and established global law firms. In our experience, engagements with these advisors rarely yield effective and cost-efficient results. In practice, many of these firms often have a difficult time piecing together the relevant laws and regulations of multiple jurisdictions.

Further complicating the situation, practitioners at U.S.-based law firms and accounting firms focus exclusively on the area of estate planning that they specialize in, often deferring to other qualified professionals' opinions when questions relating to other areas of estate planning arise. Unfortunately, this often results in the client receiving subpar outcomes, conflicting opinions and hefty fees. This is where this book could be useful. Every example illustrated this book has been understood and utilized by Wealth Creators who have similar questions and concerns.

The lead author of this book has settled numerous trusts for himself and his family. The majority of structures in this book have not only been created by the author, but they are also currently being updated, maintained, and improved upon to this day. Unlike most practitioners, who attest to their clients' successes, the author actually utilizes this book's very structures and can speak to their efficacy.

Wealth Creators should consider their succession strategy a core task and prioritize the creation of a sustainable plan to pass their assets on to their successors. While understanding key concepts can help, case studies are often the best way to truly understand estate planning and wealth succession. We include five illustrative case studies herein to help Wealth Creators with thinking about their trust planning.

3. 已將其亞洲全部或部分財富轉移到美國投資。

在完成身分變更（成為美國人）或資產轉移（到美國）時，創富者不全然能瞭解可能涉及的法律及稅務後果，因此，亞洲創富者經常透過在美國及大中華區聘請專業人士試圖解決這些問題。

有些創富者甚至會採納四大會計師事務所或大型知名的國際型律師事務所的建議。依據我們的經驗，委任這些顧問很少能產生有效且具成本效益的結果。許多前述的事務所在實務上往往很難掌握多個司法管轄區相關法律規範的全貌。

使情況更加複雜的是，美國律師事務所及會計師事務所的從業人員只專注於他們擅長的傳承規劃領域，當涉及到其他傳承規劃領域的問題時，通常會轉而尋求其他合格專業人士的意見。遺憾的是，這通常會導致客戶收到低於標準的結果、相互矛盾的意見以及高昂的費用。本書在這方面可發揮作用，書中所舉的每個案例均已實際運用在有類似情況、疑問及擔憂的創富者身上。

本書主筆已為自己及家人設立多個信託；不僅創建書中大多數的財富傳承架構，且至今也仍持續進行更新、維護及優化。有別於其他執業人士僅能證實其客戶的成功案例，本書的主要作者已實際運用書中的財富傳承架構，故得以暢談該架構的成效。

創富者應將他們的財富傳承策略視為核心任務，並優先制定永續性的計劃，得以將其資產傳承予其後代。雖然理解關鍵概念會有所助益，但案例研析通常是確實瞭解傳承規劃及財富交替的最佳方式。以下我們提供五個案例研究，以協助創富者思考其信託規劃。

Case Study 1
How can Asia-based Wealth Creators utilize U.S. trusts to their advantage?

Background:

Mr. Fang is the Founder of a large restaurant group in Shanghai (a listed company) and just turned 65. Since Mr. Fang had a modest upbringing, he has always been extremely cautious financially. He primarily invests cash generated from his operating businesses in low-risk financial investments and real estate in China. Mr. Fang's wife and children have lived in Los Angeles, CA for many years now, where he purchased a house under his wife's name in 2015. Throughout the years, he has also gifted his wife various sums, which she has since invested in an LLC that holds equity investments in U.S. office buildings and shopping malls. While Mr. Fang's wife and children have received U.S. green cards, Mr. Fang has not applied for immigration and is a non-U.S. person (a non-resident alien for U.S. tax purposes).

Below is a chart of Mr. Fang's assets prior to estate planning:

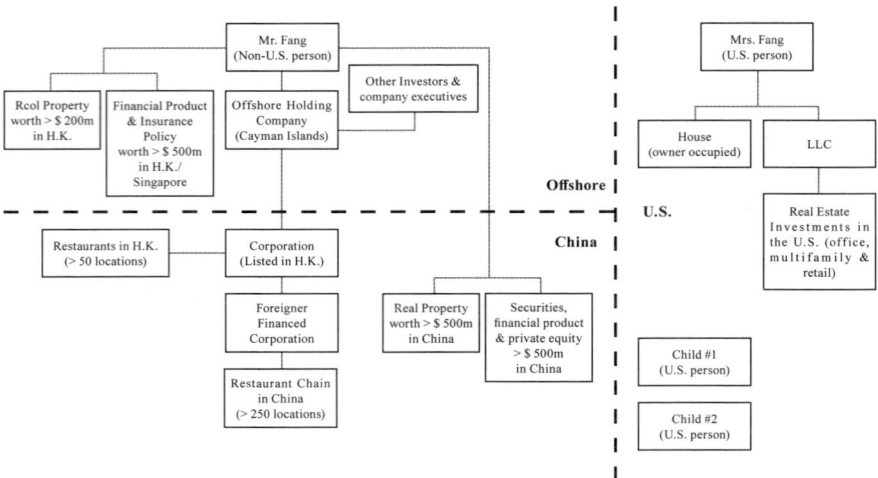

Key Planning Points:

1. Mr. Fang owns many assets in China. If China enacts an estate and transfer tax regime, a large proportion of Mr. Fang's assets may be subject to taxation. To pay this tax, his descendants may have

案例研究（一）

亞洲的創富者該如何善加利用美國信託？

案例背景：

剛滿 65 歲的方先生是一家上海大型餐飲集團（掛牌公司）的創辦人。方先生從小家境普通，因而他在財務上一直非常謹慎，他將經營業務的所得主要投資於中國的低風險金融商品及房地產。方先生在 2015 年以妻子的名義在加州購置一棟房產，其妻兒已在洛杉磯生活多年。多年來，方先生多次贈與金錢給方夫人，而方夫人將這些資金投資於一家持有美國辦公大樓及購物中心股權的有限責任公司。方先生的妻兒雖已取得美國綠卡，但目前方先生仍未申請移民，所以身分上為非美國人（即美國稅法上的非居住在美國的外國人）。

下圖為方先生在傳承規劃前的資產：

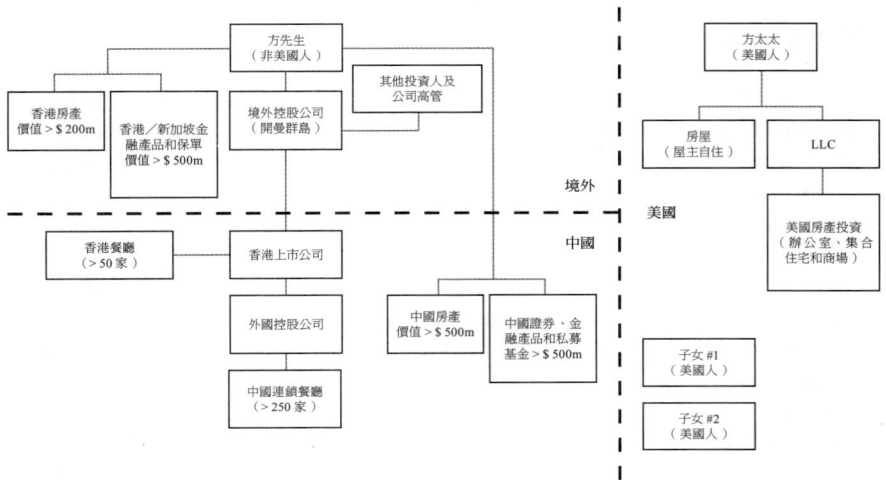

規劃要點：

1. 方先生在中國擁有多項資產。若中國實行遺產稅及贈與稅

to sell off their families' assets, potentially including shares of their listed company.

2. Since many of Mr. Fang's family members have immigrated to the U.S. over the years, Mr. Fang wishes to transfer more of his assets into the U.S. If he wishes to apply for immigration to the U.S., he should consider transferring his assets prior to immigrating. An U.S. irrevocable trust can serve as an excellent vehicle to hold his funds currently held by offshore companies in Hong Kong or Singapore. Alternatively, a U.S. revocable trust prior to Mr. Fang's death or immigration could serve as a vehicle for offshore companies that hold assets based in China or other operating companies.

3. When Mr. Fang makes gifts to his wife and children in the U.S., it is important to consider U.S. gift and estate tax implications of any such transfer. If Mrs. Fang holds enough assets in the U.S., it is likely that she will be liable for U.S. gift or estate tax if she receives additional assets from Mr. Fang over time. We recommend that Mr. Fang establish an irrevocable trust in the U.S. and transfer his assets into the trust. This would minimize the family's exposure to a U.S. estate tax and facilitate a smoother transition of assets to future generations.

4. If members of the management team in China are awarded incentive compensation in the form of shares, they should receive shares of the Foreign-Financed Chinese Corporation. If members of the management team outside of China are awarded shares, they should receive shares of the BVI holding company.

5. Mr. Fang should consider restructuring his holdings in China. Due to tightening currency controls, moving assets out of China has become difficult. If the opportunity arises, Mr. Fang should consider transferring ownership of his China-based assets to various offshore companies to facilitate the transfer of assets to his descendants. With professional assistance, this can generally be done through direct transfers, pre-planned financing events and gifts.

制度，方先生很大一部分資產可能會被課稅，故可能導致方先生為了繳稅而須出售家族資產（可能包括其掛牌公司的股份）。

2. 由於多位家族成員已移民美國多年，方先生希望能將更多資產轉移到美國。若方先生也想申請移民美國，應該考慮在移民前轉移其資產。美國不可撤銷信託可以作為一絕佳工具來持有他目前由香港或新加坡的離岸公司持有的資金。另一方面，在方先生逝世或移民之前，美國可撤銷信託亦可作為其透過離岸公司所持有中國資產或其他公司的工具。

3. 當方先生對在美國的妻兒進行贈與時，必須慎重考量其所涉及的美國贈與稅及遺產稅。若方夫人在美國持有的資產達一定規模，當她隨著時間從方先生獲得額外的資產時，她可能要負擔美國的贈與稅或遺產稅。因此，我們建議方先生在美國設立不可撤銷信託並將其資產轉移至信託，藉此最小化家族在美國遺產稅上的曝險程度，並使資產更平順地傳承給後代。

4. 若方先生擬對在中國的經營團隊成員授予股權作為激勵報酬，建議以中國的外商投資企業股份為標的；如擬對在中國境外的經營團隊成員授予股權激勵，建議以在英屬維京群島註冊的控股公司之股份為標的。

5. 方先生應考慮重組其在中國所擁有的投資資產。由於緊縮性的貨幣管制，將資產轉移出中國已變得困難。如有合適的時機，方先生應考慮將其中國資產的所有權移轉予多家離岸公司，以利於將資產轉移給後代。在專業人士的協助下，通常可藉由直接移轉、預先規劃的融資安排及贈與來達成此一目的。

Below is a chart of Mr. Fang's assets after estate planning:

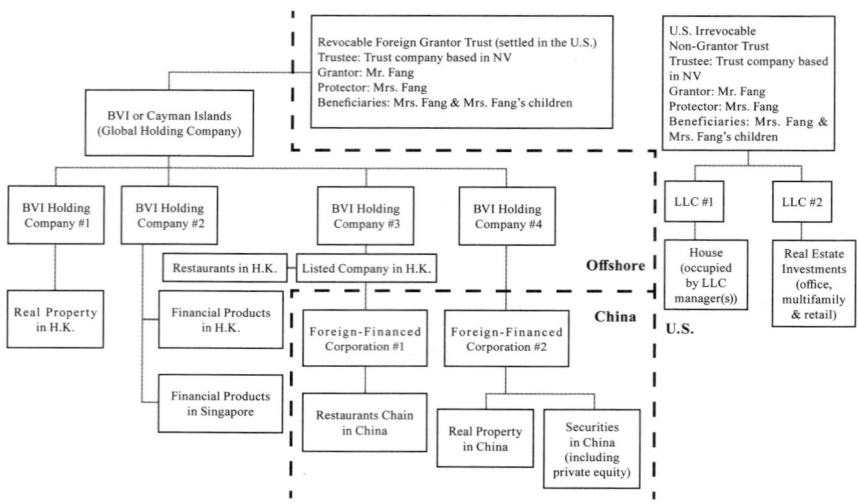

Case Study 2
How should Non-U.S. Wealth Creators transfer wealth to their descendants if their descendants are primarily U.S. Persons?

Background:
Mr. Huang, an entrepreneur based in China, owns several factories in Nanjing, Suzhou and Chengdu. His operations in China are held by W Corp., a Chinese holding company. W Corp. is owned by X Corp., a Hong Kong holding company that he holds. Over the years, he has transferred much of the profits from Chengdu to a Hong Kong bank account held by Y Corp., another wholly owned company. Periodically, he transfers funds from his Y Corp. bank account to another Hong Kong bank account held by Z Corp., a British Virgin Islands (BVI) company. Funds accumulated in Z Corp. are invested in various financial products and investments in both Hong Kong and Singapore.

While Mr. Huang is a Chinese citizen and does not have any plans of relocating to the U.S., his wife, daughter and sons are all based in the U.S. and have U.S. citizenship. Over the years, Mr. Huang has come to realize the need to formulate a plan that would

經傳承規劃後，方先生的資產如下圖所示：

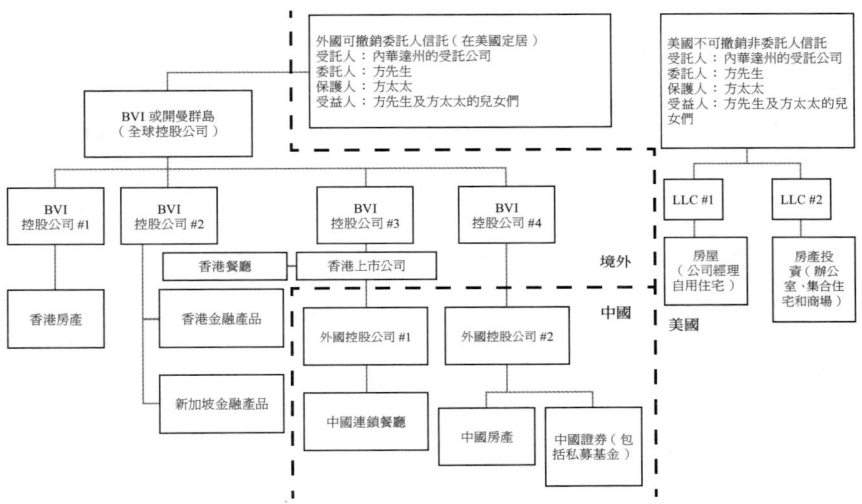

案例研究（二）

當非美國人創富者的後代主要為美國人時，該如何將財富轉移給後代？

案例背景：

黃先生是名中國企業家，在南京、蘇州及成都擁有多家工廠。他透過中國控股公司（W 公司）來持有中國的業務，而 W 公司則由他獨資的香港控股公司（X 公司）所持有。多年來，他將成都工廠大部分的利潤轉移至另一間其獨資的香港公司（Y 公司）的香港銀行帳戶。此外，他也會定期將 Y 公司銀行帳戶中的資金轉入另一家由其獨資的英屬維京群島（BVI）公司（Z 公司）的香港銀行帳戶，Z 公司積累的資金則用於投資香港及新加坡的各種金融產品。

黃先生是中國公民，沒有任何移居美國的計劃，但他的妻子

allow him to effectively transition his assets to his descendants; however, he is unsure of how to proceed given the complexity of his structures.

Specifically, he had the following questions:

1. How do I effectively delegate responsibilities between my companies' managers and my descendants?
2. How should I allocate company profits between my companies' managers and my children?
3. What is a trust? Can a trust help me achieve my succession goals?
4. Which trust jurisdiction is most suitable?
5. Who should I engage to draft the trust agreement or maintain the trust?
6. How should I transfer assets to my trust?
7. Who can manage my trust's assets once it is established?
8. Who will manage my trust assets after I pass away?
9. Which advisors can help me craft and execute my business succession plans?

Below is a chart of Mr. Huang's assets prior to estate planning:

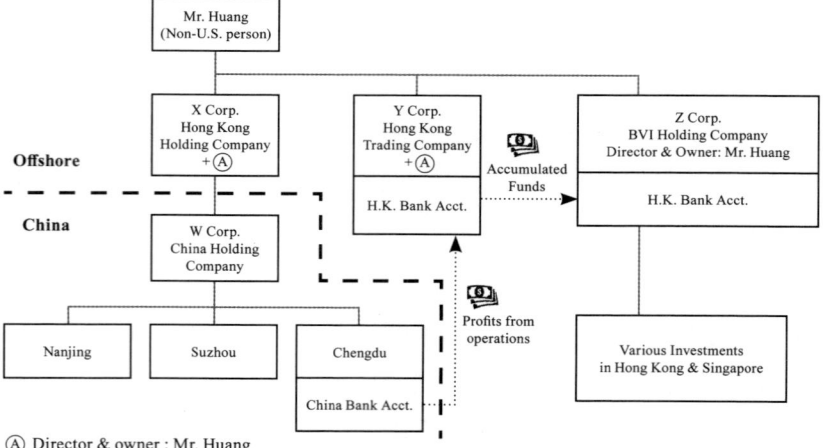

及子女們都在美國，並擁有美國國籍。多年來，黃先生逐漸意識到有必要制定計劃，使他能夠有效地將自己的資產移交給後代；然而，礙於既有投資架構的複雜性，他不確定該如何進行。

具體而言，黃先生有以下疑問：

　　1. 如何在公司經理人與我的子女們間委派責任？

　　2. 如何在公司經理人與我的子女們間妥適地分配公司的利潤？

　　3. 甚麼是信託？信託有助於我達到傳承的目標嗎？

　　4. 哪個信託司法管轄區最適合？

　　5. 我該聘任誰來撰擬信託合約或維護信託？

　　6. 我該如何將資產移轉至信託？

　　7. 信託一旦成立後，誰來管理信託資產？

　　8. 我過世之後誰來管理信託財產？

　　9. 哪些顧問可以協助我制定及執行我的事業傳承計劃？

下圖為黃先生在傳承規劃前的資產：

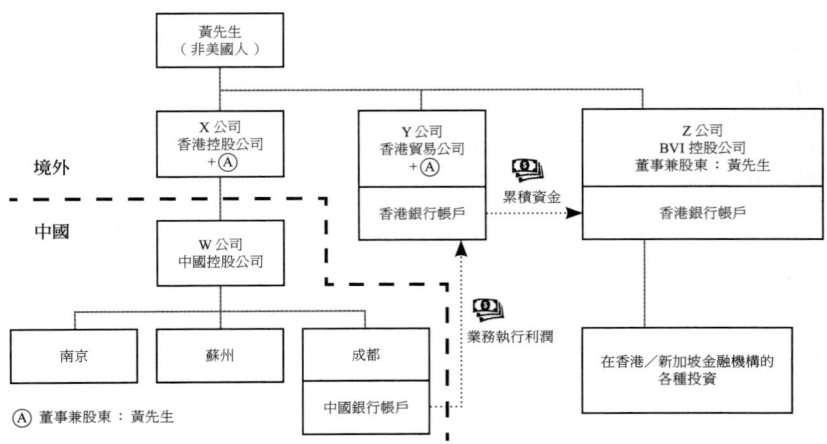

Below is a chart of Mr. Huang's assets after estate planning:

```
Mr. Huang
(Non-U.S. person)
├── X Corp. (Hong Kong Holding Company)
│   └── W Corp. (China Holding Company)
│       ├── Nanjing
│       ├── Suzhou
│       └── Chengdu
│           └── China Bank Acct.
├── Y Corp. (Hong Kong Trading Company)
│   └── H.K. Bank Acct.
└── Z Corp. (BVI Holding Company, Director: Mr. Huang)
    ├── H.K. Bank Acct.
    └── Various Investments in Hong Kong & Singapore
```

Note: Mr. Huang can also consider placing the X Corp. & Y Corp. into the revocable trust during his lifetime if he determined that they hold substantial value.

Note: Mr. Huang gifts his interest in Z Corp. to his foreign grantor trust but remains director of Z Corp. during his lifetime.

Revocable Foreign Grantor Trust (settled in the U.S.)
Trustee: Trust company based in NV
Grantor: Mr. Huang
Protector: Mrs. Huang (U.S. person)
Beneficiaries: Mr. Huang's children (U.S. persons)

Upon Mr. Huang's death ⬇

Note: The trust agreement will include language that would automatically facilitate the change of the trust structure upon Mr. Huang's death.

Irrevocable U.S. Non-Grantor Trust
Trustee: Trust company based in NV
Grantor: Mr. Huang or Huang family relative
Protector: Mrs. Huan or U.S C-corp.
Beneficiaries: Mr. Huang's children

U.S. Investment Account

Analysis:

1. Chinese Wealth Creators who wish to transfer their business interests to their descendants must first realize the importance of restructuring their holdings. Oftentimes, this is done by transferring their interest in closely held businesses to offshore companies, often based in Hong Kong, the British Virgin Islands (BVI) or the Cayman Islands. Since Mr. Huang's wife and children have immigrated to the U.S., it is important for him to consider how he will eventually move some of his assets outside of China, if he wishes to eventually transfer his assets to his family.

2. Fortunately, since Mr. Huang does not have a U.S. Green Card or U.S. citizenship, he remains a non-U.S. person for U.S. income tax purposes. This has several important tax advantages. Since Mr. Huang is generally not considered a U.S. person for income tax

經傳承規劃後，黃先生的資產如下圖所示：

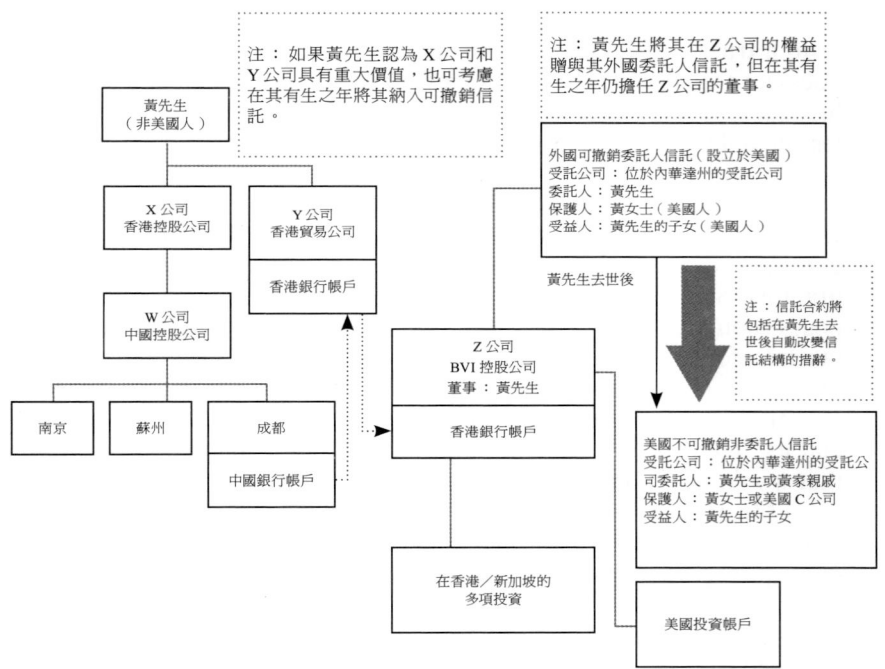

分析：

1. 中國的創富者若希望將其商業利益移轉給後代，首先必須意識到資產重組的重要性，而這通常是透過移轉其閉鎖性企業的股權給在香港、英屬維京群島或開曼群島的離岸公司來實現。由於黃先生的妻子及子女們已移民到美國，若他希望最終能將資產轉移給家人，對他而言，考慮最終如何將部分資產轉移到中國境外頗為重要。

2. 幸而因為黃先生並無美國綠卡或公民身分，他仍是美國所得稅法上的非美國人，而得享有若干重要的稅上優惠。由於黃先生在所得稅上通常不會被視為美國人，因此他自己（以及由他單

purposes, he (and any Foreign Grantor Trust settled and funded exclusively by him) would generally not be liable for U.S. income tax. In addition, gifts that Mr. Huang makes (whether to an individual or to a trust) can be planned for in advance and structured so that it does not trigger any U.S. gift taxes. Lastly, upon Mr. Huang's death, his assets would generally not be subject to U.S. estate taxation, unless he holds U.S. situs assets for estate tax purposes.

3. In this scenario, Mr. Huang should consider settling a Foreign Grantor Trust (FGT). Since the trust is a grantor trust for U.S. tax purposes, the income tax liability falls on the Mr. Huang (the trust's grantor). Since Mr. Huang is a non-U.S. person for income tax purposes, non-U.S. situs assets gifted to the trust would continue to be tax free for U.S. tax purposes. Thus, until the FGT becomes a non-grantor trust (generally upon Mr. Huang's death), non-U.S. sourced income is neither taxable to the trust itself nor to the trust's beneficiaries. The trust agreement could be drafted to include provisions that would automatically convert the trust to a U.S. non-grantor trust upon Mr. Huang death. This prevents the trust from ever becoming a foreign non-grantor trust for U.S. income tax purposes, which in turn prevents the trust from being taxed unfavorably.

4. By settling a Foreign Grantor Trust (FGT), Mr. Huang does not need to cede control of assets transferred to the trust. Even after Mr. Huang gifts shares of his businesses into a FGT, Mr. Huang can continue to retain full control over the company's management, voting and board of directors. Furthermore, upon Mr. Huang's death, assets gifted to the trust can either be (1) distributed to his beneficiaries outright or (2) held in the trust for future generations in perpetuity.

5. Mr. Huang and other Chinese Wealth Creators are frequently approached by family offices or wealth managers who wish for them to settle non-U.S. based trusts. Since Mr. Huang's spouse and descendants are U.S. persons, settling non-U.S. based trusts (such as one based in the Cayman Islands, Jersey, Guernsey, Nevis or Bahamas) may lead to unexpectedly adverse tax consequences. Distributions from Foreign Non-Grantor Trusts (FNGTs) typically face Throwback Taxes from Undistributed Net Income (UNI), leading to extremely high tax rates if distributions exceed income generated in that year. Furthermore, non-U.S. based trusts often do not have

獨設立及提供資金的外國委託人信託）通常無須負擔美國所得稅。此外，針對黃先生所為的贈與（無論是贈與給個人或信託），均可透過提前規劃及建立架構以達到不被課徵任何美國贈與稅的目的。最後，在黃先生過世時，除非他持有任何美國遺產稅上的美國資產，其資產通常非屬美國遺產稅的課徵標的。

3. 於本案的情況下，黃先生應考慮設立一個外國委託人信託。因為此信託屬於美國稅法上的委託人信託，所得稅由黃先生（即信託的委託人）負擔。由於黃先生是美國所得稅法上的非美國人，因此他將非美國資產贈與給信託在美國依然免稅。因此，在該外國委託人信託變更為非委託人信託（通常是在黃先生去世時）之前，信託的非美國來源所得對信託本身及信託受益人均為免稅。信託合約撰擬時得包含該信託於黃先生去世時將自動轉換為美國非委託人信託的條款，藉此防止該信託在美國所得稅上成為外國非委託人信託，從而避免信託被不利徵稅。

4. 透過設立外國委託人信託，黃先生無須放棄移轉給信託的資產的支配權。即便黃先生將其事業股份贈與給外國委託人信託後，他仍可持續保有對公司的管理、表決及董事會的完全控制權。此外，透過信託條款約定，於黃先生去世時，其已贈與給信託的資產得（1）直接分配予其受益人，或（2）為將來的後代而無限期由信託持有。

5. 黃先生及其他中國創富者經常接獲家族辦公室或財富管理業者的洽詢，遊說其設立美國境外信託。但由於黃先生的配偶及後代均為美國人，設立美國境外信託（例如位於開曼群島、英屬澤西島、根西島、尼維斯島或巴哈馬等地的信託）可能會導致意想不到的不利稅務後果。外國委託人信託在分配未分配淨所得

strong legal precedents protecting the trust. By settling a U.S.-based trust, whether the trust be revocable or irrevocable, wealth creators such as Mr. Huang can effectively prevent trust income from being taxed punitively by the U.S.

6. Even if Mr. Huang has already settled a non-U.S. based trust, he should consider (1) "migrating" the trust to the U.S. or (2) transferring or decanting the assets from the existing trust to a new trust based in the U.S. The majority of non-U.S. based trusts have provisions that allow for such a transfer. Though the legal and administrative hurdle of doing so may seem burdensome, a proficient team of cross-border professionals should be able to easily navigate the roadblocks and achieve the desired outcome.

Case Study 3
What happens when Foreigners Purchasing U.S. Real Property?

Background:
Mrs. Wang is a longstanding executive at a Shanghai-based construction company. Over the years, she has accumulated substantial wealth in China and overseas. Last year, she attained a Green Card through investment in the EB-5 program and moved to the United States with her children. Like many Wealth Creators, Mrs. Wang wished for her descendants to move to the U.S. and settle there permanently. Over the years, she has learned that the U.S. levies hefty taxes on the wealthy. Prior to her becoming a U.S. person (attaining a U.S. green card), she transferred funds to her mother, a Chinese citizen. She then purchased many U.S. properties in the U.S. under her mother's name.

Two years later, a close friend introduced her to a U.S. accountant, who informed her that U.S. estate taxes are levied not only on U.S. persons, but also foreigners with certain assets in the U.S. Furthermore, the gift and estate tax exemption for foreigners was a mere $60,000 and that any taxable estate in excess of the exemption would generally be subject to a 40% estate tax. Hearing this, Mrs. Wang was in disbelief. She now began searching for a way to decrease her U.S. tax exposure.

（Undistributed Net Income）時通常會面臨回溯稅，導致在分配的信託利益金額超過當年收入時，會適用極高的稅率。此外，美國境外信託在法律上往往沒有強力的判例可保護信託。相對的，藉由設立美國（可撤銷或不可撤銷）信託，與黃先生情形類似的創富者得有效地防止信託收入遭受美國懲罰性的徵稅。

6. 即便黃先生已設立美國境外信託，他仍應考慮（1）將信託遷移至美國，或（2）將資產從既有的信託移轉或轉注到美國設立的新信託（大多數美國境外信託合約中有允許此類移轉的條款）。雖然上述方案在法律上及行政上的障礙看似頗繁瑣，但一支熟稔跨境業務的專業團隊應能輕鬆克服障礙，並達成預期結果。

案例研究（三）
外國人購置美國房地產時有何影響？
案例背景：

王女士長年擔任一間上海建設公司的高管，多年來在中國及海外積累了大量財富。去年，她透過 EB-5 投資移民項目取得綠卡並帶著子女搬到美國。王女士與許多創富者一樣，希望她的後代移居並永久定居美國，她也已瞭解美國對富人徵收巨額稅款，因此在她取得美國綠卡成為美國稅法上的美國人之前，她將資金轉給其具中國公民身分的母親，接著以母親的名義在美國購置多項美國房地產。

兩年後，她的好友介紹了一個美國會計師給她，這位會計師告知她，美國的遺產稅不僅對美國人徵收，亦對在美國擁有特定資產的外國人徵收，此外，針對贈與稅及遺產稅的免稅額，外國人僅有 6 萬美元，而任何超過免稅額的應稅遺產通常適用 40%

Mrs. Wang's Structure (Prior to Restructuring)

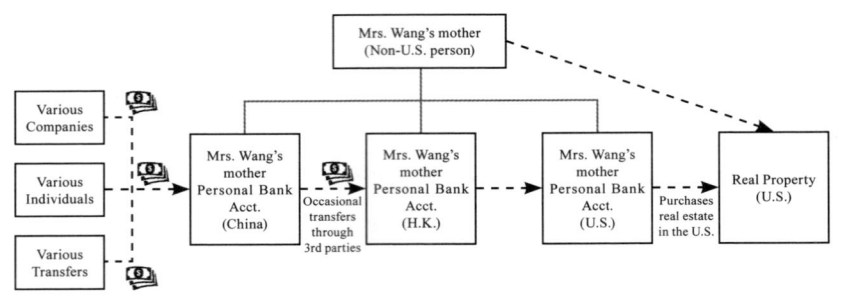

```
                        ┌─────────────────────────┐
                        │   Mrs. Wang's mother    │
                        │    (Non-U.S. person)    │
                        └─────────────────────────┘
                         │      │       │        ╲
                         │      │       │         ╲
┌──────────┐             ▼      ▼       ▼          ▼
│ Various  │       ┌─────────┬─────────┬─────────┐  ┌───────────┐
│Companies │       │Mrs.Wang'│Mrs.Wang'│Mrs.Wang'│  │Real Property│
└──────────┘──▶    │ mother  │ mother  │ mother  │──▶  (U.S.)   │
┌──────────┐       │Personal │Personal │Personal │  └───────────┘
│ Various  │──▶    │  Bank   │  Bank   │  Bank   │   Purchases
│Individuals│      │  Acct.  │  Acct.  │  Acct.  │   real estate
└──────────┘       │ (China) │ (H.K.)  │ (U.S.)  │   in the U.S.
┌──────────┐       └─────────┴─────────┴─────────┘
│ Various  │──▶       Occasional
│Transfers │          transfers
└──────────┘          through
                      3rd parties
```

Reflections on Succession:

1. The use of nominees for holding structures is common in China and may pose a number of significant obstacles to wealth preservation and transfer.

Wealth Creators in China are accustomed to holding assets under the names of others ("Nominees"), since they see minimal risks of doing so. Though nominee usage is prevalent in China, Wealth Creators who use nominees to hold assets outside of China may face considerable challenges.

Unlike in China, under U.S. laws, if the Wealth Creator were to challenge the legitimacy of the nominee's ownership over an asset, they would need to assert a reasonable legal claim over the said asset. In the U.S., an agreement to hold an asset on someone else's behalf could be viewed as insufficient to justify ownership. Thus, if the loyalty of the Nominee is at risk, the true owner of the assets can expect to face considerable odds when reasserting ownership.

Assuming the Nominee remains loyal to the Wealth Creator, the nominee's health could potentially be another concern. If the Nominee were to pass away while holding considerable assets, those assets may (1) be subject to substantial taxation in the U.S. or (2) subject to division per the Nominee's estate or last will. In many cases the Nominee's family may not be willing to cooperate or may even not be aware of arrangements between the Nominee and the "true" owner.

A last consideration would be the Nominee's legal status. In the past, we've encountered situations in which even the Wealth Creator

的遺產稅率。這番話讓王女士難以置信，因此她開始尋找降低其美國稅務風險的方法。

在傳承規劃前，王女士的資產結構如下：

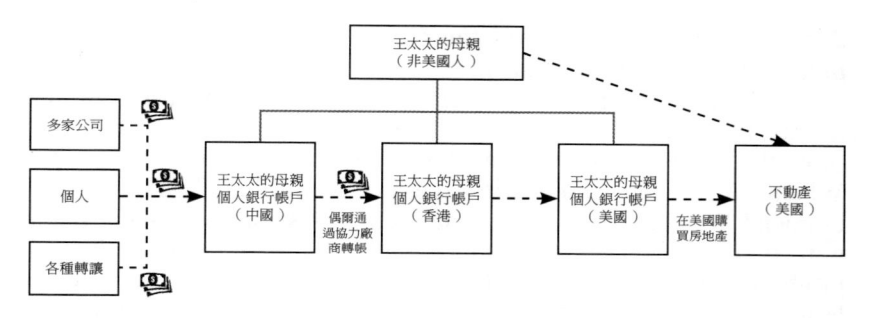

```
                            王太太的母親
                            （非美國人）
                                 │
        ┌────────────────┬───────┴───────┬────────────────┐
多家公司                                                  │
         →   王太太的母親      王太太的母親      王太太的母親    不動產
個人          個人銀行帳戶      個人銀行帳戶      個人銀行帳戶   （美國）
         →    （中國）    →   （香港）    →    （美國）    →
各種轉讓                偶爾通                            在美國購
         →              過協力廠                          買房地產
                        商轉帳
```

對傳承的省思：

1. 在中國常見借名他人持有財產的架構，但這可能對財富保全及轉移帶來一些重大障礙。

中國的創富者習慣向他人（「**出名人**」）借名持有資產，因為他們（即「**借名人**」）認為這樣做的風險極微。儘管在中國，借名的做法很普遍，但借名持有中國境外資產的創富者可能會面臨相當大的挑戰。

與中國不同的是，根據美國法律，若創富者要挑戰出名人對資產所有權的正當性，需要在法律上針對該資產提出合理的權利主張，但「代他人持有資產的協議」在美國可能被視為不足以證明借名人對資產具有所有權。因此，一旦出名人的忠誠度有疑慮，資產的實際所有權人在主張其所有權時，得預期會面臨相當大的挑戰。

假設出名人對借名的創富者保持忠誠，亦有可能因為出名人的健康狀況而有疑慮。若出名人在持有大量資產時去世，該等資

was unaware of the Nominee attaining a new citizenship or permanent residence (green card) in the U.S. or another jurisdiction. While these situations are rare, they may pose a considerable taxation risk to the Wealth Creator if improperly supervised or managed.

2. When moving assets into the U.S., Wealth Creators must explain their source(s) of wealth.

When creating U.S. accounts or moving cash into U.S. accounts, the Wealth Creator generally must declare his or her source(s) of wealth and his or her estimated total net worth at account opening. When transferring amounts in excess of $1 million (USD), we recommend Wealth Creators find qualified professionals to assist them with their transfers. Furthermore, our recommendation is to find professionals who are accustomed to assisting clients who receive large transfers from outside of the U.S. Once assets fall under U.S. jurisdiction, the financial institution itself, the U.S. Treasury Department or even the Internal Revenue Service (IRS) may question the source(s) of funds or request additional information including evidence of past transfers or income taxes paid. Competent professionals are able to both prepare the relevant documentation and assist the clients in preparing a proper written response to the questions posed.

3. Wealth Creators often wish to open bank accounts quickly in order to purchase U.S. real estate and financial products under the names of their foreign relatives, friends, or associates.

They may see this as an opportunity to invest in the U.S., while minimizing their U.S. tax exposure and disclosure obligations; however, many may falsely believe that the U.S. does not impose an estate tax on foreigners with U.S. holdings.

Furthermore, real estate brokers or investment management personnel often urge Wealth Creators to quickly transfer funds in order to further their own agendas (primarily their commissions and fees), without fully understanding or explaining the relevant tax and regulatory consequences of the proposed transactions. They may even make claims such as "don't worry, the CPA will take care of your concerns."

To minimize tax consequences and regulatory risk, we recommend that Wealth Creators find advisors who can address all aspects of wealth transfer at least 6-18 months prior to moving assets into the U.S. This team should consist of accountants who can analyze U.S.

產可能（1）在美國被課徵巨額稅款，或（2）根據出名人的遺產或遺囑而成為分割的標的。在許多情況下，出名人的家人可能不願配合或甚至對出名人與實際所有權人之間的安排一無所知。

最後一個考量點為出名人的法律地位。我們在過去曾遇過即使是創富者亦未知悉出名人在美國或其他司法管轄區已取得新的公民身分或永久居留權（綠卡）。這種情況雖然罕見，但如未適當監督或管理，可能對創富者造成相當大的稅務風險。

2. 將資產移轉到美國時，創富者必須解釋其財富來源。

在開立美國帳戶或將現金轉入美國帳戶時，創富者通常必須申報其財富來源及其開戶時的估計總資產淨值。當移轉金額超過100 萬美元時，建議創富者洽詢合格專業人士以協助該移轉。此外，亦應尋求熟稔協助客戶收受來自美國境外的大額資金移轉的專業人士。一旦資產進入美國的管轄範圍，金融機構本身、美國財政部或甚至國稅局均可能會質疑資金來源，或要求提供過往轉帳或繳納所得稅之證據等額外資料，而稱職的專業人士除得製作相關文件外，亦得協助客戶對前述機構所提出的問題提供適當的書面回覆。

3. 創富者通常希望能快速開設銀行帳戶，俾利以外國親戚、朋友或同事的名義購買美國房地產及金融產品。

創富者可能將此視為在美國投資的機會，並同時最小化其在美國稅務的曝險程度及揭露義務；然而，許多人可能誤以為美國不會對持有美國資產的外國人課徵遺產稅。

此外，房地產經紀人或投資管理從業人員常常基於達成其自身的訴求（主要是佣金及手續費收入），而催促創富者快速轉移資金，卻未先充分理解或解釋其所建議的交易在稅務及法規層面

income, estate and gift taxes, attorneys who can analyze cross-border legal structures and secretaries who can manage U.S. and overseas fund transfers (often through financial institutions in Hong Kong and Singapore) and deliver sufficient evidence of the client's source(s) of wealth.

Succession Framework Analysis:

In order to transfer the property from Mrs. Wang's mother to Mrs. Wang, her children or a U.S. trust, there may be a substantial tax consideration. Furthermore, assets held under individuals may be subject to further U.S. gift and estate taxation and can be a potential target for creditors if any legal disputes arise. Lastly, the Nominee may have other heirs, who may or may not know that the asset does not belong to the Nominee. Potential transfers and their tax and legal effects are summarized below:

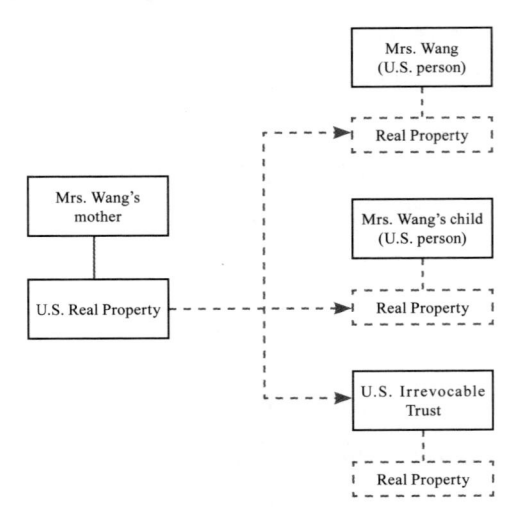

的相關後果；甚至可能會使用像是「別擔心，會計師能解決您的疑慮」的話術。

為求最小化稅負的不利影響及法規風險，我們建議創富者在轉移資產到美國的 6～18 個月前尋求能全面處理財富轉移的顧問團隊，其應配置能分析美國所得稅、遺產稅及贈與稅的會計師、能分析跨境交易法律架構的律師、以及能管理美國及海外資金移轉（通常透過香港及新加坡的金融機構）及能提供客戶財富來源充分佐證的秘書等人員。

傳承架構分析：

為了將財產從王女士的母親移轉給王女士、王女士的子女或在美國的信託，需考量許多稅務議題。此外，個人持有資產可能進一步成為美國贈與稅及遺產稅的課徵標的；且如有法律糾紛，其亦可能會成為債權人的請求標的。最後，出名人可能有其他繼承人，而繼承人可能知悉或不知悉借名財產事實上並不屬於出名人。下圖摘要本案例可能涉及的資產移轉方式及其在稅務及法律層面的影響：

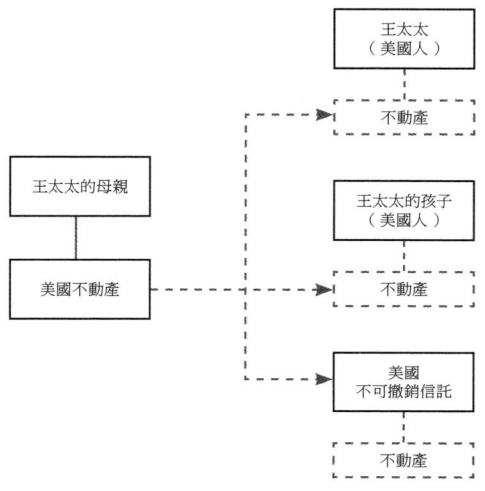

Method	Transferee	Tax and Legal Considerations
Gift	Mrs. Wang	Triggers a 40% gift tax upon transfer, as the asset (real estate) possesses a U.S. situs for gift tax purposes; uses up Mrs. Wang's lifetime exemption when the property is transferred to her descendants through a gift or her estate.
Sale		Triggers U.S. capital gains tax for Mrs. Wang's mother; uses up Mrs. Wang's lifetime exemption when the property is transferred to her descendants through a gift or her estate.
Estate		Triggers a 40% estate tax upon transfer, as the asset (real estate) possesses a U.S. situs for estate tax purposes; potential issues regarding the Nominee and the division of her estate among her heirs; uses up Mrs. Wang's lifetime exemption when the property is transferred to her descendants through a gift or her estate.
Gift	Mrs. Wang's Children	Triggers a 40% gift tax upon transfer, as the asset (real estate) possesses a U.S. situs for gift tax purposes; potential target for future creditors (including divorce).
Sale		Triggers U.S. capital gains tax for Mrs. Wang's mother; uses up the child's lifetime exemption when the property is transferred to his or her descendants through a sale or the child's estate; potential target for future creditors (including divorce).
Estate		Triggers a 40% estate tax upon transfer, as the asset (real estate) possesses a U.S. situs for estate tax purposes; potential issues regarding the Nominee and the division of her estate among her heirs; potential target for future creditors (including divorce).
Gift	A U.S. Irrevocable Non-Grantor Trust	Triggers a 40% gift tax upon transfer, as the asset (real estate) possesses a U.S. situs for gift tax purposes.
Sale		Triggers U.S. capital gains tax for Mrs. Wang's mother; does not use up any lifetime gift or estate exemption as long as the property is held in trust and not distributed to the trust's beneficiaries.
Estate		Triggers a 40% estate tax upon transfer, as the asset (real estate) possesses a U.S. situs for estate tax purposes; potential issues regarding the Nominee and the division of her estate among her heirs.

Note 1: Taxes are generally taxed at market value and not cost basis, based on the timing of the gift or estate. Typically, valuations of real estate are conducted by licensed real estate appraisers based in the property's jurisdiction.

Note 2: Lifetime exemption mentioned above refers to the unified lifetime gift and estate tax exemption available to U.S. persons.

資產移轉方式	移轉對象	稅務及法律考量
贈與	王女士	移轉時會引發 40% 的贈與稅，因為該資產（房地產）屬贈與稅上的美國資產；當王女士透過贈與或遺產繼承將財產移轉予其後代時，將用盡王女士的終身免稅額。
買賣	王女士	王女士的母親會產生美國資本利得稅；當王女士透過贈與或遺產繼承將財產移轉予其後代時，將用盡王女士的終身免稅額。
繼承遺產	王女士	移轉時會引發 40% 的遺產稅，因為該資產（房地產）屬遺產稅上的美國資產；另涉及出名人還有繼承人之間遺產分割的潛在問題。當王女士透過贈與或遺產繼承將財產移轉予其後代時，將用盡王女士的終身免稅額。
贈與	王女士的子女	移轉時會引發 40% 的贈與稅，因為該資產（房地產）屬贈與稅上的美國資產；此資產未來可能成為債權人（包括因離婚而產生之債權人）的請求標的。
買賣	王女士的子女	王女士的母親會產生美國資本利得稅；當王女士的子女將財產通過出售或遺產繼承等方式，將財產移轉予其後代時，會用盡該子女的終身免稅額；此資產未來可能成為債權人（包括因離婚而產生之債權人）的請求標的。
繼承遺產	王女士的子女	移轉時會引發 40% 的遺產稅，因為該資產（房地產）屬遺產稅上的美國資產；另有涉及出名人還有繼承人之間遺產分割的潛在問題；此資產未來可能成為債權人（包括因離婚而生之債權人）的請求標的。
贈與	美國不可撤銷非委託人信託	移轉時會引發 40% 的贈與稅，因為該資產（房地產）屬贈與稅上的美國資產。
買賣	美國不可撤銷非委託人信託	王女士的母親會產生美國資本利得稅；只要財產以信託方式持有且不分配予信託的受益人，就不會用盡任何贈與稅或遺產稅的終身免稅額。
繼承遺產	美國不可撤銷非委託人信託	移轉時會引發 40% 的遺產稅，因為該資產（房地產）屬遺產稅上的美國資產；另涉及出名人還有繼承人之間遺產分割的潛在課題。

注1：稅負通常是按贈與或繼承時的市價（而非成本）計算，而房地產通常是由其所在地司法管轄區的執業房地產估價師進行鑑價。

注2：上述提到的終身免稅額是指美國人可享有的統一贈與稅及遺產稅終身免稅額。

Mrs. Wang's Structure (After Restructuring)

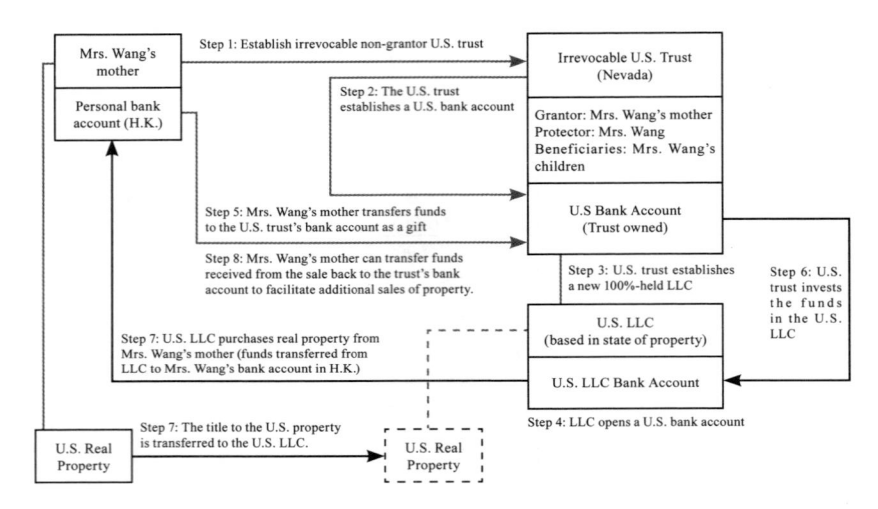

```
Mrs. Wang's mother          Step 1: Establish irrevocable non-grantor U.S. trust         Irrevocable U.S. Trust (Nevada)

Personal bank               Step 2: The U.S. trust establishes a U.S. bank account       Grantor: Mrs. Wang's mother
account (H.K.)                                                                            Protector: Mrs. Wang
                                                                                          Beneficiaries: Mrs. Wang's children

                            Step 5: Mrs. Wang's mother transfers funds                    U.S Bank Account
                            to the U.S. trust's bank account as a gift                    (Trust owned)

                            Step 8: Mrs. Wang's mother can transfer funds
                            received from the sale back to the trust's bank               Step 3: U.S. trust establishes      Step 6: U.S.
                            account to facilitate additional sales of property.           a new 100%-held LLC                 trust invests
                                                                                                                              the funds
                                                                                          U.S. LLC                            in the U.S.
                            Step 7: U.S. LLC purchases real property from                 (based in state of property)        LLC
                            Mrs. Wang's mother (funds transferred from
                            LLC to Mrs. Wang's bank account in H.K.)                      U.S. LLC Bank Account

                            Step 7: The title to the U.S. property                        Step 4: LLC opens a U.S. bank account
U.S. Real                   is transferred to the U.S. LLC.         U.S. Real
Property                                                            Property
```

If Mrs. Wang's mother gifts the real estate to either Mrs. Wang or a U.S. Irrevocable Trust, the gift is taxed at 40% of the property's market value. If Mrs. Wang chooses to leave the existing structure as is, her mother's heir would be subject to a 40% estate tax upon her mother's death. To eliminate U.S. transfer taxes, Mrs. Wang should seek to unwind the previous transaction.

1. In these situations, we recommend that Mrs. Wang's mother first establish a U.S. Irrevocable Non-Grantor Trust. Mrs. Wang, a U.S. person, can serve as the Trust Protector of this trust. Her children and / or other persons determined by Mrs. Wang can be selected as beneficiaries of the trust.

2. The Trust can then establish a U.S. bank account.

3. The Trust can then establish a 100% owned U.S. Limited Liability Company (LLC)

4. The LLC can then open U.S. LLC bank checking account(s), after applying for an Employer Identification Number (EIN) with the IRS through Form SS-4.

5. Mrs. Wang's mother gifts funds from her personal bank account outside of the U.S. (typically in Hong Kong or Singapore) into a bank account set up by the U.S. Trust.

6. A direction letter is drafted by Mrs. Wang to instruct the

經傳承規劃後，王女士的資產結構如下：

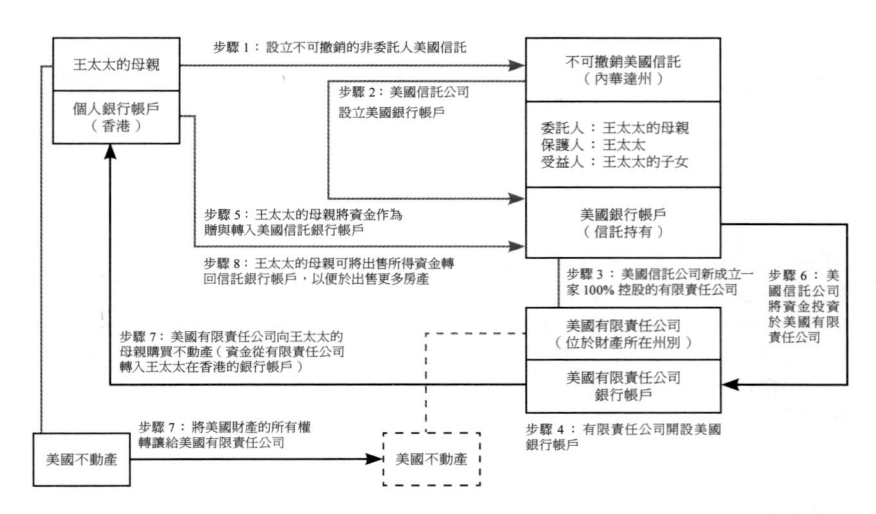

```
王太太的母親 ──步驟1：設立不可撤銷的非委託人美國信託──→ 不可撤銷美國信託
                                                    （內華達州）
個人銀行帳戶
（香港）      ──步驟2：美國信託公司設立美國銀行帳戶──→
                                                    委託人：王太太的母親
                                                    保護人：王太太
                                                    受益人：王太太的子女

              ──步驟5：王太太的母親將資金作為──────→ 美國銀行帳戶
                  贈與轉入美國信託銀行帳戶            （信託持有）

              ──步驟8：王太太的母親可將出售所得資金轉─
                  回信託銀行帳戶，以便於出售更多房產    步驟3：美國信託公司新成立一   步驟6：美
                                                    家100%控股的有限責任公司      國信託公司
                                                                                將資金投資
              步驟7：美國有限責任公司向王太太的                                   於美國有限
              母親購買不動產（資金從有限責任公司      美國有限責任公司              責任公司
              轉入王太太在香港的銀行帳戶）          （位於財產所在州別）

                                                    美國有限責任公司
                                                    銀行帳戶

              ──步驟7：將美國財產的所有權────→         步驟4：有限責任公司開設美國
                  轉讓給美國有限責任公司              銀行帳戶

美國不動產                                           美國不動產
```

若王女士的母親將房地產贈與給王女士或美國不可撤銷信託，則房地產贈與稅按其市價計收並適用 40% 稅率。若王女士選擇維持原本的資產架構，王女士母親去世時，其繼承人將被課徵 40% 的遺產稅。為避免被課徵美國的移轉稅，王女士應該設法從先前的交易解套。

1. 在這些情況下，我們建議王女士的母親先設立一個美國不可撤銷的非委託人信託，身為美國人的王女士可擔任該信託的保護人，而她的子女及／或由王女士選定的其他人可成為信託的受益人。

2. 信託可隨後開設一個美國銀行帳戶。

3. 信託可隨後成立一家由其完全持有的美國有限責任公司。

4. 美國有限責任公司以 SS-4 表向美國國稅局申請並取得雇主識別號碼（EIN）後，即可開設美國銀行支票帳戶。

5. 王女士的母親將她在美國境外（通常在香港或新加坡）個

Nevada trustee to transfer the funds from the trust's bank account to the LLC's U.S. bank account.

7. The U.S. LLC hires a real estate appraiser and appraises the property that will be sold. The U.S. LLC then purchases the property from Mrs. Wang's mother at the value determined through a property's appraisal, transferring proceeds from the sale to a bank account held by Mrs. Wang's mother.

8. If proceeds are transferred to Mrs. Wang's mother's bank account outside the U.S., the funds can be transferred back to the U.S. after the transaction is complete. The funds, now in the LLC's U.S. bank account, can then be used to purchase additional real estate (or stakes of real estate) held by Mrs. Wang's mother. If proceeds are transferred to Mrs. Wang's mother's bank account in the U.S., we recommend that funds be transferred from her U.S. bank account back to her offshore bank account prior to transferring the funds back into the U.S. LLC.

9. Since the U.S. real estate is now held by the U.S. irrevocable non-grantor trust, Mrs. Wang's mother's death would no longer trigger U.S. estate tax for the real estate sold to the trust-owned LLC.

Case Study 4
What happens if an offshore trust does not adequately protect the trust's assets? What is an illusory trust?

Background:
In the past decades, Wealth Creators often used offshore trusts settled in various jurisdictions to protect their assets. Otto Poon, the founder of Analogue Holdings, settled an irrevocable discretionary Jersey Trust in July 1995. He served as the Trust's Grantor, the Trust Protector, and one of the Trust's Beneficiaries. HSBC's Trust Company was appointed as trustee of his trust. After the Trust was established, he gifted 85% of his holdings in Analogue to his trust.

Since Mr. Poon still retained effective control over to the trust assets, the Hong Kong Court of Final Appeal held that the trust assets were includible in his matrimonial assets. The trust thus did not serve its intended purpose.

人銀行帳戶的資金捐贈到美國信託的銀行帳戶。

6. 由王女士擬定一封指示信，藉以指示內華達州的信託受託人將資金從信託的銀行帳戶轉移到前述美國有限責任公司的美國銀行帳戶。

7. 美國有限責任公司聘請房地產估價師對擬出售的財產進行鑑價。之後美國有限責任公司按房地產鑑價後的價值向王女士的母親購買該房地產，並將買賣價金轉入王女士母親持有的銀行帳戶。

8. 若買賣價金是轉入王女士母親在美國境外的銀行帳戶，則可在交易完成後將資金以前述方式轉回美國。待資金進入美國有限責任公司的美國銀行帳戶後，得用來購買王女士母親持有的其他房地產（或房地產股份）。若買賣價金是轉入王女士母親在美國的銀行帳戶，我們建議在將資金轉回美國有限責任公司之前，先將資金從她的美國銀行帳戶轉至其離岸銀行帳戶。

9. 由於美國房地產自此由美國不可撤銷非委託人信託所持有，故王女士母親去世時，已出售予該信託持有的美國有限責任公司的房地產將不會產生美國遺產稅。

案例研究（四）
若離岸信託未能充分保護信託資產，會有甚麼後果？甚麼是偽信託？
案例背景：

在過去幾十年裡，創富者經常使用在不同司法管轄區設立的離岸信託來保護他們的資產。安樂工程集團的創始人潘樂陶先生在 1995 年根據澤西島法律設立一個不可撤銷的裁量型信託。他

Reflections on Succession:

At the time of the ruling, the court decision shocked many Wealth Creators, who previously believed that their assets would be thoroughly protected by offshore trusts no matter whether they held substantial control over the trust's assets or not.

1. There are generally three types of offshore trust structures:
   (1) A client's private bank representative or wealth advisor creates a trust structure to facilitate investment of the client's assets.
   (2) A client retains a professional trust company and establishes a trust for the primary purpose of asset protection or succession planning.
   (3) A client retains attorneys and a trust company for assistance with settling a private trust company (PTC).

When establishing an offshore trust, the Wealth Creator should evaluate the pros and cons of each jurisdiction. Typically, if there is a dispute, complaints would be filed in the jurisdiction that the trust company is situated and not where the trust assets are situated. Wealth Creators that seek to protect their assets through establishing a trust should seek jurisdictions with strong case law as a basis for providing those protections.

In Structure (1), described above, private bankers and wealth managers attempt to recommend trusts that (A) maximize the investment advisor's control over the trust, (B) minimize the trust's tax liability and (C) maximize the grantor's retained powers. As the grantor often retains substantially all powers (including the power to invest the trust assets, the power to distribute the trust assets and the power to determine trust beneficiaries), these types of trusts typically suffer from a lack of independence. Since the trust lacks independence, many competent courts would and have ruled that these trusts never existed and that the grantor has retained his interest in assets "gifted" to the trust, thus opening the trust's assets up for distribution to the grantor's creditors. These trusts are often referred to as "Illusory Trusts."

是該信託的委託人、保護人及多位受益人之一,而滙豐國際信託有限公司是該信託的受託人。信託設立後,他將其持有的約85%安樂工程集團股權贈與給此信託。

然而,由於潘先生對信託資產仍然保持有效控制,香港終審法院裁定該些信託資產應計入他的婚姻財產。因此,該信託未能達到他預期的資產保護的目的。

對傳承的省思:

前述的法院判決震驚了許多創富者,因為他們以前認為無論他們是否對信託資產持有高度控制,其資產都將受到離岸信託的徹底保護。

1. 離岸信託架構通常有三種類型:
(1)客戶的私人銀行代表或財富顧問創建信託架構,以便於客戶資產的投資。
(2)客戶聘請專業信託公司並設立信託,主要目的是資產保護或傳承規劃。
(3)客戶聘請律師及信託公司協助設立私人信託公司(PTC)。

在設立離岸信託時,創富者應評估各個司法管轄區的利弊。若因信託關係而涉訟,通常是在信託受託公司所在地(而非信託資產所在地)的司法管轄區起訴。尋求透過設立信託以保護其資產的創富者應尋求具強有力判例法的司法管轄區作為提供這些保障的基礎。

在架構(1)中,私人銀行家及財富管理公司會試圖推薦以下信託:(A)最大化投資顧問對信託的控制權,(B)最小化信託的納稅義務,及(C)最大化委託人保留的權力。由於委託人通常保

In Structure (2), since the primary purpose of such trusts is to protect the trust's assets and to pass these assets on to the trust's beneficiaries, powers are more often clearly delineated, with the grantor retaining minimal to no powers. We advise that families seeking to create these structures find competent legal counsel in all applicable jurisdictions in order to ensure that the assets held in these trusts would be protected and that the trust would be treated as an entity independent from the trust's grantor, protector, and beneficiaries.

In Structure (3), Wealth Creators may be persuaded to establish a Private Trust Company (PTC) either in an offshore jurisdiction or even in the U.S. While a PTC can and often do provide certain protections, they often also come with immense and immediate setup and maintenance costs (often exceeding US$200,000 per year). Highly customized and extremely complex, PTCs may not be suitable for most families and certainly can make the process of cross-border wealth transfers an even more daunting task.

2. While many jurisdictions offer grantors flexibility to retain certain powers in a bid to win their business, offshore trusts, generally settled on offshore islands or territories, often provide the maximum amount of flexibility. For many years, this was seen as a boon for professionals (especially attorneys specializing in offshore trusts); however, as clearly illustrated in this case, a high degree of control may lead other jurisdictions to disregard the trust structure in its entirety. The risk of a trust being recognized as an "illusory trust" is increasing, as more and more competent jurisdictions realize that an offshore trust is only a trust in name and not in substance.

留絕大多數的權力（包含投資暨分配信託資產的權力及決定信託受益人的權力），這些類型的信託通常缺乏獨立性。由於缺乏獨立性，許多管轄法院可能會認定該類信託不存在，且因為設立人仍保留其在「已贈與」給信託的資產上的權益，會導致信託資產得被分配給委託人的債權人。這些信託通常被稱為「偽信託」。

在架構（2）中，由於此類信託的主要目的是保護信託資產並將資產轉移給信託的受益人，因此權力通常被明確界定，而委託人僅保留最少的權力甚至沒有權力。我們建議尋求建立此類架構的家族在所有適用的司法管轄區內諮詢稱職的法律顧問，以確保信託持有的資產得到保護，並且信託會被視為獨立於信託委託人、保護人及受益人的獨立實體。

在架構（3）中，創富者可能會被說服在離岸司法管轄區甚至在美國設立私人信託公司（PTC）。雖然 PTC 可以，且通常確實提供特定保障，但它們通常隨之而來的就是巨額的設立及維護成本（通常每年超過 20 萬美元）。由於 PTC 的高度客製化且極其複雜，可能不適合大多數家族，且無疑會使跨境財富轉移過程變得更加艱巨。

2. 雖然許多司法管轄區為委託人提供保留特定權力的彈性以爭取業務，但離岸信託（通常在離岸島嶼或領土上設立）通常提供最大的彈性。多年來，這被視為專業人士（尤其是專門從事離岸信託的律師）的福音；然而，本案顯示，高度的控制可能導致其他司法管轄區全然無視於信託架構的存在。信託被認定為「偽信託」的風險正在增加，因為越來越多的司法管轄權區認知到，離岸信託僅是名義上的信託，而非實質上的信託。

Succession Framework Proposal:
The Offshore Trust (Prior to Restructuring)

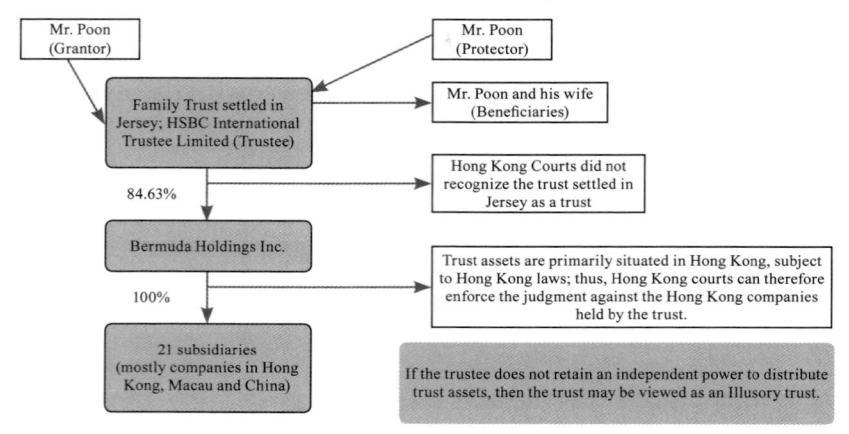

```
Mr. Poon                                    Mr. Poon
(Grantor)                                   (Protector)
    │                                           │
    ▼                                           ▼
Family Trust settled in  ──────────►  Mr. Poon and his wife
Jersey; HSBC International              (Beneficiaries)
Trustee Limited (Trustee)
    │                         ──────►  Hong Kong Courts did not
    │ 84.63%                           recognize the trust settled in
    ▼                                  Jersey as a trust
Bermuda Holdings Inc.
    │                                  Trust assets are primarily situated in Hong Kong, subject
    │ 100%                             to Hong Kong laws; thus, Hong Kong courts can therefore
    ▼                                  enforce the judgment against the Hong Kong companies
21 subsidiaries                        held by the trust.
(mostly companies in Hong
Kong, Macau and China)                 If the trustee does not retain an independent power to distribute
                                       trust assets, then the trust may be viewed as an Illusory trust.
```

Suggested Structure

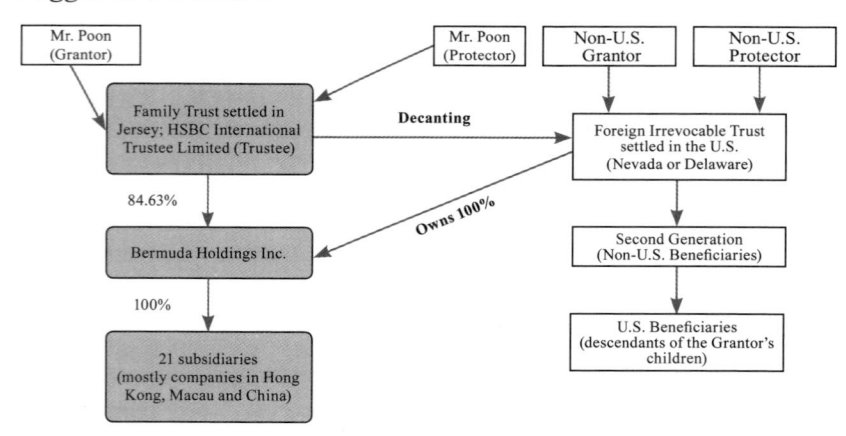

```
Mr. Poon              Mr. Poon          Non-U.S.        Non-U.S.
(Grantor)             (Protector)       Grantor         Protector
    │                     │                 │               │
    ▼                     ▼                 ▼               ▼
Family Trust settled in      Decanting    Foreign Irrevocable Trust
Jersey; HSBC International ──────────────► settled in the U.S.
Trustee Limited (Trustee)                  (Nevada or Delaware)
    │                                           │
    │ 84.63%           Owns 100%                ▼
    ▼                                      Second Generation
Bermuda Holdings Inc. ◄──────────          (Non-U.S. Beneficiaries)
    │                                           │
    │ 100%                                      ▼
    ▼                                      U.S. Beneficiaries
21 subsidiaries                            (descendants of the Grantor's
(mostly companies in Hong                  children)
Kong, Macau and China)
```

Succession Framework Analysis:

While offshore trusts have long been a mainstay for wealthy families, balancing the need for control with the asset protection qualities of a trust is important to keep in mind. If the trust's grantor retains many powers over the trust, courts may view the trust skeptically or, in a worst-case scenario, deny that the trust ever existed. This could potentially cause assets to be seized by creditors. The

傳承架構建議：
調整前的離岸信託架構

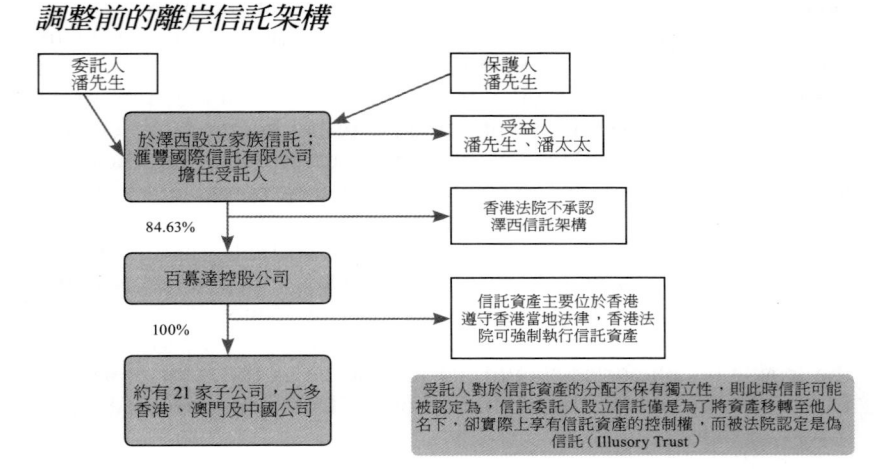

```
委託人                                      保護人
潘先生                                      潘先生
    │                                         │
    ▼                                         ▼
於澤西設立家族信託；  ──────►  受益人
滙豐國際信託有限公司              潘先生、潘太太
擔任受託人
    │      │
    │      └──────►  香港法院不承認
    │                 澤西信託架構
 84.63%
    │
    ▼
百慕達控股公司  ──────►  信託資產主要位於香港
    │                     遵守香港當地法律，香港法
   100%                   院可強制執行信託資產
    ▼
約有 21 家子公司，大多    受託人對於信託資產的分配不保有獨立性，則此時信託可能
香港、澳門及中國公司      被認定為，信託委託人設立信託僅是為了將資產移轉至他人
                          名下，卻實際上享有信託資產的控制權，而被法院認定是偽
                                        信託（Illusory Trust）
```

建議架構

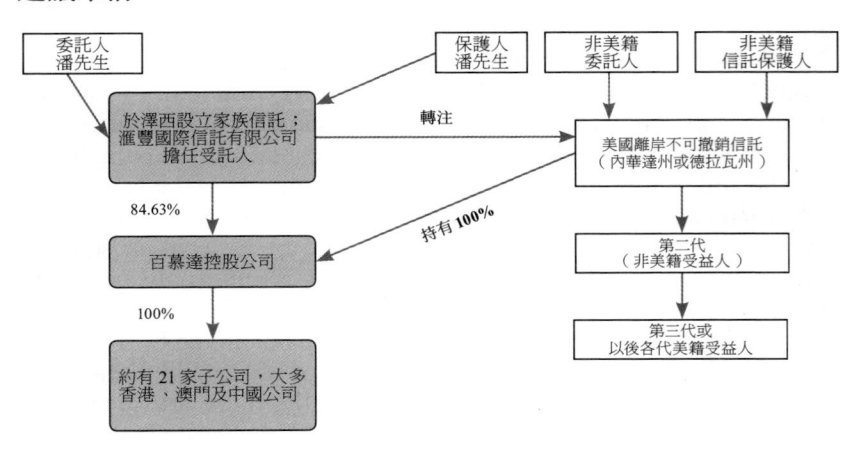

```
委託人                     保護人        非美籍       非美籍
潘先生                     潘先生        委託人       信託保護人
    │                        │             │            │
    ▼                        ▼             ▼            ▼
於澤西設立家族信託；  ◄────  轉注    美國離岸不可撤銷信託
滙豐國際信託有限公司                   （內華達州或德拉瓦州）
擔任受託人                                   │
    │                                        ▼
 84.63%         ◄──── 持有 100% ────    第二代
    │                                    （非美籍受益人）
    ▼                                        │
百慕達控股公司                               ▼
    │                                    第三代或
   100%                                  以後各代美籍受益人
    ▼
約有 21 家子公司，大多
香港、澳門及中國公司
```

傳承架構分析：

儘管富裕家族長期以來一直非常仰賴離岸信託，但仍需謹記在追求對信託的掌控之際，亦應兼顧信託資產的保障。若信託的委託人對信託保留許多權力，法院可能會對信託持懷疑態度，或

following steps are crucial for determining whether a trust is able to serve its function and protect assets from potential creditors:

1. When reviewing a trust agreement, advisers typically focus on the grantor's intent. Typically, trusts are settled either to protect the Grantor's assets or reduce tax-related risks. Another important aspect to consider are the grantor and his or her descendants' current and future tax residencies. We especially recommend families that are drafting trusts with U.S. beneficiaries seek competent U.S. tax counsel to determine the tax effects of offshore trusts.

2. Trust agreements should be drafted so that grantors do not have powers that would jeopardize the trust's independence. If the trust agreement provides for a trust protector (generally a fiduciary in charge of the most impactful functions of a trust), the grantor and the trust's beneficiaries should not also serve as the trust protector. Doing so may reduce the likelihood of the trust being deemed an illusory or ineffective trust.

3. When preparing a structure that includes a trust, advisers should consider potential gift and estate tax consequences for the grantor, the trust protector, the beneficiaries, and the trust itself. Failure to do so may result in adverse tax consequences.

4. For families with any U.S. nexus (one or more U.S. grantor, protector, beneficiary, or asset), we would recommend evaluating the pros and cons of U.S. trusts versus offshore trust structures. For families with existing offshore trust(s), we recommend looking to see whether migrating the trust to the U.S. or decanting the assets to a U.S. trust is possible. While this often requires the assistance of U.S. and non-U.S. counsel, the relative stability of a U.S. legal jurisdiction and its consistent set of protective trust laws is almost always worth the effort.

5. U.S. trusts (including foreign trusts settled in the U.S. for U.S. income tax purposes) are typically drafted or reviewed by attorneys in the state that the trust is settled. Typically, those attorneys also give an opinion regarding the independence of the trust. Tax counsel would also usually a separate opinion regarding potential U.S. tax consequences.

者在最壞的情況下，否認信託的存在。這可能會導致債權人向法院聲請扣押資產。以下步驟對於確定信託是否能夠發揮其功能並保護資產免受潛在債權人的侵害至關重要：

1. 在審閱信託合約時，顧問通常著重信託委託人的意向。通常設立信託是為了保障委託人的資產或降低稅務相關風險。另一個需要考慮的重要面向是信託委託人及其後代當前及未來的稅務居住地。我們特別建議有美國受益人的家族在擬定信託合約時應尋求稱職的美國稅務顧問，以確定離岸信託的稅務影響。

2. 信託合約擬定時，應使信託委託人不具有危及信託獨立性的權力。若信託合約訂有信託保護人（通常是負責信託最有影響力職能的受託責任人），則信託委託人及信託受益人不應同時擔任信託保護人，以降低信託被視為偽信託或無效信託的可能性。

3. 在籌劃包含信託在內的家族傳承架構時，顧問應考量對信託委託人、信託保護人、受益人及信託本身的潛在贈與稅及遺產稅後果，否則可能會導致不利的稅務後果。

4. 對於與美國有連結的家族（例如家族有一個或多個美國信託委託人、信託保護人、受益人或資產），我們會建議其評估美國信託與離岸信託架構的利弊。對於擁有離岸信託的家族，我們會建議其評估將信託遷移至美國或將資產轉注到美國信託的可能性。雖然這通常需要美國及非美國律師的協助，但由於美國司法管轄區的相對穩定性及其信託法律保障的一致性，在絕大多數的情況下是值得創富者作此努力的。

5. 美國信託（包含為美國所得稅目的而在美國設立的外國信託）通常由信託設立地該州的律師撰擬或審閱。該些律師通常亦會對信託的獨立性提供意見；稅務律師則通常也會針對潛在的美國稅務影響另行提供意見。

Case Study 5
Planning prior to immigrating to the U.S.

Background:
Mr. Jiang and Mrs. Jiang, a married couple residing in China, finally received notices that they were granted their U.S. Permanent Resident Cards (Green Cards) after more than a decade. As they were not sure that they were going to ever receive their green cards, they never considered the tax consequences of their U.S. residency status. When they came to the U.S., they consulted with trusted U.S. CPAs, who informed them that their worldwide assets would now be subjected to U.S. income, gift, and estate taxes, much to their disbelief.

Reflections on Succession:
1. Over the past couple of years, Hong Kong, Australia, and Canada have increasingly tightened their immigration policies. The enactment of EB-5 in the U.S. came as a relief to many Chinese families seeking to permanently relocate their families. Tax advisors often advised Wealth Creators to retain their original citizenships and tax residency, while their spouses applied for Green Cards, since the U.S. generally taxes its residents more heavily. However, since many Chinese nationals believe that a married couple should stay together indefinitely and never separate, we frequently see both the Wealth Creator and their spouses attain Green Cards.

2. Once a foreign national obtains a Green Card and becomes a U.S. tax resident, he or she is liable for not only U.S. income taxes on his or her worldwide income, but also subject to disclosure requirements of his or her offshore assets in accordance with numerous U.S. laws and regulations. Many wonder whether there is a way to attain U.S. permanent residency, without the enormous tax and disclosure responsibilities that come with it. For those that created their wealth outside of the U.S., is there a path to U.S. citizenship without payment of considerable income, estate and gift taxes?

案例研究（五）
移民美國前的規劃
案例背景：

　　江先生及江夫人是居住在中國的一對夫婦；在申請綠卡十多年後，他們終於收到取得美國永久居民卡（綠卡）的通知。由於過往不確定是否會取得綠卡，因此從未考慮過美國居留身分的稅務後果。當他們來到美國時，他們諮詢了值得信賴的美國註冊會計師。會計師告訴他們，他們的全球資產現在將有義務申報美國所得稅、贈與稅及遺產稅，這使其難以置信。

對傳承的省思：

　　1. 在過去幾年裡，香港、澳大利亞及加拿大的移民政策越來越嚴格。美國頒布的 EB-5 讓許多尋求永久定居的中國家庭鬆了一口氣。稅務顧問經常建議創富者保留他們原來的公民身分及稅務居民身分，而讓他們的配偶申請綠卡，因為美國通常對其居民徵收更重的稅。然而，由於許多中國人認為已婚夫婦應該永不分離，因而常見創富者及其配偶都取得綠卡。

　　2. 一旦外國人獲得綠卡並成為美國稅務居民，不僅要對其全球收入繳納美國所得稅，還須根據許多美國法律及法規對其離岸資產進行揭露。許多人想知道是否有辦法取得美國永久居留權而不需負擔隨之而來的巨額稅款及揭露責任。對於那些在美國境外創造財富的人來說，有沒有一條途徑是可以在不支付可觀的所得稅、遺產稅及贈與稅的情況下取得美國公民身分？

Timeline

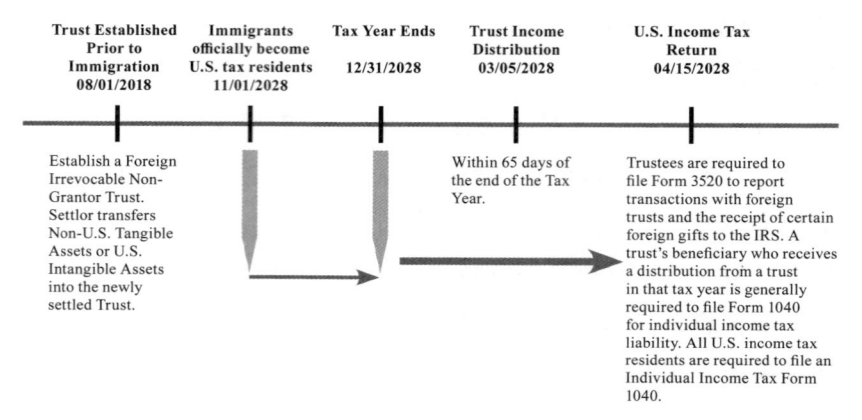

Trust Established Prior to Immigration 08/01/2018	Immigrants officially become U.S. tax residents 11/01/2028	Tax Year Ends 12/31/2028	Trust Income Distribution 03/05/2028	U.S. Income Tax Return 04/15/2028
Establish a Foreign Irrevocable Non-Grantor Trust. Settlor transfers Non-U.S. Tangible Assets or U.S. Intangible Assets into the newly settled Trust.			Within 65 days of the end of the Tax Year.	Trustees are required to file Form 3520 to report transactions with foreign trusts and the receipt of certain foreign gifts to the IRS. A trust's beneficiary who receives a distribution from a trust in that tax year is generally required to file Form 1040 for individual income tax liability. All U.S. income tax residents are required to file an Individual Income Tax Form 1040.

Succession Framework Proposal

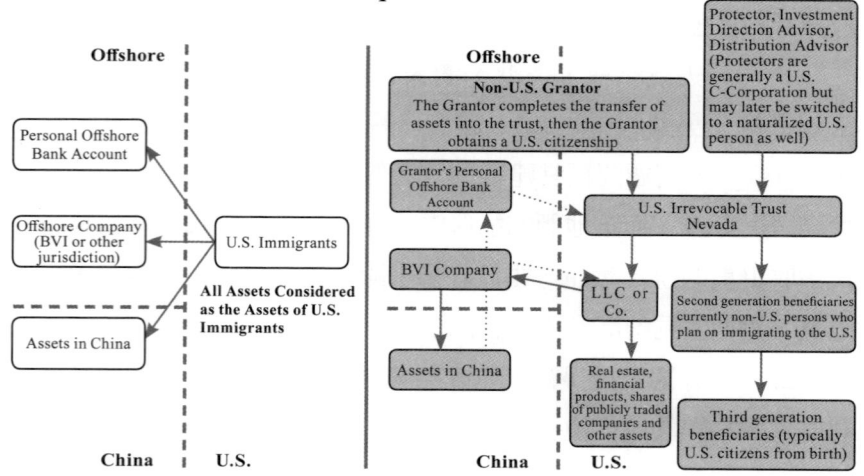

Offshore (China side):
- Personal Offshore Bank Account
- Offshore Company (BVI or other jurisdiction)
- Assets in China

All Assets Considered as the Assets of U.S. Immigrants → U.S. Immigrants

Offshore / U.S. side:
- Non-U.S. Grantor: The Grantor completes the transfer of assets into the trust, then the Grantor obtains a U.S. citizenship
- Grantor's Personal Offshore Bank Account
- BVI Company
- Assets in China
- U.S. Irrevocable Trust Nevada
- LLC or Co.
- Real estate, financial products, shares of publicly traded companies and other assets
- Protector, Investment Direction Advisor, Distribution Advisor (Protectors are generally a U.S. C-Corporation but may later be switched to a naturalized U.S. person as well)
- Second generation beneficiaries currently non-U.S. persons who plan on immigrating to the U.S.
- Third generation beneficiaries (typically U.S. citizens from birth)

Succession Framework Analysis:

1. Wealthy families planning on immigrating to the U.S. often consider investing in U.S. real estate. Prior to becoming U.S. persons, Wealth Creators should consult with tax and legal advisors and discuss the options available to achieve both the taxes minimization and asset protection.

時間軸

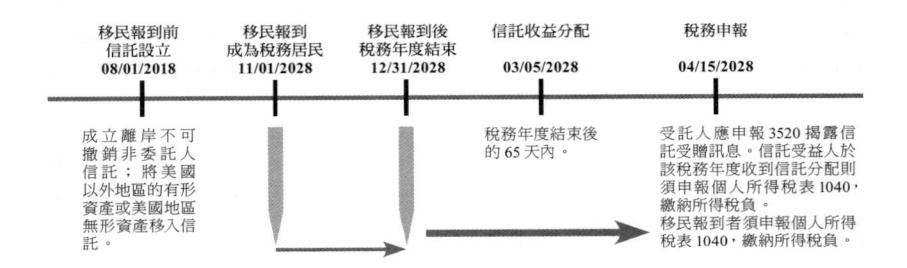

- **移民報到前信託設立 08/01/2018**：成立離岸不可撤銷非委託人信託；將美國以外地區的有形資產或美國地區無形資產移入信託。
- **移民報到成為稅務居民 11/01/2028**
- **移民報到後稅務年度結束 12/31/2028**
- **信託收益分配 03/05/2028**：稅務年度結束後的65天內。
- **稅務申報 04/15/2028**：受託人應申報3520揭露信託受贈訊息。信託受益人於該稅務年度收到信託分配則須申報個人所得稅表1040，繳納所得稅負。移民報到者須申報個人所得稅表1040，繳納所得稅負。

傳承架構建議

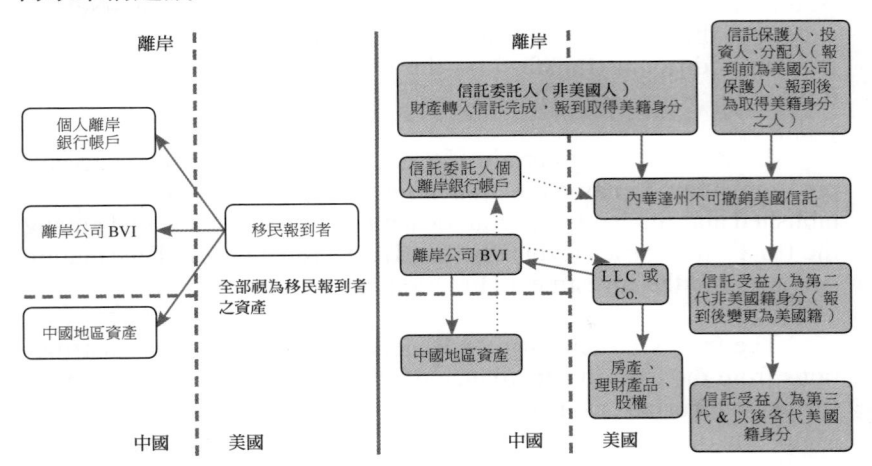

（左圖：中國 / 美國）
- 個人離岸銀行帳戶
- 離岸公司 BVI
- 中國地區資產
- 移民報到者（全部視為移民報到者之資產）

（右圖：離岸 / 中國 / 美國）
- 信託委託人（非美國人）：財產轉入信託完成，報到取得美籍身分
- 信託委託人個人離岸銀行帳戶
- 離岸公司 BVI
- 中國地區資產
- 內華達州不可撤銷美國信託
- LLC 或 Co.
- 房產、理財產品、股權
- 信託保護人、投資人、分配人（報到前為美國公司保護人、報到後為取得美籍身分之人）
- 信託受益人為第二代非美國籍身分（報到後變更為美國籍）
- 信託受益人為第三代 & 以後各代美國籍身分

傳承架構分析：

1. 計劃移民美國的富裕家族通常會考慮投資美國房地產。在成為美國人之前，創富者應諮詢稅務及法律顧問，商議達到兼顧稅負最小化及資產保障的可行選項。

2. 移民到美國的家族通常希望將其部分或全部財富從國外司法管轄區轉移到美國。我們通常建議擬移轉超過200萬美元的家族尋求有執照的專業人士的指導，以增加對美國稅務及法律制度

2. Families immigrating to the U.S. often wish to transfer part or all of their wealth from foreign jurisdictions into the U.S. We generally recommend families bringing in excess of $2 million seek guidance from licensed professionals to increase their understanding of the U.S. tax and legal systems.

3. For U.S.-bound individuals with significant wealth, settling a U.S. non-grantor trust may help with both minimizing applicable taxes and asset protection. Individuals with assets in excess of the lifetime U.S. gift and estate tax exemption may be subject to a 40% estate tax for assets above that threshold. The tax is levied on both assets attained before and after an individual immigrates to the U.S. Additionally, individuals who wish to make gifts or leave assets in excess of their lifetime exemption to those 37.5 years younger may face an additional transfer tax, the U.S. Generation-Skipping Tax (GST).

4. When settling certain U.S. trusts, both individuals and corporations may be named as fiduciaries. U.S. trusts are typically established and funded by its grantor with governance allocated among the trust's fiduciaries (typically, the Trust Protector, the Distribution Advisor, and the Investment Direction Advisor, among others).

The trust's Beneficiary (or Beneficiaries) may receive distributions from the trust in accordance with the trust agreement, which is further categorized as income distributions or principal distributions. Many trust agreements are drafted so that the Beneficiaries are not legally entitled to any distributions for asset protection purposes. It can be drafted so that the trust's Distribution Advisor has full discretion as to the amount of any distribution paid to the trust's Beneficiaries (or even if the Beneficiaries receive any distribution at all). Doing this would generally protect the trusts' assets from any creditors of the Beneficiaries of the trust.

Note: For a detailed explanation of the various roles and responsibilities in a U.S. Trust, please refer to the section of Chapter 2 that discusses Determining the Roles in a Nevada Irrevocable Trust.

In Directed Trusts, the Trustee generally handles the administrative and secretarial functions of the trust. It is generally advis-

的理解。

3. 對於將前往美國且擁有大量財富的個人，設立美國非委託人信託可能有助於兼顧稅負最小化及資產保護。資產超過美國贈與稅及遺產稅終身免稅額的個人，就超過額度部分的資產可能需要繳納 40% 的遺產稅。此項稅負對個人在移民美國以前及之後獲得的資產均予以課徵。此外，如果個人希望將超過終身免稅額的資產贈與或留給比自己小 37.5 歲的人，可能要另外負擔額外的美國隔代移轉稅（GST）。

4. 在設立特定類型的美國信託時，個人及公司均得被指定為受託責任人。美國信託通常由其委託人設立及資助，治理權則分配給信託的受託責任人（通常是信託保護人、分配顧問及投資指示顧問等）。

信託的受益人可根據信託合約的規定自信託獲得分配（進一步分類為分配收入或分配本金）。為保全資產，許多信託合約設計使受益人在法律上無權獲得任何分配，並且置入信託的分配顧問對支付給信託受益人的任何分配金額有絕對裁量權的條款。如此通常得保障信託資產使其免受信託受益人之債權人的主張。

注：有關美國信託中各種角色及責任的詳細說明，請參閱第二章有關「決定內華達州不可撤銷信託中的角色」的段落。

在指示型信託中，受託人通常負責信託的行政及秘書職能。我們多會建議創富者尋求有專業執照的信託公司作為受託人。如此可以確保信託受到持續的管控，且各種秘書職能受到監督。擔任指示型信託受託人的信託公司通常收取固定的年費，而非按所管理資產的一定百分比收取費用。

5. 由於來自非美國人所獲之贈與通常免稅，考慮贈與超過

able for Wealth Creators to seek out the services of a licensed Trust Company to act as the Trustee. Doing so ensures that there is ongoing oversight of the trust and that the various secretarial functions are being monitored. Trust companies serving as Trustee of directed trusts typically charge a flat annual fee rather than a percentage of assets under administration.

5. While gifts from non-U.S. persons are often tax-free, Wealth Creators who are considering gifts above $2 million (USD) should consider making the gift to a trust for the intended Beneficiary, rather than making a gift directly to the Beneficiary. Since the recipient of the gift is the trust itself rather than an individual, the trustee of the trust would file Form 3520 to report the gift. As a trust receiving large sums is more common, it is less likely to be scrutinized than if an individual were to receive the large gift.

6. U.S. persons receiving distributions from or controlling foreign trusts often face unfavorable or even punitive U.S. income tax consequences. As such, Wealth Creators seeking to immigrate the U.S. should consider unwinding their non-U.S. trusts in favor of U.S. trusts. Even Wealth Creators who are not personally seeking to immigrate to the U.S. but have U.S. descendants should consider shifting their assets into U.S. trusts, as they are generally more protective of U.S. descendants both from an asset protection perspective and from a U.S. tax perspective. When structured properly, moving assets into a U.S. trust can lead to (1) a clearer wealth transfer structure, (2) preferable tax treatment, (3) stronger asset protection and (4) lower ongoing maintenance costs (relating to both Trustee fees and accounting and disclosure requirements).

200萬美元的創富者應考慮贈與給指定受益人信託，而不是直接贈與給該受益人；由於受贈人是信託本身而不是個人，信託的受託人須填寫3520表申報此項贈與。相較於個人接受大額贈與，信託接受大額資金較為常見，因而在此情況下受到審查的可能性較小。

6. 從外國信託獲得分配或控制外國信託的美國人經常面臨不利或甚至懲罰性的美國所得稅後果。因此，尋求移民美國的創富者應考慮解除其外國信託而改採美國信託。即使是個人不打算移民美國但後代具有美國身分的創富者，亦應該考慮將其資產轉移到美國信託，因為從資產保護及美國稅務的角度來看，美國信託通常更保護具美國身分的後代。若妥當規劃，將資產轉移到美國信託可帶來（1）更清晰的財富轉移架構，（2）較有利的稅務待遇，（3）較有力的資產保護，及（4）較低的維持成本（與受託人費用、會計及揭露要求有關）。

NOTE :

第二章

美國不可撤銷朝代信託
U.S. Irrevocable Dynasty Trusts

What is a Dynasty Trust and how is it relevant to me?

A Dynasty Trust is a trust settled with the primary purpose of transitioning wealth from one generation to one or more future generations. An irrevocable Dynasty Trust simply implies that gifts made by the Grantor to the trust are not distributable back to the Grantor at the Grantor's discretion, but rather controlled by fiduciaries appointed by the Grantor to protect and manage for the benefit of the trust's beneficiaries, often the Grantor's U.S.-based descendants or relatives.

Few vehicles can compare to a U.S. Dynasty Trust when it comes to passing down familial wealth from one generation to future generations. This is especially true in countries with a transfer tax (a tax on wealth transfers between individuals). Transferring wealth in the U.S. is especially pricey, generally costing 40% or more of the wealth being transferred either through a gift tax or through an estate tax. As such, Wealth Creators based in the U.S. often must consider ways to maximize their lifetime gift and estate tax exemption ($13.61 million for individuals and double for married couples in 2024).

Fortunately for first generation non-U.S. Wealth Creators, the U.S. tax code has built in certain exceptions from U.S. transfer taxes. In addition, they may also be exempt from U.S. income tax if income derived is sourced from non-U.S. sources. When properly structured, a Dynasty Trust should serve the purposes of transferring wealth and minimizing transfer taxes.

Why should I establish an irrevocable trust, rather than a revocable one? Does it make a difference where I settle my U.S. trust?

The U.S. Irrevocable Trust is one such vehicle that, when properly structured, has the ability to shelter assets from U.S. transfer taxes almost indefinitely. It does so by having the Grantor transfer assets to the trust irrevocably, thereby completing a gift. After the gift is completed, the Grantor is no longer the legal owner of the assets transferred.

Non-U.S. Wealth Creators should consider seeking counsel

甚麼是朝代信託？它與我有何相關？

朝代信託（Dynasty Trust）是以財富傳承到下一代或多個世代為主要目的的信託。不可撤銷的朝代信託是指，委託人一旦贈與資產給信託，委託人即無法任意將該資產分配回給委託人。該資產將在委託人所指派的受託責任人的控制下為信託受益人（通常是委託人在美國的後代或親屬）之利益進行保護及管理。

在家族財富世代傳承的工具中，很少有工具可以與美國朝代信託相比擬，尤其在實施轉讓稅（就個人間轉讓財富所課徵的稅）制度的國家更為顯著。在美國轉讓財富的代價高昂，通常須負擔轉讓財產價值40%或更高的贈與稅或遺產稅。因此，在美國的創富者須經常思考如何最大化使用其贈與稅及遺產稅的終生免稅額（2024年個人遺產稅終生免稅額為1,361萬美元，夫妻免稅額則是個人免稅額的兩倍）。

幸而美國稅法給予非美籍第一代創富者在特定例外狀況下無須負擔美國的轉讓稅，且如果該創富者之所得非屬美國來源所得，亦可免除美國所得稅的負擔。藉由適當的規劃，朝代信託應能幫助創富者達成財富傳承及避免轉讓稅的目標。

為甚麼要選擇設立不可撤銷信託，而不是可撤銷信託呢？在美國哪個州設立美國信託有何差別？

美國的不可撤銷信託是一種財富傳承工具，如果規劃得當，幾乎可以無限期地使資產在美國不被課徵轉讓稅。其運作方式是由委託人將資產不可撤銷地移轉給信託，進而完成贈與。在贈與完成後，委託人將不再是該轉讓資產法律上的所有權人。

非美國創富者在進行贈與時應考慮尋求法律諮詢，尤其是涉

when making gifts, especially as it relates to completed gifts because they are irrevocable by definition and can quite easily trigger a gift tax (40%+ of the value of the gift) when the gift consists of U.S.-situs assets. In contrast, gifting non-U.S. situs assets into a U.S. Irrevocable Trust generally does not incur any gift tax. Furthermore, even if these non-U.S. situs assets are liquidated and reinvested in U.S. situs assets, the Grantor's death should not trigger any U.S. estate tax for assets previously gifted.

Each U.S. state has different regulations regarding the governance of trusts, with certain states being more favorable trust jurisdictions than others. In certain states, rules against perpetuities are in place, defining a definite lifespan for trusts; in other states, trust income may be taxed at high rates. Many Asian Wealth Creators choose to establish their trusts in Nevada or Delaware.

This chapter explores the U.S. irrevocable trust in detail; specifically, it addresses the purpose(s) of establishing a U.S. irrevocable trust, the tax ramifications of a U.S. irrevocable trust and how control of the U.S. irrevocable trust is distributed.

In summary, U.S. irrevocable trusts, when structured as directed trusts, often allow non-U.S. persons to make gifts to U.S. descendants while (1) allowing for the assets to be controlled and protected by trusted persons assigned as fiduciaries and (2) protecting future generations from U.S. transfer taxes. Wealth Creators who seek to permanently transfer assets into the U.S. for the benefit of U.S. beneficiaries should evaluate the merits of such a trust.

Why do Grantors select directed trusts when passing down their wealth?

Many irrevocable Dynasty Trusts are structured as directed trusts, especially those settled by Asian Wealth Creators. In the U.S., the Trustees have historically held many of the key management powers within Dynasty Trusts, including the power to allocate the trust's investments and the power to determine the trust's distributions. Over time, however, many Wealth Creators realized that they would rather have trusted and named fiduciaries make those deci-

及到完全贈與時,因為完全贈與本質上是不可撤銷的,且當贈與的資產包含美國境內資產時,很容易引發贈與稅(可能高達贈與資產價值的 40% 以上)。相反地,將非美國境內資產贈與給美國不可撤銷信託通常不會產生任何贈與稅。此外,即使被贈與的非美國境內資產被變現並重新投資於美國境內資產,委託人去世時也不會使之前贈與給信託的非美國境內資產被課徵美國遺產稅。

美國每個州對於信託管理的規定不同,特定幾州在信託法方面的規範相較下更有利於傳承規劃,例如某些州的信託法訂有反永續規則(Rule against Perpetuality),因而限制信託的存續期間;某些州以高稅率就信託所得徵稅。總括考量下,許多亞洲創富者選擇在內華達州或德拉瓦州設立信託。

本章將詳細探討美國不可撤銷信託,具體說明設立美國不可撤銷信託的目的、稅務影響以及如何配置對信託的控制權。

綜上所述,被建構為指示型信託的美國不可撤銷信託通常能讓非美國人士在向美籍後代移轉資產的同時,(1)讓資產在值得信賴而被指派為受託責任人的控制及保護之下,且(2)讓後代免於承擔美國轉讓稅。若創富者有意為美籍受益人的利益永久性地將資產轉移到美國,應將此類信託的優點納入考量。

委託人如何利用指示型信託達成財富世代傳承的目的?

亞洲創富者多半利用指示型信託來建構不可撤銷朝代信託。在美國,受託人過往在朝代信託中握有許多關鍵管理權,包括信託投資決策權及決定信託收益的分配權。然而隨著時間的演進,許多創富者意識到,他們更希望由值得信賴的指定受託責任人,而非與他們的價值觀不見得一致的受託人來做決定。此外,當受

sions, rather than Trustees that may or may not have similar values aligned with their beliefs. Furthermore, when Trustees must make investment or distribution decisions on behalf of trusts, the potential legal liabilities of Trustees are noticeably increased, which leads to higher maintenance fees usually pegged as a percentage of total assets under administration.

While Wealth Creators who set up trusts in the U.S. typically seek to transfer their assets to their descendants or family members, trusts in Asia are often settled with the sole intent of directing assets towards investments. Many Asia-based financial advisors at large financial institutions sell trusts as a way to market their investment products. In the vast majority of these trusts, the trustee holds a tremendous amount of power over the trust and the trust agreement is almost always drafted to benefit the trustee or its affiliate, which frequently earns revenue as a percentage of assets held. Furthermore, financial advisors typically have little to no room for modifications in the trust agreement's templated language, reducing the clients' ability to tailor the contract to their needs.

In contrast to their Asian counterparts, U.S. trusts are typically drafted by qualified attorneys for the sole benefit of the clients themselves. While this process requires a separate legal fee (billed either as a flat fee or an hourly fee), as attorneys do not earn revenue based on assets managed like an investment manager does, the trust agreement is tailored to the client's specific needs. This usually means that the Wealth Creators have more say as to who will hold the powers to invest and distribute the trust's assets.

As such, U.S. trusts may suit the needs of these Wealth Creators more. In U.S. directed trusts, the Grantor gets to appoint fiduciaries that can control substantially all operations of the trust, often leaving trustees with purely administrative functions such as keeping track of the trust's paperwork and signing off on the trust's tax forms. As the trustee's control over the trust is minimized, the trustee's liability is also minimized, leading to lower fees (often a flat annual fee, rather than a fee based on a percentage of assets).

託人必須為信託做出投資或分配決策時,受託人潛在的法律責任會明顯增加,進而導致受託人收取更高的信託維護費用(通常以信託資產的一定百分比計算)。

　　許多創富者在美國設立信託的主要目的是為了順利傳承其資產予後代或家族成員,但在亞洲的信託通常會被引導為以投資為目的而設立。許多亞洲大型金融機構的財務顧問向客戶銷售信託服務,並將信託做為推銷其投資產品的管道。這些信託中的絕大多數,受託人對信託持有極大的權力,且信託合約幾乎都是為受託人或其關聯方(通常賺取受託資產一定百分比作為收入)的利益而撰擬。此外,財務顧問通常僅有極小或甚至沒有權限修改信託合約的制式條款,從而降低客戶根據自身需求制定信託合約的可能性。

　　相較於亞洲的信託,美國信託的合約通常是由具備該州執照的律師專為客戶的利益而撰擬。雖然此過程需要支付額外的法律費用(按固定費用或鐘點計費),但由於律師不同於銀行的投資經理人藉由管理信託資產來賺取收入,因此信託合約會根據客戶的具體需求進行客製化,而這通常意味著創富者對於誰能握有信託資產的投資及分配的決策權有更大裁量空間。

　　綜上所述,美國信託可能更合適創富者的資產傳承需求。在美國的指示型信託架構下,委託人可以指派受託責任人(保護人、投資指示顧問及分配顧問)控制信託絕大部分的運作,而受託人通常僅剩單純的行政功能,如掌握信託的書面文件及核可信託的稅務表格。由於受託人對信託的控制權限縮,受託人所承擔的責任也因此降低,連帶讓信託維護費用下降(通常是固定的年費,而不是按受託資產價值百分比計算費用)。

Relevant Considerations

A trust is generally established for the benefit of its Beneficiaries. The trust's Grantor appoints a Trustee to manage the administration of trust assets. Typically, at the time the trust is formed, the Grantor appoints relevant fiduciaries and assigns various powers to each fiduciary.

This structure allows the Grantor's descendants and / or other named Beneficiaries to benefit from trust distributions (as determined by the Distribution Advisor), without the trust assets being directly includible in the Beneficiaries' personal assets. When structured properly, creditors of trust Beneficiaries are not able to enforce their claims against the assets held in a trust.

A Dynasty Trust may be structured as a Grantor Trust or Non-Grantor Trust for U.S. income tax purposes. A trust is generally considered a "Grantor Trust" if the Grantor is liable for paying income taxes on the trust's income. A trust is considered a "Non-Grantor trust" if the trust's Grantor is not liable for income taxes attributable to the trust's income.

Under the U.S. Federal Income Tax regime, a U.S. trust is generally treated as a U.S. income tax resident. The IRC clearly defines a U.S. trusts for U.S. income tax purposes under IRC §§ 7701(a)(30)(E) and (31)(B), effected in 1996. A trust is a U.S. trust when both of the following conditions are satisfied. A trust is considered a foreign trust if either of the two following conditions are not satisfied.

1. A court within the U.S. is able to exercise primary supervision over the administration of the trust (commonly referred to as the "Court Test") AND

2. One or more U.S. persons have the authority to control all substantial decisions of the trust (commonly referred to as the "Control Test").

Thus, by definition, a U.S. trust is a trust governed by U.S. courts and has a U.S. person controller. Furthermore, a foreign trust, by definition, is a trust that does not fulfill either the Court Test or the Control Test and thus, cannot be considered a U.S. trust. To establish a U.S. trust, the Court and Control Tests are often satisfied by trust agreements that:

相關考量

信託通常是為了受益人的利益而設立，信託的委託人會任命受託人來管理信託資產的行政事務。通常在信託成立時，委託人會任命相關的受託責任人（保護人、投資指示顧問以及分配顧問）並分配各種權力給每位受託責任人。

這種架構安排使委託人的後代及／或其他指定受益人從信託的分配中受益（由分配顧問決定），但信託資產不會直接納入受益人的個人資產。如果信託的架構安排得當，受益人的債權人將無法對信託中的資產進行追償。

從美國所得稅法角度，朝代信託可以被架構為委託人信託或非委託人信託。如果委託人需要為信託的所得負責申報納稅，則該信託通常被認定為「委託人信託」；如果委託人不就信託所得負責申報納稅，則該信託會被認定為「非委託人信託」。

美國聯邦所得稅體制下，美國信託通常被視作美國所得稅法上的居民。自1996年起，《美國聯邦稅法》在第7701(a)(30)(E)及(31)(B)條為美國所得稅目的明確定義了何謂「美國信託」。當信託通過以下兩個測試時，該信託會被認定為美國信託；如果信託無法通過以下任一個測試，則該信託會被認定為外國信託：

1. 美國法院能夠對信託的管理進行主要監督（通常稱作「法院測試」）和

2. 一個或多個美國人有權控制信託的所有重大決策（通常稱作「控制測試」）。

因此，根據定義，美國信託是受美國法院管轄並由美國人控制的信託。此外，根據定義，外國信託因為不符合法院測試或控制測試，所以不能被認為是美國信託。為了設立美國信託，通常

1. state explicitly that a U.S. court has jurisdiction;
2. have one or more U.S.-based Trustee, whom together, have substantial control over the administration of the trust; and
3. have one or more U.S. persons or U.S.-based corporations (generally U.S. LLCs or C-Corporations) control all substantial decisions.

When these conditions are met, a trust is considered to be a U.S. trust and governed by both U.S. Federal laws and State laws (usually in the state the trust is established). For U.S. taxpayers, a U.S. trust is frequently preferable to a Foreign Trust, especially as it relates to income tax purposes (with a limited exceptions for certain Foreign Trusts settled by non-U.S. persons). In trust agreements where the Trust Protector holds substantially all relevant powers, the Trust Protector must be a U.S. person (or U.S. corporation) for the trust to be a U.S. trust.

In accordance with Treasury Reg. 301-7701-7(d)(2), if a U.S. Trustee is replaced by a foreign Trustee, the trust is allotted 12 months to replace the Foreign Trustee with a U.S. Trustee to maintain U.S. trust status. If the change is not made within the 12 months specified, the trust will be treated as a Foreign Trust from the date the Trustee changes.

How does an Irrevocable Trust established in the U.S. compare with an Irrevocable Trust established outside of the U.S.?

In prior decades, numerous Wealth Creators, often persuaded by their private bankers and financial advisors, have settled irrevocable trusts outside of the U.S. These trusts are frequently settled in less established jurisdictions (the Cayman Islands, BVI, Bermuda or Cook Islands, among others) and may have ambiguous legal situs. While often marketed as tools to help safeguard and invest assets for the next generation, these trusts often failed to accomplish its preset goals.

Over the years, descendants of these Wealth Creators have immigrated to the U.S., either receiving a U.S. citizenship or green card; however, this information is rarely if ever considered when

會藉由信託合約的設計來通過法院測試及控制測試,因此信託合約必須有以下條款:

1. 明確載明美國法院具有管轄權;

2. 任命一個或多個美國受託人,其共同對信託的管理具有實質性控制權;及

3. 任命一個或多個美國人或美國公司(通常是美國有限責任公司或股份公司)來控制所有重大決策。

當這些條件滿足時,信託即被認定為美國信託,並受美國聯邦法律及州法(通常是信託設立的州)管轄。對於美國納稅人而言,當涉及所得稅議題時,美國信託通常比外國信託更受青睞(少數由非美國人設立的特定外國信託除外)。提醒注意,在信託合約中,如果信託保護人握有管理信託的大部分權力,則信託保護人必須是美國人(或美國公司)才能使信託成為美國信託。

此外,根據《財政部法規》第 301-7701-7(d)(2) 條規定,如果美國受託人被外國受託人取代,信託得在 12 個月內重新指派美國受託人取代外國受託人,以維持其美國信託的地位。如果在指定的 12 個月內未能更換為美國受託人,則該信託將從受託人變更成外國受託人之日起被視為外國信託。

美國境內設立的不可撤銷信託與美國境外設立的不可撤銷信託有何不同?

在過去幾十年中,許多創富者常在私人銀行家及財務顧問的勸說下,於美國境外設立不可撤銷信託。這些信託通常設立在建置較不完善的司法管轄區(例如開曼群島、英屬維京群島、百慕達或庫克群島等),且其法律管轄權地也可能不明確。雖然這些

crafting the family's estate plan. Unbeknownst to many of these Wealth Creators, trusts established outside of the U.S. often do not serve the needs of their U.S.-based descendants and could potentially have calamitous tax consequences for their U.S. beneficiaries.

By decanting assets from an offshore irrevocable trust (one established outside of the U.S.) to a U.S.-based one, the Wealth Creator's family can protect the trust's assets more thoroughly and reduce its annual trust maintenance expenditures.

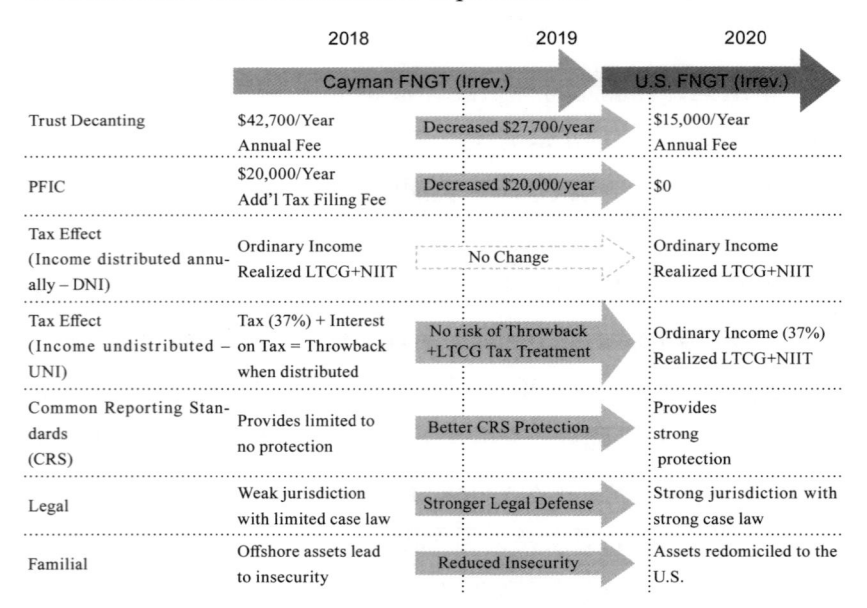

	2018 — Cayman FNGT (Irrev.)	2019	2020 — U.S. FNGT (Irrev.)
Trust Decanting	$42,700/Year Annual Fee	Decreased $27,700/year	$15,000/Year Annual Fee
PFIC	$20,000/Year Add'l Tax Filing Fee	Decreased $20,000/year	$0
Tax Effect (Income distributed annually – DNI)	Ordinary Income Realized LTCG+NIIT	No Change	Ordinary Income Realized LTCG+NIIT
Tax Effect (Income undistributed – UNI)	Tax (37%) + Interest on Tax = Throwback when distributed	No risk of Throwback +LTCG Tax Treatment	Ordinary Income (37%) Realized LTCG+NIIT
Common Reporting Standards (CRS)	Provides limited to no protection	Better CRS Protection	Provides strong protection
Legal	Weak jurisdiction with limited case law	Stronger Legal Defense	Strong jurisdiction with strong case law
Familial	Offshore assets lead to insecurity	Reduced Insecurity	Assets redomiciled to the U.S.

*LTCG refers to long-term capital gains, generally taxed at 20% for trusts
*NIIT refers to net investment income tax, generally taxed at 3.8% for trusts

境外信託通常被標榜為幫下一代保護及投資資產的工具,但這些境外信託往往未能達到原先預設的目標。

在前述境外信託設立並經過多年營運後,這些創富者的後代可能已取得綠卡或美國公民身分並移民美國;然而,在擬訂家族傳承計劃時卻很少或從未考慮到此變化。許多創富者不瞭解在美國境外設立的信託通常不能滿足其美國後代的需求,並可能對其美國受益人產生災難性的稅務後果。

此時,如果能進行信託資產轉注,亦即將資產從美國境外設立的不可撤銷信託轉移至美國境內的信託,創富者的家族可以更徹底地保護信託資產,並降低其年度信託維護費用。

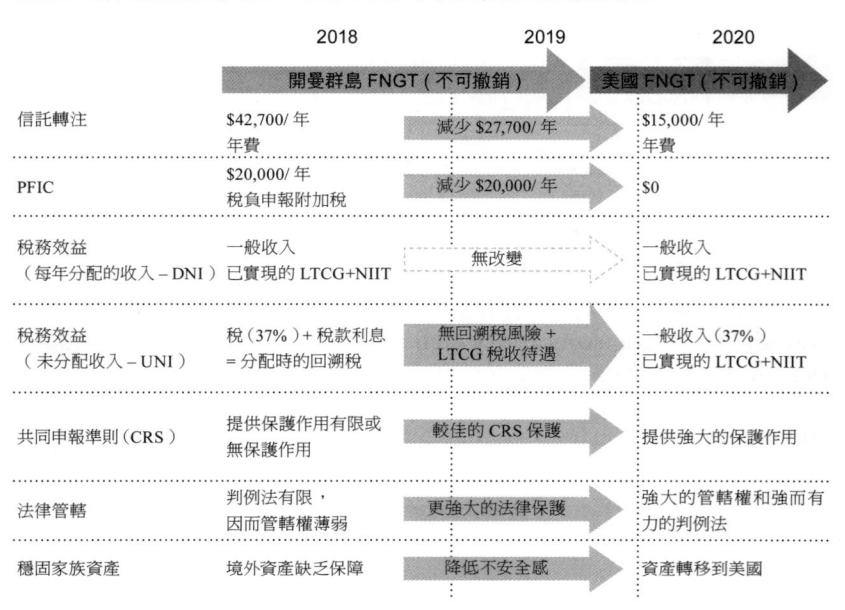

	2018 開曼群島 FNGT（不可撤銷）	2019	2020 美國 FNGT（不可撤銷）
信託轉注	$42,700/年 年費	減少 $27,700/年	$15,000/年 年費
PFIC	$20,000/年 稅負申報附加稅	減少 $20,000/年	$0
稅務效益（每年分配的收入 – DNI）	一般收入 已實現的 LTCG+NIIT	無改變	一般收入 已實現的 LTCG+NIIT
稅務效益（未分配收入 – UNI）	稅(37%)+稅款利息 = 分配時的回溯稅	無回溯稅風險 + LTCG 稅收待遇	一般收入(37%) 已實現的 LTCG+NIIT
共同申報準則(CRS)	提供保護作用有限或無保護作用	較佳的 CRS 保護	提供強大的保護作用
法律管轄	判例法有限, 因而管轄權薄弱	更強大的法律保護	強大的管轄權和強而有力的判例法
穩固家族資產	境外資產缺乏保障	降低不安全感	資產轉移到美國

*LTCG（Long-Term Capital Gains）是指長期資本利得,信託的 LTCG 通常按 20% 的稅率徵稅
*NIIT（Net Investment Income Tax）是指淨投資收入稅,信託的 NIIT 通常按 3.8% 的稅率徵稅

Illustrative Nevada Irrevocable Trust

* Managers or Directors of LLCs and Corporations may be the fiduciaries or beneficiaries of the irrevocable trust.

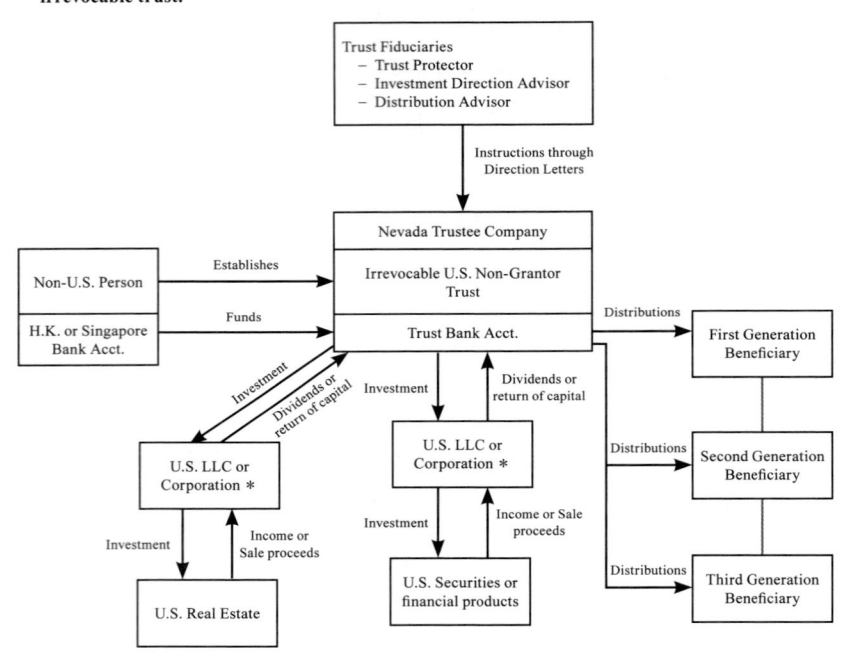

The above trust is settled by a non-U.S. person in Nevada. A Nevada Trust Company is selected as Trustee. The trust's beneficiaries, designated by the grantor, are all U.S. persons. The trust invests in multiple wholly-owned LLCs and / or C-Corporations. These companies are invested in U.S. securities, time deposits and real estate.

內華達州不可撤銷信託示例

＊有限責任公司和公司的經理或董事可以是不可撤銷信託的受託責任人或受益人。

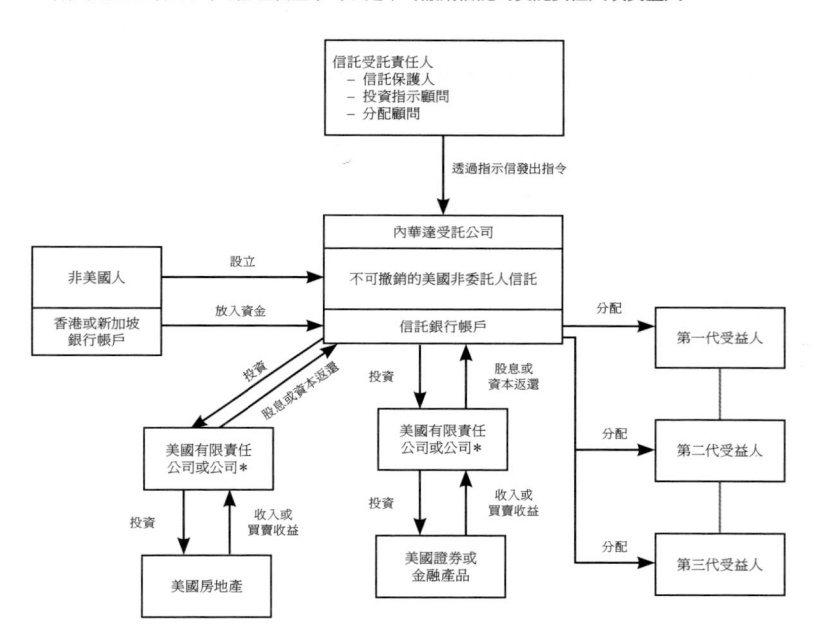

```
                    ┌─────────────────┐
                    │  信託受託責任人   │
                    │  - 信託保護人    │
                    │  - 投資指示顧問  │
                    │  - 分配顧問      │
                    └────────┬────────┘
                             │ 透過指示信發出指令
                             ▼
┌──────────┐   設立   ┌─────────────────┐
│  非美國人 │────────▶│   內華達受託公司  │
├──────────┤         │  不可撤銷的美國   │   分配   ┌──────────┐
│香港或新加坡│ 放入資金 │   非委託人信託   │────────▶│第一代受益人│
│ 銀行帳戶 │────────▶│   信託銀行帳戶   │         └──────────┘
└──────────┘         └─────────────────┘              │
        ▲投資  股息或    投資▼ ▲股息或              分配│
        │     資本返還        資本返還           ┌──────────┐
        │                                       │第二代受益人│
   ┌──────────┐              ┌──────────┐       └──────────┘
   │美國有限責任│              │美國有限責任│            │
   │公司或公司＊│              │公司或公司＊│         分配│
   └──────────┘              └──────────┘       ┌──────────┐
     投資│ ▲收入或           投資│ ▲收入或       │第三代受益人│
         │ │買賣收益             │ │買賣收益     └──────────┘
         ▼ │                    ▼ │
   ┌──────────┐              ┌──────────┐
   │ 美國房地產 │              │ 美國證券或 │
   │           │              │ 金融產品   │
   └──────────┘              └──────────┘
```

　　上圖的信託是由一位非美籍人士在內華達州設立，並選任一家內華達州信託公司為受託人，此外，由委託人指定的信託受益人全部為美國人。該信託持有多家獨資有限責任公司及／或股份公司，再由這些公司持有美國證券、定期存款及房地產的投資。

Should I still consider establishing a U.S.-based trust if I have no U.S.-based descendants?

Wealth Creators with no U.S.-based descendants should consider establishing a Foreign Non-Grantor Trust in the U.S (see structure below).

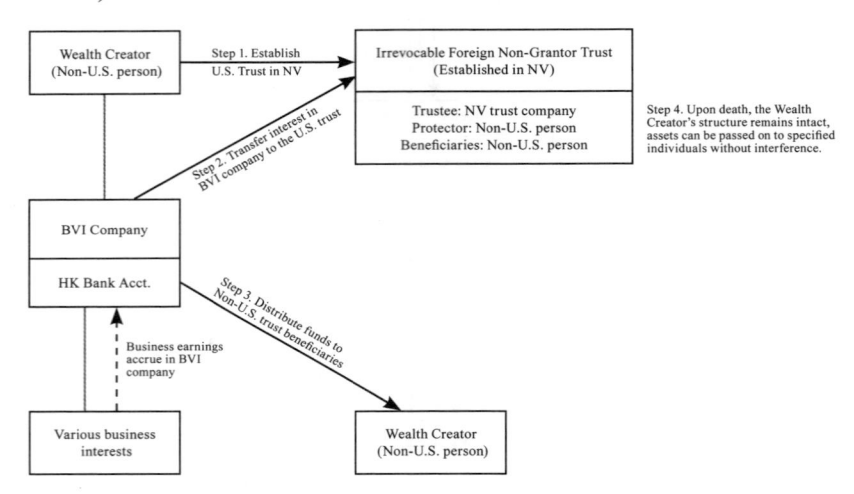

```
Wealth Creator          Step 1. Establish        Irrevocable Foreign Non-Grantor Trust
(Non-U.S. person)       U.S. Trust in NV         (Established in NV)

                        Step 2. Transfer         Trustee: NV trust company        Step 4. Upon death, the Wealth
                        interest in BVI          Protector: Non-U.S. person       Creator's structure remains intact,
                        company to the U.S.      Beneficiaries: Non-U.S. person   assets can be passed on to specified
                        trust                                                     individuals without interference.

BVI Company

HK Bank Acct.           Step 3. Distribute funds to
                        Non-U.S. trust beneficiaries

    Business earnings
    accrue in BVI
    company
                                                 Wealth Creator
Various business                                 (Non-U.S. person)
interests
```

By using this structure, the Wealth Creator attains several key benefits, without incurring additional expenses.

(1) The Wealth Creator is able to continue to operate his or her business(es) as if the trust were not created. Even though ownership of the BVI company has already been transferred to the trust, the Wealth Creator can continue to serve as the company's director and control the company's operations.

(2) The Wealth Creator is able to make distributions from his or her BVI company to the trust's non-U.S. beneficiaries, without incurring U.S. income tax. The only form that is required by the U.S. is FINCEN Form 114 (FBAR); additional information regarding the FBAR can be found in Chapter 4.

(3) The Wealth Creator is able to choose the trust's beneficiaries. After transferring assets into the trust, the assets would no lon-

如果我沒有美籍後代，我仍須考慮設立美國信託嗎？

創富者若沒有美籍後代則應該考慮在美國設立外國非委託人信託。

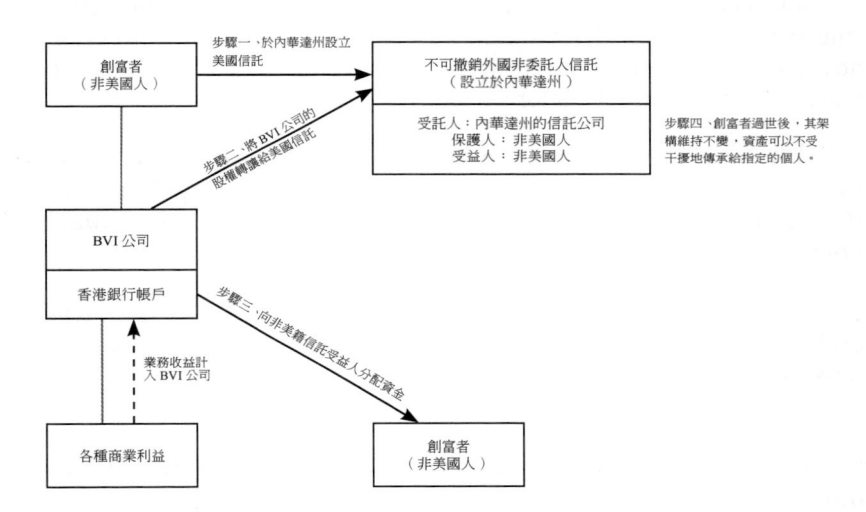

```
創富者                步驟一、於內華達州設立      不可撤銷外國非委託人信託
（非美國人）           美國信託                  （設立於內華達州）

                                              受託人：內華達州的信託公司      步驟四、創富者過世後，其架
                     步驟二、將BVI公司的          保護人：非美國人              構維持不變，資產可以不受
                     股權轉讓給美國信託          受益人：非美國人              干擾地傳承給指定的個人。

BVI公司

香港銀行帳戶                      步驟三、向非美籍信託受益人分配資金

         業務收益計
         入BVI公司                              創富者
                                              （非美國人）
各種商業利益
```

藉由以上的信託架構，創富者得保有以下多項主要利益，並避免產生額外費用：

（1）儘管 BVI 公司的所有權已經轉移給信託，創富者仍可繼續擔任公司董事並控制公司的運營，猶如信託並未設立一般。

（2）創富者能從其 BVI 公司向信託的非美籍受益人進行分配，而不會產生美國所得稅。唯一需要提交的表格是美國財政部金融犯罪執法網的 114 號表格（FBAR）；有關 FBAR 的更多資訊請參見第四章。

（3）創富者得選擇信託的受益人。轉入信託的資產將不再被認定為創富者遺產的一部分，因此通常不受規範遺產分配的法律約束。

ger be considered part of the Wealth Creator's estate and thus would generally not be subject to laws that regulate the distribution of one's estate.

(4) The Wealth Creator is able to choose the trust's fiduciaries (the trust protector, distribution advisor and investment direction advisor), thereby determining who will have the power to direct the trust after the Wealth Creator's death.

(5) Since the trust is based in the U.S. (usually in Nevada) and the U.S. does not participate in the Common Reporting Standards (CRS), the trust's beneficial ownership interest information would not be shared to other countries.

(6) The cost of maintaining the structure is relatively low, generally less than US$10,000 per year. This is significantly lower than most structures created outside of the U.S.

1 – Establishing a Nevada Irrevocable Trust (General Procedures)

While there are numerous benefits to settling an Irrevocable Trust, Wealth Creators, especially non-U.S. ones, often face considerable difficulty when selecting a firm to work with. When non-U.S. Wealth Creators set out to create a trust, they usually must contact the following service providers:

(1) A law firm or attorney that specializes in drafting trust agreements, frequently called the "drafter"

(2) A law firm or attorney that specializes in cross-border taxation and estate planning, usually called the "tax attorney"

(3) An accounting firm or accountant that can assist with specific disclosures, tax forms and tax returns required of the IRS and other U.S. agencies

(4) A secretarial company that can assist with the creation or transfer of offshore or U.S. companies into U.S. trusts

(5) A secretarial company that can work closely with banks in Hong Kong, Singapore or other jurisdictions on transfers of funds into U.S. accounts

（4）創富者得選擇信託的受託責任人（信託保護人、分配顧問及投資指示顧問），從而決定在創富者去世後，誰將有權管理信託。

（5）由於信託設立在美國（通常在內華達州），而美國未參與共同申報準則（CRS），因此信託的受益所有權資訊不會與其他國家共用。

（6）此信託架構的維持成本通常每年不到 1 萬美元，相較大多數設立在美國境外的信託架構來得低。

1 – 設立內華達州不可撤銷信託（一般程序）

雖然設立不可撤銷信託有諸多好處，但對非美籍創富者而言，在選擇合作的事務所時往往會面臨相當大的困難，因為非美籍創富者在設立信託時，通常必須聯繫以下專業服務提供者：

（1）專門撰擬信託合約的律師事務所或律師（通常稱為「合約撰擬者」）。

（2）專門從事跨境稅務及資產規劃的律師事務所或律師（通常稱為「稅務律師」）。

（3）協助處理美國國稅局或其他政府單位所要求之特殊揭露申報、稅務表格及稅務申報的會計師事務所或會計師。

（4）協助設立離岸／美國公司，或將這類公司轉入美國信託的秘書公司。

（5）與香港、新加坡或其他司法管轄區的銀行密切合作，協助將資金轉入美國帳戶的秘書公司。

由於這些服務提供者通常都會對客戶的需求、資金來源以及與現有客戶（特別是律師事務所）是否存在利益衝突進行盡職

Each of these service providers will typically conduct their own due diligence on the clients' needs, source of funds and any conflicts with existing clients (for the law firms). As a result, many non-U.S. Wealth Creators may find the process quite daunting. This is especially true when the wealth transfer process takes a number of years or when clients have drastic changes in their life circumstances.

The complexities of the structures necessary for non-U.S. persons to optimize their estate planning may also frequently result in miscommunication, delays in the setup process, difficulties in maintaining various holding structures and even the creation of inoperable structures, if the different service providers are communicating directly with the client only and not with each other.

The authors of this book are all managers of a global accounting and law firm headquartered in Taiwan. Over the past decade, we have worked with numerous U.S. and non-U.S. Wealth Creators on creating their succession plans, establishing over 150 trusts. As an integrated firm with offices in the U.S. and licensed professionals across Asia, we provide clients with services encompassing essential functions necessary for planning cross-border wealth transfer.

The above chart illustrates the steps necessary to establishing a U.S. irrevocable trust. While each client situation may require substantial customizations, the timeline is generally an estimate of the time each step will take.

調查，許多非美籍創富者面對這些繁瑣的調查程序可能會備感艱辛。這種精神上的消耗，在費時數年的財富移轉過程中，或在創富者的生活發生劇烈變化時尤為明顯。

非美籍人士若是為滿足其資產規劃而使用複雜的信託架構，也常常會衍生出溝通不良、設立期程延誤、以及難以維持各種持股架構等問題，甚而，如果不同的服務提供者僅與客戶進行縱向溝通而未與其他服務提供者進行橫向聯繫，還可能導致設立的信託無法順利運作。

本書的主筆舉家為總部設立於台灣的全球性會計暨法律事務所之專業經理人。過去十多年期間，與許多美籍與非美籍創富者合作，為其制定傳承計劃，並設立超過 150 個信託。作為一家在美國設有辦事處並在亞洲配置專業證照人員的整合型事務所，我們為客戶提供的服務兼具規劃跨境財富轉移所必備的主要功能。

前述圖表說明設立美國不可撤銷信託所需的步驟。由於可能須針對每位客戶的狀況對信託架構量身訂製，下頁時間表僅對每個步驟所需時間進行概括估計。

Party						Detailed Description	1
Client	Multifamily Office / CPA	U.S. Trust Attorney (in State of Trust)	U.S. Corporate Attorney (in State of Company)	U.S. Tax Attorney	Trustee		1 2 3 4 5 6 7 (days)
O	O					Confirm engagement and client representation.	
O	O					Collect client information through trust questionnaire(s) and identification document(s).	
O	O					Collect company setup information through questionnaires.	
		O	O			Draft client KYC paperwork and organize client's source of wealth documentation.	
		O				Complete Form W-8BEN and Form W-9 for non-U.S. persons and U.S. persons, respectively.	
		O				Based on information collected, draft initial structure and trust agreement(s).	
O	O	O				Discuss client's structure and preliminary trust agreement(s).	
	O	O	O			Further customize trust agreements to client's specific structural, legal and tax requirements.	
O	O			O		Discuss the tax implications of the client's structure and trust agreement(s).	
	O				O	Send applicable setup documentation to the trust company.	
O	O				O	Receive notarized trust agreement and other relevant doucments and complete trust setup.	
	O				O	Open a trust custodial account at the trust company for each trust.	
	O				O	Apply for the trust's Employment Identification Number (EIN) from the U.S. Internal Revenue Service (IRS).	
	O				O	Provide the trust's EIN to the trustee.	
	O	O				Draft deed of gift and direction letter.	
O	O				O	Transfer funds into trust's custodial account.	
	O				O	Send direction letter to trustee for each gift made to the trust.	
	O				O	Transfer funds from the trust's custodial account to the wholly-owned LLC or C-Corp.	

第二章 美國不可撤銷朝代信託

Timeline for Establishing a Protector Company

Party						Detailed Description	1
Client	Multifamily Office / CPA	U.S. Trust Attorney (in State of Trust)	U.S. Corporate Attorney (in State of Company)	U.S. Tax Attorney	Trustee		1 2 3 4 5 6 7 (days)
O	O					Collect company setup information through company setup questionnaires.	
		O	O			Register a new company with the applicable Secretary of State in the U.S. (typically in Nevada).	
	O					Apply for the Company's Employment Identification Number (EIN) from the U.S. Internal Revenue Service (IRS).	
	O		O			Prepare corporate documents (such as bylaws, annual report, stock ledger and / or operating agreement).	
O	O					Request client signatures for applicable documents for company setup.	
	O	O				Fill in the company's name as the initial trust protector in the trust agreement.	

Timeline for Establishing an Operating Company

Party						Detailed Description	1
Client	Multifamily Office / CPA	U.S. Trust Attorney (in State of Trust)	U.S. Corporate Attorney (in State of Company)	U.S. Tax Attorney	Trustee		1 2 3 4 5 6 7
O	O					Collect company setup information through company setup questionnaires.	
		O	O			Register a new company within the U.S. to hold investments (typically a C-Corp. or a LLC).	
	O					Apply for the Company's Employment Identification Number (EIN) from the U.S. Internal Revenue Service (IRS).	
	O					Prepare corporate documents (such as bylaws, annual report, stock ledger and / or operating agreement).	
	O		O			Request client signatures for applicable documents for company setup.	
	O					Open bank account(s) for U.S. C-Corp. or LLC(s).	

第二章 美國不可撤銷朝代信託　　89

2	3	4	5	6	7	8
8 9 10 11 12 13 14 (days)	15 16 17 18 19 20 21 (days)	22 23 24 25 26 27 28 (days)	29 30 31 32 33 34 35 (days)	36 37 38 39 40 41 42 (days)	43 44 45 46 47 48 49 (days)	50 51 52 53 54 55 56 (days)

2	3	4	5	6	7	8
8 9 10 11 12 13 14	15 16 17 18 19 20 21	22 23 24 25 26 27 28	29 30 31 32 33 34 35	36 37 38 39 40 41 42	43 44 45 46 47 48 49	50 51 52 53 54 55 56

參與人員						工作事項說明	1
客戶	聯合家族辦公室／會計師	美國信託律師（信託設立州）	美國公司律師（公司設立州）	美國稅務律師	受託人		1234567（天）
O	O					確認客戶委任及其代表窗口	
O	O					透過信託設立問卷及客戶身分證明文件收集客戶資訊	
O	O					透過問卷調查收集公司設立資訊	
		O	O			撰寫客戶的 KYC 報告並釐清客戶財富來源	
	O					填寫 W-8BEN 表格（適用於非美國人士）或填寫 W-9 表格（適用於美國人士）	
		O				根據收集的資訊草擬信託架構圖及信託合約初稿	
O	O	O				向客戶解說信託架構圖以及信託合約初稿	
		O	O	O		根據客戶的具體架構、法律及稅務需求進一步客製化信託合約	
O	O			O		與客戶討論信託架構以及信託合約的稅務影響	
	O				O	將信託設立文件送交受託公司	
O					O	接收經過公證的信託合約及其他相關文件，並完成信託設立	
	O				O	在受託公司開設信託的託管帳戶	
	O				O	向美國國稅局申請信託的雇主識別號碼（EIN）	
	O				O	提供信託的 EIN 給受託公司	
	O	O				草擬贈與合約及指示信	
O	O				O	將資產移入信託的託管帳戶	
	O				O	就每筆贈與給信託的資金向受託公司寄發指示信	
	O				O	將資金從信託的託管帳戶中轉入信託持有的獨資公司（LLC 或是 C-Corp.）	

第二章 美國不可撤銷朝代信託

2	3	4	5	6	7	8
8 9 10 11 12 13 14（天）	15 16 17 18 19 20 21（天）	22 23 24 25 26 27 28（天）	29 30 31 32 33 34 35（天）	36 37 38 39 40 41 42（天）	43 44 45 46 47 48 49（天）	50 51 52 53 54 55 56（天）

設立保護人公司之時間表

參與人員						工作事項說明	1
客戶	聯合家族辦公室／會計師	美國信託律師（信託設立州）	美國公司律師（公司設立州）	美國稅務律師	受託人		1 2 3 4 5 6 7（天）
O	O					透過公司設立問卷收集公司設立資訊	
	O		O			向美國州政府（通常在內華達州）註冊一家新公司作為信託的保護人	
	O					向美國國稅局（IRS）申請公司的雇主識別號碼（EIN）	
	O		O			準備公司文件（如章程、年度報告、股東名冊及／或運營協議）	
O	O					請客戶簽署公司設立的相關文件	
	O	O				在信託合約中填入公司名稱作為首任信託保護人	

設立營運公司之時間表

參與人員						工作事項說明	1
客戶	聯合家族辦公室／會計師	美國信託律師（信託設立州）	美國公司律師（公司設立州）	美國稅務律師	受託人		1 2 3 4 5 6 7
O	O					透過公司設立問卷收集公司設立資訊	
	O		O			在美國註冊一家新公司（通常是 C-Corp. 或 LLC）以持有投資	
	O					向美國國稅局（IRS）申請公司的雇主識別號碼（EIN）	
	O					準備公司文件（如章程、年度報告、股東名冊及／或運營協議）	
	O		O			請客戶簽署公司設立的相關文件	
	O					為 U.S. C-Corp. 或 LLC 開立銀行帳戶	

第二章 美國不可撤銷朝代信託

2	3	4	5	6	7	8
8 9 10 11 12 13 14 （天）	15 16 17 18 19 20 21 （天）	22 23 24 25 26 27 28 （天）	29 30 31 32 33 34 35 （天）	36 37 38 39 40 41 42 （天）	43 44 45 46 47 48 49 （天）	50 51 52 53 54 55 56 （天）

2	3	4	5	6	7	8
8 9 10 11 12 13 14	15 16 17 18 19 20 21	22 23 24 25 26 27 28	29 30 31 32 33 34 35	36 37 38 39 40 41 42	43 44 45 46 47 48 49	50 51 52 53 54 55 56

2 – Determining the Roles in a Nevada Irrevocable Trust

When establishing a U.S. trust, the Wealth Creator must take into consideration the roles that must be assigned and their powers in the trust. Generally, a trust has the following roles:
- Trustee (typically a licensed trust company)
- Grantor (otherwise known as Settlor)
- Fiduciaries
  - Protector
  - Investment Direction Advisor
  - Distribution Advisor
- Beneficiaries

When selecting a trust company, the Wealth Creator should do research on the types of trusts the trust company services, the services they offer and their credibility and reputation. While trustees can be individuals residing in the trust's jurisdiction, we highly recommend that Wealth Creators engage the services of a professional and licensed trust company. Individuals may not understand the inner workings of a trust, may not adequately service the family's needs, or handle the trustee's legal responsibilities and may not even comply with the legal requirements set forth by the trust jurisdiction.

The structure below introduces the trust agreement and the roles defined by a trust agreement:

2 – 決定內華達州不可撤銷信託中的角色

當創富者在設立美國信託時,必須考慮需要指派的角色及其在信託中所具有的權力。一般而言,信託架構中會有以下角色:

- 受託人(通常是具備專業執照的信託公司)
- 委託人(也稱為設立人)
- 受託責任人
    - 保護人
    - 投資指示顧問
    - 分配顧問
- 受益人

在選擇信託公司時,創富者應研究該信託公司提供的信託種類、提供的服務內容及其信譽與聲望。雖然居住在信託管轄地的個人得擔任受託人,但我們仍強烈建議創富者聘請專業、具備執照的信託公司提供服務,因為個人可能不瞭解信託的內部運作,無法充分滿足創富者家族的需求或處理受託人應負的法律責任,甚至可能未遵循信託管轄地的法律規定。

下圖概述信託合約的架構及其定義的角色:

Trustee
- Article 7 Trustee's Powers
- Article 8 Exclusive Duties of Trustee
- Article 14 Trustee's Commissions
- Article 15 Resignation, Removal and Appointment of Trustees
- Article 22 Liability of Trustee
- Article 25 Acknowledgment By Trustee

Trust
- Article 1 Trust Management
- Article 2 Grantor / Non-Grantor Trust Status
- Article 3 Rule Against Perpetuities
- Article 4 Incapacity of Beneficiary
- Article 5 Alienation
- Article 6 Trust Additions and Mergers
- Article 12 Payment of Death Taxes and Administration Expenses
- Article 16 Subchapter S Stock
- Article 18 Definitions
- Article 19 Controlling Law
- Article 20 United States Trust
- Article 23 Bonds, Accountings, and Privacy Provisions
- Article 24 Binding Effect
- Article 26 Agreement in Counterparts
- Article 27 No Contest Provision

Fiduciaries
- Article 9 Investment Direction Adviser
- Article 10 Trust Protector
- Article 11 Distribution Adviser
- Article 13 Waiver of Prudent Investor Rule
- Article 17 Interested Fiduciary
- Article 21 Limitation on Powers

Grantor

Beneficiaries

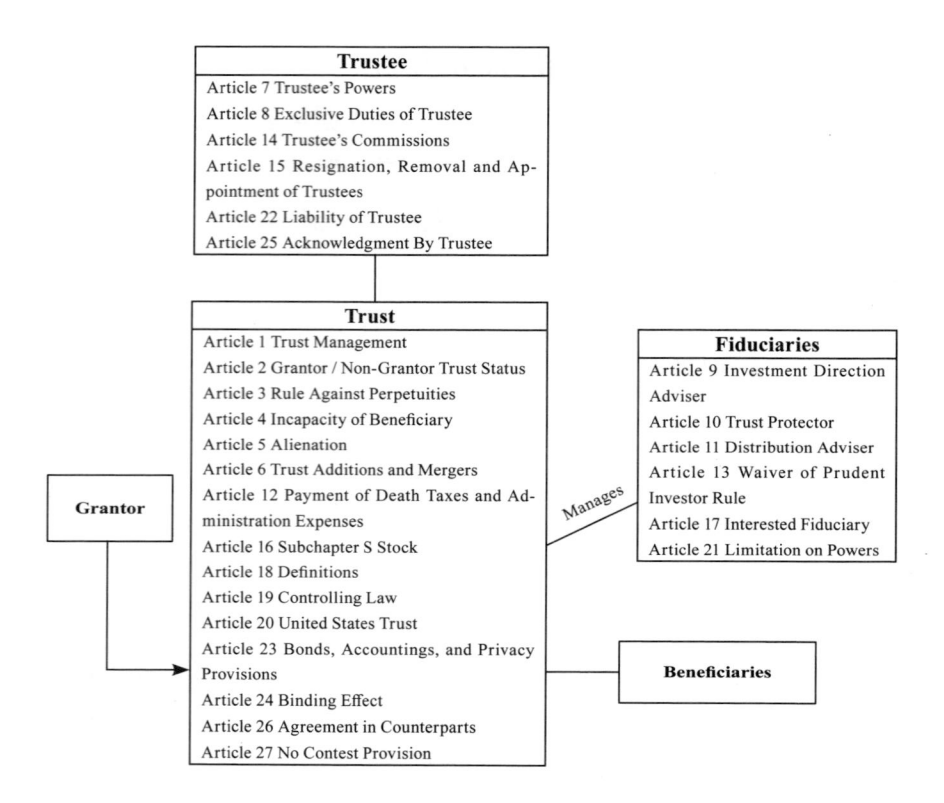

Manages

Most trust agreements are drafted so that each power holder (each of the roles) is independent of both the grantor and the beneficiaries. The main purpose of this independence is to separate the trust assets from the assets of both the grantor and the beneficiaries. By doing so, the structure minimizes the risk of triggering various taxes. Primarily, trust attorney(s) would consider the following factors when determining whether a trust can maintain independence (though other rules may apply for specific situations):

1. The trust should be so drafted so that the trust's grantor(s) and beneficiaries are not allocated powers, that could result in the trust either being treated as a sham trust or being deemed as a certain grantor or beneficiary's assets for both U.S. income tax purposes and / or U.S. estate tax purposes.

2. In many irrevocable trust agreements, the grantor(s) and beneficiaries of the trust are prohibited from determining the trust's

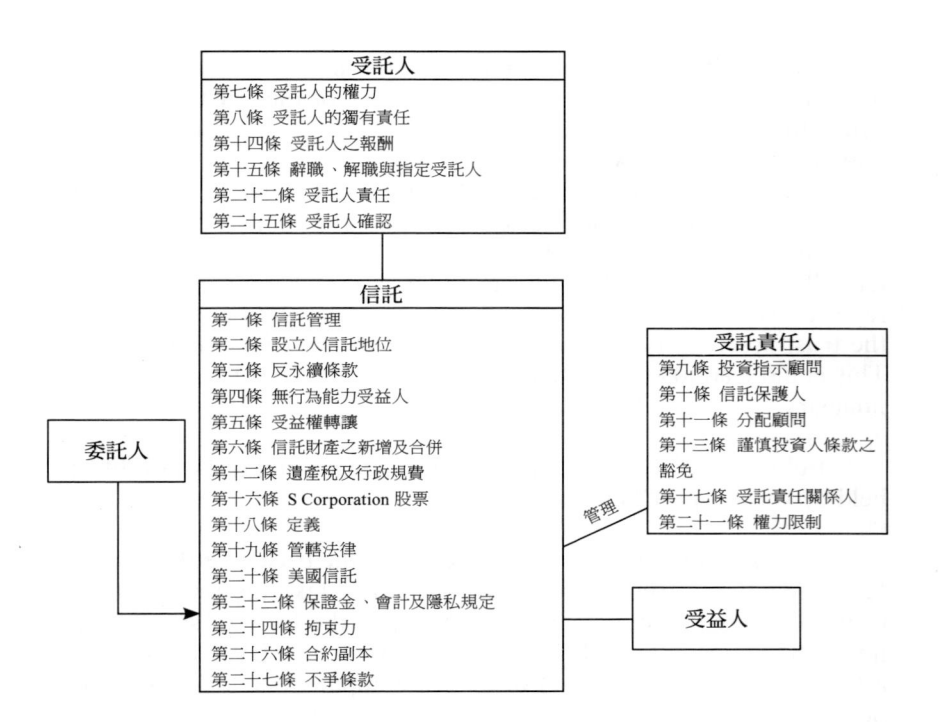

```
┌─────────────────────────────────┐
│           受託人                  │
├─────────────────────────────────┤
│ 第七條  受託人的權力              │
│ 第八條  受託人的獨有責任          │
│ 第十四條 受託人之報酬             │
│ 第十五條 辭職、解職與指定受託人    │
│ 第二十二條 受託人責任             │
│ 第二十五條 受託人確認             │
└─────────────────────────────────┘
```

```
┌─────────────────────────────────┐          ┌─────────────────────────────┐
│           信託                    │          │        受託責任人            │
├─────────────────────────────────┤          ├─────────────────────────────┤
│ 第一條  信託管理                  │          │ 第九條  投資指示顧問          │
│ 第二條  設立人信託地位            │          │ 第十條  信託保護人            │
│ 第三條  反永續條款                │          │ 第十一條 分配顧問             │
│ 第四條  無行為能力受益人          │          │ 第十三條 謹慎投資人條款之      │
│ 第五條  受益權轉讓                │          │         豁免                 │
│ 第六條  信託財產之新增及合併      │          │ 第十七條 受託責任關係人       │
│ 第十二條 遺產稅及行政規費         │          │ 第二十一條 權力限制           │
│ 第十六條 S Corporation 股票       │          └─────────────────────────────┘
│ 第十八條 定義                     │
│ 第十九條 管轄法律                 │
│ 第二十條 美國信託                 │
│ 第二十三條 保證金、會計及隱私規定 │
│ 第二十四條 拘束力                 │
│ 第二十六條 合約副本               │
│ 第二十七條 不爭條款               │
└─────────────────────────────────┘
```

委託人 → 信託 → （管理）→ 受益人

　　　大多數信託合約在撰擬時會讓每個受託責任人在委託人及受益人間保持獨立，此獨立性的架構設計是為了讓信託資產與委託人及受益人的資產實質分離，如此便可將引發各種稅負的風險降至最低。信託律師在決定信託是否能保持獨立性時，主要會考慮以下因素（但在特定情況下須考慮其他法規對信託的影響）：

　　1.在撰擬信託合約時，應避免賦予委託人及受益人任何可能導致信託被視作虛偽信託的權力，或從美國所得稅及／或遺產稅角度，可能讓信託被視為特定委託人或受益人資產的權力。

　　2.在許多不可撤銷信託合約中，信託的委託人及受益人不得決定信託分配。雖有少數特例，但較為理想的設計應該是當前的

distributions. Preferably, the current grantor and beneficiaries would not also simultaneously serve as a fiduciary of the trust (the Trust Protector, Investment Direction Advisor or Distribution Advisor), with a few limited exceptions.

3. If the Trust Protector or Distribution Advisor are the legal parents of the trust's beneficiaries, they should not make distribution to the beneficiaries until the beneficiaries turn 21. Doing so could potentially be deemed as the fiduciary (the parent) using trust assets to replace his or her legal responsibility to raise the child and thus have the trust assets to be deemed as assets of the fiduciary (the parent). This could lead to adverse tax consequences for the trust and / or the fiduciary.

Below, we give an example of roles, powers and responsibilities held by various parties to the trusts:

The **Grantor** (sometimes referred to as the trust's Settlor) transfers assets to the trust. Assets transferred can take the form of cash (typically wired from outside the U.S.) or in the form of shares of a non-U.S. company (an offshore company, such as a BVI company or a Cayman Islands company) or a U.S. company (such as a C-Corporation or interest in an LLC). In an irrevocable trust, the Grantor typically does not have any powers that would allow him or her to manage the operations of the trust. In a revocable trust (as discussed in Chapter 3), a Grantor would typically retain the power to revoke the trust and the power to distribute trust assets to any person during his or her lifetime.

The **Trust Protector** typically holds the most power in the trust, effectively allowing him or her to determine all substantial decisions made by the trust. The Trust Protector's powers typically include the powers to:
- Replace the trust's trustee.
- Add charitable beneficiaries.
- Direct a decanting of the trust's assets.
- Direct a division of the trust into separate trusts (held for the same or different beneficiaries).
- Add individual beneficiaries (subject to certain limitations).
- Change the trust's jurisdiction (subject to certain limitations).

委託人及受益人不得同時擔任信託的受託責任人（信託保護人、投資指示顧問或分配顧問）。

3. 如果信託的保護人或分配顧問是受益人的法定父母，則不應該在受益人滿 21 歲之前進行信託資產的分配，因為任何分配可能會被認定是受託責任人（即父母）使用信託資產以替代其撫養子女的法定責任，從而使信託資產被視為是該受託責任人（即父母）的資產。此一認定可能對信託及／或受託責任人帶來不利的稅務後果。

以下我們彙整信託架構下各個角色及其權力與責任的概要說明：

委託人（有時稱為信託的設立人）：主要任務是將資產轉移到信託中。轉移的資產得為現金（通常從美國境外電匯）、非美國公司的股份（離岸公司，例如 BVI 公司或開曼群島公司）或美國公司的股份（例如股份公司或有限責任公司的權益）。在不可撤銷信託中，委託人通常沒有管理信託運作的權力；在可撤銷信託中（在第三章中討論），委託人通常保留撤銷信託的權力以及在生前將信託資產分配給任何人的權力。

信託保護人：通常在信託中擁有最大的權力，使其能有效裁決所有與信託有關的重大決定。信託保護人的權力通常包括：

- 更換信託的受託人。
- 新增慈善機構／組織作為受益人。
- 指示將信託資產轉注至其他信託。
- 指示將信託分割為多個信託（被相同或不同的受益人所持有）。
- 新增個人受益人（有一定限制）。

- Assign a successor trust protector, upon the resignation or passing of the Trust Protector.
- Add, remove, or replace the trust's Investment Direction Advisor(s) or Distribution Advisor(s).

The **Investment Direction Advisor** typically determines the trust's investments. This can include directing the trust to make investments and injecting capital into LLCs held by the trust. In certain situations, a beneficiary may be able to serve as the Investment Direction Advisor as the position does not have any say in regard to the distribution of trust assets.

The **Distribution Advisor** has the power to determine the amount and frequency of distributions to the trust's beneficiaries. As such, the trust's beneficiaries are typically forbidden from serving as the trust's Distribution Advisor.

In many trusts, the Trust Protector also serves as the Investment Direction Advisor and the Distribution Advisor. In many trusts, the Trust Protector may also have the power to determine compensation for the Investment Direction Advisor(s) and Distribution Advisor(s).

When establishing a trust, the trust company typically conducts the most diligence on the grantor. The trustee will typically request the grantor's basic information, including but not limited to:
- a copy of the grantor's passport and identification card.
- the grantor's current address.
- the grantor's phone number.
- the grantor's email.
- the name of the grantor's spouse.
- the grantor's place of birth.
- the grantor's citizenship or permanent residency (including those with dual residency or dual nationalities).

In addition, the trustee must also conduct independent diligence on the grantor's source of wealth. This often involves requesting:
- a statement regarding the grantor's intent and the trust's purpose. The statement should include how frequently the trust will distribute to its beneficiaries and the nature of such distributions (income or principal).

- 更改信託的司法管轄區（有一定限制）。
- 在信託保護人辭任或去世時指定繼任的信託保護人。
- 新增、移除或更換信託的投資指示顧問或分配顧問。

投資指示顧問： 通常決定信託的投資，得包括指示信託進行投資並向信託持有的有限責任公司注入資金。因為該職位不涉及信託資產的分配，所以在特定情況下，受益人得擔任投資指示顧問。

分配顧問： 有權決定分配給信託受益人的金額及頻繁程度，也因此，通常信託合約禁止信託受益人擔任信託的分配顧問。

在許多信託中，信託保護人也同時擔任投資指示顧問及分配顧問；在為數不少的信託中，信託保護人也有權決定投資指示顧問及分配顧問的報酬。

設立信託時，信託公司通常會對委託人進行最深入的盡職調查。受託人通常會要求委託人提供基本資訊，包括但不限於：

- 委託人的護照及身分證複印件
- 委託人目前的地址
- 委託人的電話號碼
- 委託人的電子郵件
- 委託人的配偶姓名
- 委託人的出生地
- 委託人的國籍或永久居留權（包括雙重居留權或雙重國籍）

此外，受託人還必須對委託人的財富來源進行獨立的盡職調查，故通常需要委託人提供：

- 關於委託人設立信託意向及目的的聲明書。聲明書應包括信託向受益人分配的頻繁程度以及該分配的性質（收入

- the grantor's employer.
- the grantor's job title.
- a list of companies that the grantor currently owns or manages.
- the value of assets that will be transferred into the trust.
- the grantor's resume or CV is required
- the grantor's education and or employment background.
- a written statement of the grantor's source(s) of wealth:
  - If inheritance or gift, the statement should name the grantor's giftor or ascendant and their source(s) of wealth.
  - If investment, the statement should include detailed information regarding the type and market value of the investments (if current) or date of sale and total proceeds (if past). The statement should explain when and how the investment was made.
  - If operating company, the statement should include the name of the business and a general description of the business.
  - if anyone other than the grantor were to fund the trust, the trustee would ask for information regarding the additional grantor's source(s) of wealth.

The trustee will also request information regarding the trust's beneficiaries, typically including:
- a copy of the beneficiary's passport and identification card.
- a copy of the beneficiary's social security card (if available).
- the beneficiary's place of birth.
- the beneficiary's current address (a U.S. one, if available).
- the beneficiary's phone number (a U.S. one if available).
- the beneficiary's email.
- the beneficiary's green card issuance date (if one has been issued).
- the beneficiary's citizenship or permanent residency (including those with dual residency or dual nationalities).

或本金)。
- 委託人的雇主
- 委託人的職位
- 委託人當時擁有或管理的公司名單
- 將轉入信託的資產價值
- 委託人的簡歷或履歷
- 委託人的教育及/或工作背景
- 委託人財富來源的書面聲明:
    - 如果資金來自於繼承或贈與,聲明書應包括委託人的贈與人或祖先以及其財富來源。
    - 如果資金來自於投資,聲明書應包括關於投資的類型及市場價值(若當前有投資)或出售日期及總收入(若為過去投資)的詳細資訊。聲明書應解釋投資的時間及方式。
    - 如果資金來自於經營公司的獲利,聲明書應包括公司名稱及業務的概況說明。
    - 如果資金來自委託人以外的其他人,受託人會要求該位新增委託人提供資金的來源資訊。

受託人也會索取信託的受益人資訊,通常包括:
- 受益人的護照及身分證複本
- 受益人的社會安全卡複本(如有)
- 受益人的出生地
- 受益人目前的地址(如有美國地址,則須提供)
- 受益人的電話號碼(如有美國號碼,則須提供)
- 受益人的電子郵件

Lastly, the trustee will request information from the trust's fiduciaries (including the trust protector, investment direction advisor and distribution advisor). While the trust's grantor and beneficiaries are required to provide the bulk of the information, the trust's fiduciaries must also provide certain information and documentation:
- a copy of the fiduciary's passport and identification card.
- a copy of the fiduciary's social security card (if available).
- the fiduciary's current address (a U.S. one, if available).
- the fiduciary's phone number (a U.S. one if available).
- the fiduciary's email.

While different trust companies often request information in different ways, the Wealth Creator should prepare (or have a secretarial company prepare) the documents and information above. Trust companies typically also request that a formal questionnaire be filled out by their clients.

3 – *Maintaining a Nevada Irrevocable Trust*

After the trust agreement is notarized, the Nevada Irrevocable Trust is officially settled. While this is a major milestone in the process, the fiduciaries of the trust (namely, the Protector, Distribution Advisor and Investment Direction Advisor) must now direct the Trustee and the trust's legal and accounting advisors to maintain and operate the trust. This section gives specific guidance as to how a typical irrevocable trust is operated.

- 受益人綠卡的發放日期（如已經發放）
- 受益人的國籍或永久居留權（包括雙重居留權或雙重國籍）

最後，受託人還會向信託的受託責任人（包括信託保護人、投資指示顧問及分配顧問）索取資訊。雖然信託的委託人及受益人需要提供大部分資訊，但信託的受託責任人也必須提供特定資訊及文件：

- 受託責任人的護照及身分證複本
- 受託責任人的社會安全卡複本（如有）
- 受託責任人目前的地址（如有美國地址，則須提供）
- 受託責任人的電話號碼（如有美國號碼，則須提供）
- 受託責任人的電子郵件

儘管不同的信託公司會以不同的方式索取資訊，創富者應備妥（或請秘書公司準備）上述文件及資訊。信託公司通常還會要求客戶填寫正式的問卷。

3 – 維護內華達州不可撤銷信託

信託合約經公證後，內華達州不可撤銷信託即正式成立。儘管這是過程中的重大里程碑，但信託的受託責任人（即保護人、分配顧問及投資指示顧問）必須開始指示受託人以及信託的法律及會計顧問以維護及營運信託，本節將就如何運作不可撤銷信託提出具體指引。

3A – *Applying for the Trust's EIN*

In order to perform several basic functions, the trust must apply for an Employee Identification Number (EIN) with the U.S. Internal Revenue Service (IRS). After the trust receives an EIN, it can then:
(1) open U.S. bank account(s)
(2) establish and own U.S. companies (typically LLCs and C-Corporations)
(3) file annual tax filings with the IRS

There are three frequently used methods of applying for an EIN:
(1) by completing an online application
(2) by completing an application and faxing it to the IRS
(3) by calling the IRS directly and applying over the phone

Note: For a detailed explanation of EIN application, please refer to the section of Chapter 4 that discusses the Form SS-4.

3B – *Creating and Funding a Trust Bank Account*

Once the trust's EIN is obtained, the Trustee may set up an account on behalf of the trust. The process usually takes a number of weeks, depending on the Trustee's familiarity with the client and the clients' sources of funds. At this stage, KYC (Know Your Client) is typically conducted on the client and the clients' sources of wealth. After the account is established, the Grantor(s) of the trust will generally be able to wire funds from their personal bank accounts into the trust's bank account.

If the Grantor wishes to contribute funds held by a closely held business entity, the Grantor would generally be required to distribute the funds to his or her personal account before making a gift to a trust. Wealth Creators who are unable or unwilling to do so should consult with advisors who can provide alternative ways of making the gift.

3A – 申請信託的雇主識別號碼

為使信託能順利發揮基本功能，信託必須向美國國稅局（IRS）申請雇主識別號碼（EIN）。收到 EIN 後，信託得：

（1）開設美國銀行帳戶

（2）設立美國公司（通常是有限責任公司及股份公司）並擁有其股權

（3）向美國國稅局提交年度稅務報表

申請 EIN 常用的方法有三種：

（1）線上完成申請

（2）填寫申請表並將其傳真給美國國稅局

（3）直接致電美國國稅局並透過電話申請

注：有關 EIN 申請的詳細說明，請參閱第四章中有關 SS-4 表的段落。

3B – 開立信託銀行帳戶並匯入款項

信託取得 EIN 後，受託人即可代表信託開設銀行帳戶。視受託人對客戶及其資金來源的瞭解程度，整個過程通常需要數週時間。在此階段，銀行通常會對客戶及其資金來源進行客戶身分驗證（KYC）。銀行帳戶開立後，信託委託人即得從其個人銀行帳戶將資金匯入信託的銀行帳戶。

如果委託人希望用閉鎖性企業持有的資金進行注資，委託人通常需要先將資金分配到其個人帳戶，再贈與給信託。無法或不希望按照上述方式進行的創富者應諮詢專業顧問尋求替代的贈與方式。

3C – Creating and Funding a New LLC (held by the Trust)

Upon receiving the Trust's EIN, the Investment Direction Advisor may direct the Trustee to establish an LLC held by the Trust through a direction letter. The LLC is generally set up as a single-member LLC, meaning that it has a single owner (the Trust). Depending on the state, the LLCs manager(s) may be required to complete additional paperwork.

An LLC's member is typically an LLC's legal owner or shareholder. LLCs may be set up as either manager-managed LLCs or member-managed LLCs. In manager-managed LLCs, the decision-making power is held by the managers of the LLC. Managers are usually assigned by the member upon the creation of the LLC. If managers need to be added or replaced, the member generally must sign off on any changes. In member-managed LLCs, the member (owner) is typically in charge of the operations and decision-making of the LLC.

Any decision made by a member-managed LLC that is trust-owned would require the sign off of the Trustee. As such, LLCs held by Directed Trusts are most often manager-managed to maximize operational flexibility and minimize ongoing trustee fees (apart from annual trust fees, many trustees charge a per service or per signature fee). In certain circumstances, the trust's fiduciaries or even beneficiaries may serve as manager(s) of the trust-owned LLCs.

Once the LLC is established, the LLC's manager (or member) may fill out an SS-4 Form to apply for the LLC's EIN. Upon receiving the EIN, the LLC's manager (or member) can generally create a bank account for the LLC at most U.S. commercial banks.

The funds held in the trust's bank account can then be transferred into the LLC's newly created bank account. Prior to completing a funds transfer (especially a larger one), it is typical for the Trustee to require the authentication and authorization of the Trust's Investment Direction Advisor through email or phone.

Once the LLC's bank account is funded, the LLC's manager can proceed to invest the funds in securities, real estate or other in-

3C – 新設一家有限責任公司（由信託持有）並注入資金

取得信託的 EIN 後，投資指示顧問得發出指示信要求受託人設立由信託持有的有限責任公司。此有限責任公司通常會以單一成員有限責任公司的形式設立，意即該公司只有單一所有權人（即信託）。由於各州對於設立有限責任公司的規範有別，有限責任公司的管理者可能需要完成額外的文件作業。

有限責任公司的成員（member）通常是有限責任公司的法律上所有權人或股東。有限責任公司得設定為由管理者管理（Manager-Managed LLCs）或由成員管理（Member-Managed LLCs）。在管理者管理的有限責任公司中，管理者擁有決策權；管理者通常於公司設立時由成員指派。如果需要增加或更換管理者，通常必須經由成員批准。反之，在成員管理的有限責任公司中，通常由成員（所有者）負責公司的營運及決策。

由信託持有且屬於成員管理的有限責任公司，其任何決定均應經過受託人的批准。因此，由指示型信託持有的有限責任公司通常會設計成管理者管理的有限責任公司，以將公司營運的彈性最大化；信託維持費用最小化（除了年度信託管理費外，許多受託人會依每項服務或每次簽字另外收費）。在特定情況下，信託的受託責任人，甚至信託的受益人亦得擔任信託持有的有限責任公司的管理者。

一旦有限責任公司成立，有限責任公司的管理者（或成員）得填寫 SS-4 表格為有限責任公司申請 EIN。在取得 EIN 後，有限責任公司的管理者（或成員）通常得在大多數美國商業銀行為有限責任公司開設銀行帳戶。

信託在銀行帳戶中的資金得轉入有限責任公司新開設的銀行

vestments as he or she deems appropriate. Manager-managed LLC's investments generally do not require any notification to or approval by the Trustee.

3D – Processing Trust Distributions to Beneficiaries

When a trust makes a distribution to its beneficiaries, the trust can generally do so by distributing (1) the trust's principal, (2) the trust's income or (3) a mixture of both. The categorization of income vs. principal is quite complicated and varies depending on a number of factors.

Distributions of a trust's principal is generally not taxable. Upon receipt of a principal distribution, neither the beneficiary nor the trust would be liable for Federal Income Tax. If the assets in the trust do not appreciate, the trust (and its beneficiaries) would generally not owe income tax.

If the Grantor makes a gift to the trust, the gift would be considered the trust's principal. If the trust then distributes the principal to the trust's beneficiaries immediately (prior to the principal appreciating in value or generating any income), the distribution would typically not trigger U.S. income tax.

Generally, when trust income is not distributed to its beneficiaries during a given tax year, the trust must pay income tax on that income. If the trust's income is paid to the trust's beneficiaries, the trust itself would not pay income tax on the income distributed. Beneficiaries receiving income distributions from the trust will generally receive a K-1 from the trust, indicating the amount of income received.

Trusts reach the highest federal marginal income tax rate at much lower thresholds than individual taxpayers ($14,451 for trusts vs. $578,126 for individuals in 2023), and therefore generally pay higher Federal income taxes. As such, it is generally advisable that the trust's fiduciaries evaluate distributing an irrevocable trust's income to its beneficiaries, as doing so could lower the effective income tax rate.

帳戶。在進行資金轉帳前（特別是大額資金轉帳），受託人通常會要求透過電子郵件或電話取得信託投資指示顧問的認證及授權。

當有限責任公司的銀行帳戶資金到位後，有限責任公司的管理者即得進行投資有價證券、房地產或其他其認為適當的標的。有限責任公司管理者的投資決策通常不需要通知受託人或取得受託人的批准。

3D – 處理信託對受益人的分配

當信託向其受益人進行分配時，通常可以（1）分配信託的本金、（2）分配信託的所得、或（3）同時分配本金與所得。信託所得與本金如何區分相當複雜，會因為多項因素而有所不同。

信託本金的分配通常不須納稅；在收到信託本金分配時，無論是受益人還是信託都不須繳納聯邦所得稅。如果信託內的資產沒有增值，信託（及其受益人）通常不須繳納所得稅。

如果委託人贈與資產給信託，該贈與將被視為信託的本金。如果信託在收到贈與後立即將本金分配給受益人（在本金增值或產生任何收入之前），此分配通常不會引發美國所得稅。

一般而言，如果信託在特定稅務會計年度內未向受益人分配信託所得，信託必須就該信託所得繳納聯邦所得稅。如果信託將信託所得支付給受益人，信託本身就不須對已分配的所得繳納所得稅。受益人從信託收到所得分配時，通常會一併收到來自信託的 K-1 表，該表會載明該受益人所收到的分配金額。

相較於個人納稅人，信託所適用聯邦所得稅的最高邊際稅率門檻比個人來的低（2023 年信託最高稅率的門檻為 14,451 美元，個人最高稅率的門檻則為 578,126 美元），因此，在所得相同的

3E – Complying with Disclosure Requirements

Under U.S. laws and regulations, trusts established in the U.S. must comply with certain income tax and disclosure requirements. These are described in length in Chapter 4.

3G – Transferring Assets from Another Trust

From time to time, Wealth Creators may want to transfer assets from one trust to another trust. While there are many ways of transferring assets, the most common methods are:

(1) Selling the assets from one trust to another trust.

When selling assets from one trust to another trust, Wealth Creators must make note of which asset type they are selling. For example, if the trust is selling real estate, the trust would ordinarily require the services of a title company; however, if the trust is selling the LLC that owns the real estate, the transaction is significantly simpler and can be structured as a sale of the LLC interest itself. In the U.S., the sale of certain assets generally involves a purchase agreement. In addition, the buyer would ordinarily be making the payment to the previous owner of the asset. In most situations, it is advisable for attorneys, CPAs, appraisers and / or business valuation experts to give advice regarding the value of the assets being sold.

(2) Decanting the assets from one trust to another trust.

When decanting assets from one trust to another, Wealth Creators must communicate their needs to their advisors and trustee(s). Decanting often involves a direct transfer of ownership interest from one trust to another trust. Depending on the trust and the jurisdiction, decanting assets may or may not be possible. While it is possible to decant assets from a non-U.S. trust to a U.S. trust, this can prove to be quite cumbersome and may require certain approvals and indemnities. In some situations, the Trust Protector may be able to decant assets from one trust to another trust as a way to amend certain unfavorable terms of the original trust agreement.

(3) Domesticating a trust from one jurisdiction to another jurisdiction.

In certain situations, the Wealth Creator may want to change

情況下，信託通常須繳納比個人更多的聯邦所得稅。基於節稅考量，通常會建議信託的受託責任人評估是否分配不可撤銷信託的收入給受益人，以降低所得稅的有效稅率。

3E – 遵守揭露要求

根據美國法律規定，在美國設立的信託除了應履行所得稅法上之義務，還須完成特定法律對於資訊揭露之要求，這些遵循義務將於第四章詳細介紹。

3G – 信託間的資產轉移

創富者有時可能希望將資產從一個信託移轉至另一個信託。在多種移轉信託資產的方法中，最常見的是：

（1）一個信託將資產出售給另一個信託

當一個信託出售資產給另一個信託時，創富者必須注意出售資產的類型。例如，如果信託是出售房地產，通常會需要產權公司的服務；但如果信託是出售擁有房地產的有限責任公司，則交易會簡單得多，因為可以以出售有限責任公司權益的方式完成。在美國，出售特定資產通常需要買賣契約，此外，買方通常會向賣方支付對價。在大多數情況下，我們會建議聘請律師、註冊會計師、鑑價師及/或商業估價專家就所出售資產的價值提供建議。

（2）將資產從一個信託轉注到另一個信託

當資產從一個信託轉注到另一個信託時，創富者必須將需求與顧問及受託人進行溝通。轉注通常是指將資產所有權直接從一個信託轉移到另一個信託。由於信託類型及準據法差異，資產轉注有可能無法實現。雖然將資產從非美國信託轉注到美國信託是

trust jurisdictions but continue to use the same trust agreement. In this case, the Wealth Creator can consider domesticating a non-U.S. trust or changing the trust's jurisdiction from one U.S. state to another U.S. state.

(4) Dividing one trust into two or more separate trusts (trust division).

Many trusts are designed with more than one beneficiary in mind. When the Trust Protector deems that the different beneficiaries of the trust would be served by two separate sets of fiduciaries, the Trust Protector should consider dividing the original trust. This is most commonly done if the beneficiaries of the trust consist of more than one family unit. The chart below illustrates a division in action.

可行的，但轉注的過程相當繁瑣，並且可能需要特定批准及賠償。某些情況下，信託保護人得藉由將資產從一個信託轉注到另一個信託，達到修訂原信託合約中某些不利條款的目的。

（3）將信託從一個司法管轄區遷移到另一個司法管轄區

在某些情況下，創富者可能希望使用同一份信託合約，但變更信託的司法管轄區。在這種情況下，創富者可以考慮將非美國信託美國化或將信託的司法管轄區從美國一個州變更至另一個州。

（4）將一個信託拆分成兩個或多個獨立信託（信託分割）

許多信託在設計時已考慮到多個受益人。如果信託保護人認為信託的不同受益人應由兩組不同的受託責任人管理，則保護人應考慮將原信託分割。信託分割常見於信託的受益人包含不只一個家庭單位時。下圖具體說明分割的過程。

Trust Division/Decanting

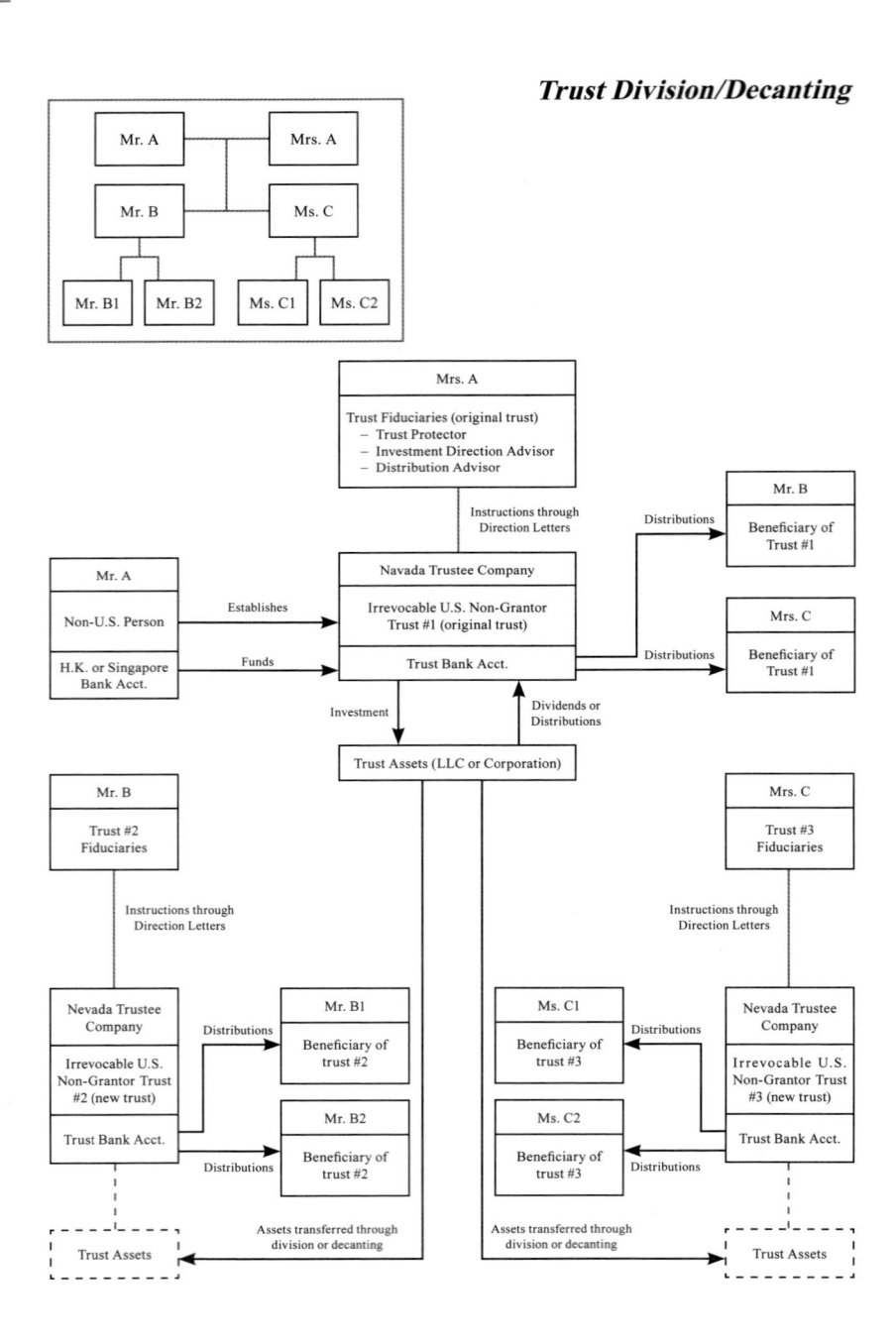

第二章 美國不可撤銷朝代信託　117

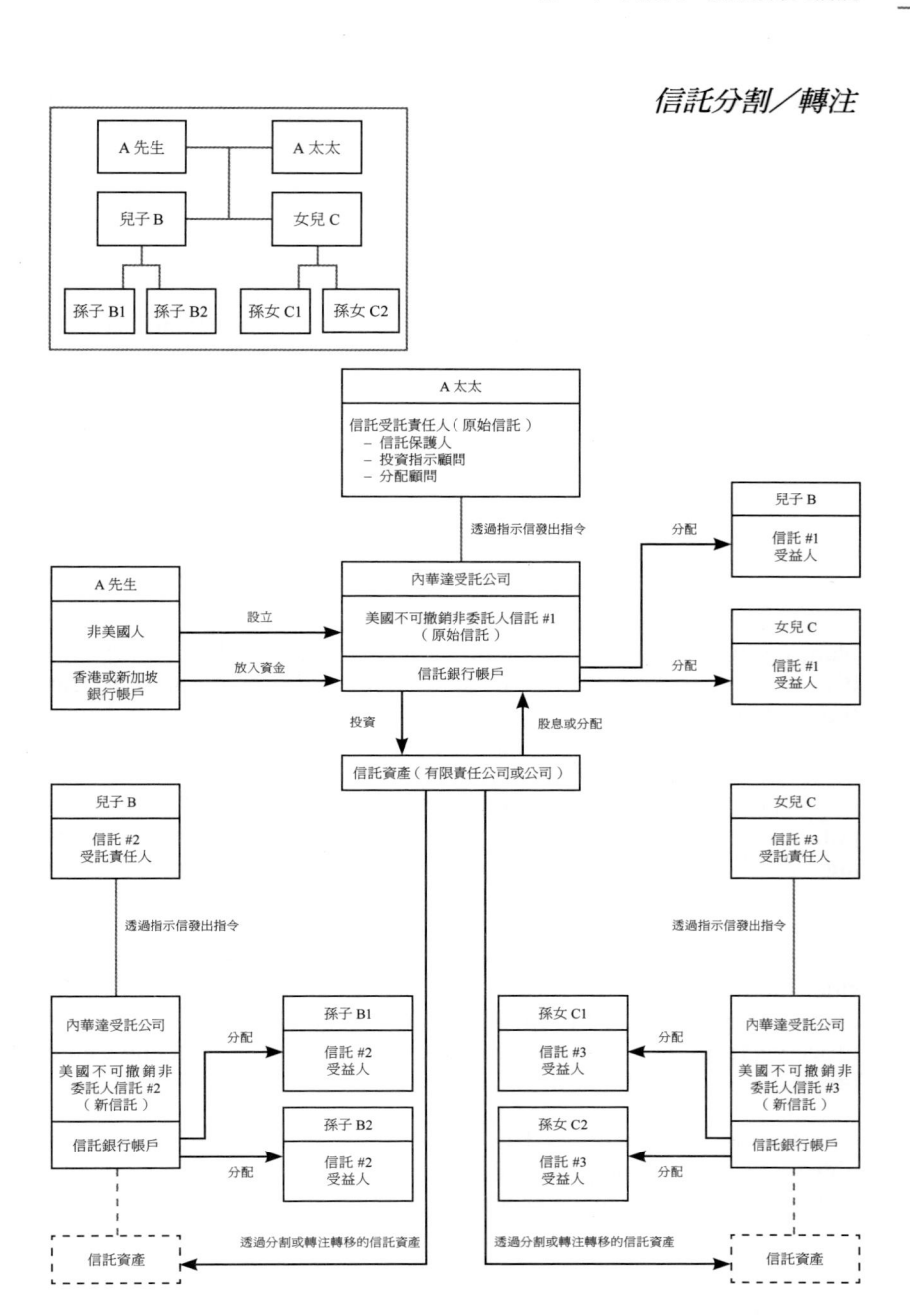

信託分割／轉注

家族關係圖：
- A 先生 — A 太太
- 兒子 B、女兒 C
- 孫子 B1、孫子 B2（兒子 B 之子女）
- 孫女 C1、孫女 C2（女兒 C 之子女）

A 太太
信託受託責任人（原始信託）
- 信託保護人
- 投資指示顧問
- 分配顧問

↓ 透過指示信發出指令

A 先生
- 非美國人
- 香港或新加坡銀行帳戶

→ 設立／放入資金 →

內華達受託公司
美國不可撤銷非委託人信託 #1（原始信託）
信託銀行帳戶

分配 →
- 兒子 B：信託 #1 受益人
- 女兒 C：信託 #1 受益人

↓ 投資　↑ 股息或分配

信託資產（有限責任公司或公司）

兒子 B
信託 #2 受託責任人
↓ 透過指示信發出指令

內華達受託公司
美國不可撤銷非委託人信託 #2（新信託）
信託銀行帳戶

分配 →
- 孫子 B1：信託 #2 受益人
- 孫子 B2：信託 #2 受益人

← 透過分割或轉注轉移的信託資產 — 信託資產

女兒 C
信託 #3 受託責任人
↓ 透過指示信發出指令

內華達受託公司
美國不可撤銷非委託人信託 #3（新信託）
信託銀行帳戶

分配 →
- 孫女 C1：信託 #3 受益人
- 孫女 C2：信託 #3 受益人

← 透過分割或轉注轉移的信託資產 — 信託資產

What is an ILIT (Irrevocable Life Insurance Trust)? How can an ILIT play a role in my estate planning?

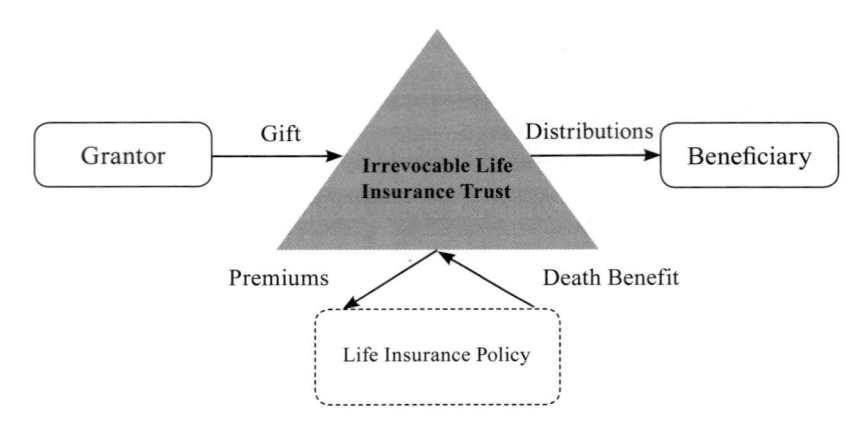

```
                          Gift                    Distributions
    ┌─────────┐  ──────────────▶   ▲   ──────────────▶  ┌─────────────┐
    │ Grantor │                   ╱ ╲                    │ Beneficiary │
    └─────────┘              Irrevocable Life            └─────────────┘
                              Insurance Trust

               Premiums                    Death Benefit
                          ┌─────────────────────┐
                          │ Life Insurance Policy │
                          └─────────────────────┘
```

Irrevocable Life Insurance Trusts (ILITs) are a popular estate planning tool in the United States, especially for high-net-worth individuals seeking to minimize estate taxes and provide liquidity for their estates. An ILIT is an irrevocable trust that contains provisions specifically designed to facilitate the ownership of insurance policies.

The ILIT is the owner and the beneficiary of the life insurance policy. If the trust is structured and managed properly, the life insurance death benefit received by the ILIT will not be subject to income or estate tax upon the insured's death.

Non-U.S. Wealth Creators with U.S. descendants should consider naming a U.S. irrevocable dynasty trust as their ILIT's beneficiary. When structured properly, this can generally effectively shield proceeds from the life insurance policy both from U.S. gift and estate taxation and creditors of the beneficiaries.

During the grantor's life, the trustee will often hold certain powers (including the power to distribute). Upon the grantor's death, distributions will be made according to the trust agreement's terms.

甚麼是不可撤銷人壽保險信託？不可撤銷人壽保險信託在遺產規劃上可以扮演甚麼樣的角色？

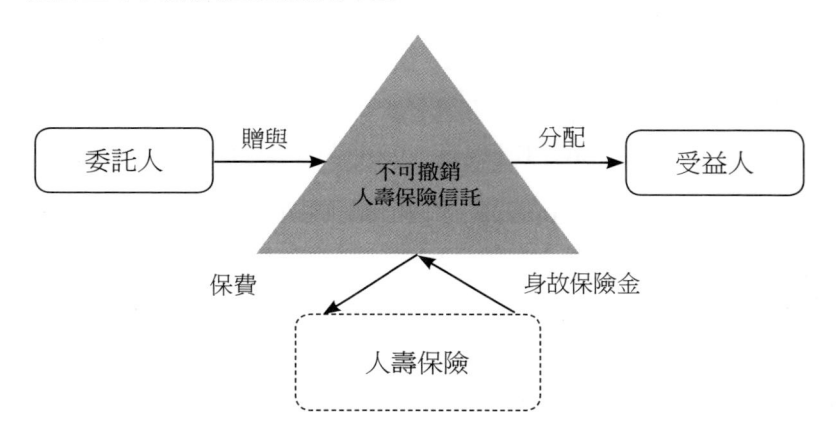

```
委託人 —贈與→ 不可撤銷人壽保險信託 —分配→ 受益人
                   ↑保費↓  ↑身故保險金
                   人壽保險
```

不可撤銷人壽保險信託（Irrevocable Life Insurance Trusts，ILITs）是一種美國流行的遺產規劃工具，特別適合那些希望減少遺產稅並為其遺產提供流動性的高淨值人士。ILIT 是一種不可撤銷的信託，信託合約會有專門為強化保單所有權而設計的條款。

不可撤銷人壽保險信託會是人壽保險單的所有人和受益人。如果信託的結構和管理得當，在被保險人死亡時，ILIT 獲得的人壽身故保險金無須繳納所得稅或遺產稅。

擁有美國籍後代的非美籍創富者應考慮讓美國不可撤銷朝代信託成為 ILIT 的受益人。如果規劃得當，這通常可以有效地保護人壽保單的保險給付，使其免於繳納美國贈與稅和遺產稅，及受益人之債權人的追索。

在委託人在世時，受託人通常會持有某些管理信託的權力（包括分配的權力）。在委託人去世後，分配將根據信託合約的條款進行。

Benefits of ILITs

1. Estate Tax Mitigation: Non-U.S. persons with U.S.-based assets may still be subject to U.S. estate taxes. U.S. persons with assets above the lifetime gift and estate tax exemption would generally also be subject to U.S. estate taxes. An ILIT can help reduce the taxable estate by removing the life insurance policy from the individual's estate.

2. Asset Protection: ILITs can provide a level of protection for assets against creditors.

3. Liquidity: Life insurance proceeds can provide liquidity to pay estate taxes, debts, and other expenses without the need to sell other assets.

Key Non-Tax Considerations

1. U.S. Situs Assets: Non-U.S. persons owning U.S.-situs assets, such as real estate or tangible personal property located in the U.S., may benefit from using an ILIT to minimize U.S. estate tax exposure.

2. Trustee Selection: The choice of trustee is critical. The trustee can generally be anyone other than the insured person. Naming an "independent trustee," such as a third-party independent trust company, may offer greater flexibility for estate planning.

3. Compliance and Reporting: ILITs established by non-U.S. persons may have additional compliance requirements, including reporting under the Foreign Account Tax Compliance Act (FATCA) and the Foreign Bank and Financial Accounts (FBAR) regulations.

不可撤銷人壽保險信託的好處

1. 降低遺產稅：擁有美國資產的非美籍人士可能仍須繳納美國遺產稅。資產超過終生贈與稅和遺產稅免稅額的美國人通常也要繳納美國遺產稅。經由設立一個 ILIT，被繼承人可以透過人壽保單將部分資產從個人遺產中移除，來減少應稅遺產。

2. 資產保護：ILIT 可以為資產提供一定程度的保護，使其免受債權人的追索。

3. 流動性：人壽保單的保險給付可以為遺產提供流動性來支付遺產稅、債務和其他費用，而無需出售其他資產。

關鍵的非稅務因素

1. 美國境內資產：非美籍人士擁有美國境內資產（例如位於美國的房地產或有形個人財產）可能會受益於使用 ILIT，來減少美國遺產稅的風險。

2. 受託人的選擇：受託人的選擇至關重要。通常受託人可以是被保險人以外的任何人。指定「獨立受託人」（例如第三方獨立信託公司），可以為遺產規劃提供更大的靈活性。

3. 法律遵循以及申報：由非美國人設立的 ILIT 可能會面臨額外的法規遵循要求，包括依《外國帳戶稅收遵從法》（FATCA）和《外國銀行和金融帳戶申報》（FBAR）進行申報。

Key Tax Considerations for U.S. Policies

Policy Issue Location	Insurer (Owner)	Insured Person	Trust Protection	U.S. Tax Consequences	Gift Tax	Income tax	Estate Tax	Remarks
U.S. Policy	U.S. Person	Same as Owner	With Trust	Owner gifts policy to trust: gift tax; Owner = insured; At death: no income or estate tax when income from policy is paid to trust	V			
			No Trust	Owner = insured; At death: there is estate tax on policy claims			V	
		Not Same as Owner	With Trust	Owner gifts policy to trust: gift tax; At owner's death: no tax	V			
				Owner gifts policy to trust: gift tax; At insured's death: no income or estate tax when income from policy is paid to trust	V			
			No Trust	At insured's death: estate tax (value of policy)				
				At Insured's Death — Beneficiary = insured; No tax				
				At Insured's Death — Beneficiary = others; there is gift tax	V			The beneficiary can be an individual or a trust
	Non-U.S. Person	Same as Owner	With Trust	Owner gifts policy to trust: No gift tax; Owner = insured; At death: no gift tax on policy claims				1. A non-U.S. gift 2. The gift transferred is in a non-U.S. jurisdiction
			No Trust	Owner = Insured; At death: No estate tax				
		Not Same as Owner	With Trust	Owner gifts policy to trust: no gift tax; At owner's death: no gift tax				
				Owner gifts policy to trust: gift tax; At insured's death: no income or estate tax when income from policy is paid to trust:			V	
			No Trust	At insured's death: estate tax (value of policy)				
				At insured's death — Beneficiary = insured: no tax				
				At insured's death — Beneficiary = someone other than the insured; no gift tax				

購買美國人壽保險的稅務考量

保單發行地點	要保人	被保人	信託保護	面臨美國稅稅務情況	贈與稅	所得稅	遺產稅	備註
美國境內保單	擁有美籍	同於要保人	使用信託	要保人有贈與稅（移入保單給信託）；要保人死亡（等同被保人死亡）；信託受益分配無所得稅、無遺產稅	V			
			無信託	要保人死亡（等同被保人死亡）：理賠金有遺產稅			V	
		不同於要保人	使用信託	要保人有贈與稅（移入保單給信託）；要保人死亡：無稅務疑慮	V			
				要保人有贈與稅（移入保單給信託）；被保人死亡：信託受益分配無所得稅、無遺產稅	V			
			無信託	要保人死亡：有遺產稅為保單價值				
				被保人死亡 — 受益人為要保人：理賠金無稅務疑慮				
				被保人死亡 — 受益人為他人：理賠金有贈與稅	V			受益人可為個人或信託
	非美籍人士	同於要保人	使用信託	要保人贈與保單給信託：無贈與稅；要保人死亡（等同被保人死亡）：無贈與稅（理賠金無贈與稅）				1. 非美籍海外贈與 2. 贈與地點在非美國本土境內
			無信託	要保人死亡（等同被保人死亡）：無遺產稅問題				
		不同於要保人	使用信託	要保人贈與保單給信託：無贈與稅；要保人死亡：無贈與稅				
				要保人贈與保單給信託：無贈與稅；被保人死亡：信託受益分配無所得稅、無遺產稅			V	
			無信託	要保人死亡：有遺產稅（保單價值）				
				被保人死亡 — 受益人為要保人：理賠金無稅務疑慮				
				被保人死亡 — 受益人為他人：理賠金無贈與稅				

Key Tax Considerations for Non-U.S. Policies

Policy Issue Location	Insurer (Owner)	Insured Person	Trust Protection	U.S. Tax Consequences	Gift Tax	Income tax	Estate Tax	Remarks
Non-U.S. Policy	U.S. Person	Same as Owner	With Trust	Owner gifts policy to trust: gift tax; At insured's death: no income or estate tax when income from policy is paid to trust.	V			1. Rev trust: policy claims are included in the estate tax 2. ILIT trust: no estate tax
			No Trust	Owner = insured; At death: there is estate tax on policy claims			V	
		Not Same as Owner	With Trust	Owner gifts policy to trust: gift tax; At owner's death: no tax	V			
			No Trust	Owner gifts policy to trust: gift tax; At insured's death: no income or estate tax when income from policy is paid to trust	V			
				At owner's death: estate tax (value of policy)			V	
			No Trust	At Insured's Death: Beneficiary = Insured; no tax				
				Beneficiary = someone other than the insured; there is gift tax on policy claims	V			
	Non-U.S. Person	Same as Owner	With Trust	Owner gifts policy to trust: no gift tax; Owner = insured; At death: no gift tax on policy claims				
			No Trust	Owner = Insured; At death: no gift or estate tax				
		Not Same as Owner	With Trust	Owner gifts policy to trust: no gift tax; At owner's death: no income or estate tax when income from policy is paid to trust				
			No Trust	Owner gifts policy to trust: no gift tax; At insured's death: no gift or estate tax when income from policy is paid to trust				
			With Trust	At owner's death: no estate tax				
			No Trust	Beneficiary = someone other than the insured; At insured's death: no gift or estate tax				

Structuring the ILIT

1. Establishing the Trust: The ILIT must be properly drafted, typically under the laws of a jurisdiction that is favorable for trust creation, such as Nevada. As an ILIT is treated as a separate entity, it apply for its own separate taxpayer identification number (typically referred to as an "EIN" or "FEIN"). All policies purchased in the name of the ILIT or transferred to the ILIT should reference the ILIT's taxpayer identification number (and not the insured's social security number) on the ownership and beneficiary forms for the life insurance policy.

2. Funding the Trust: Gifting cash or other assets to an ILIT is a common and simple funding method. U.S. persons often need to consider their lifetime gift exemptions ($13.6 million per person in 2024). When funded properly, non-U.S. persons can make gifts to an

購買非美國人壽保險的稅務考量

保單發行地點	要保人	被保人	信託保護	面臨美國稅稅務情況	贈與稅	所得稅	遺產稅	備註
美國境外保單	擁有美籍	同於要保人	使用信託	要保人有贈與稅（移入保單給信託）；要保人死亡（等同被保人死亡）；信託受益分配無所得稅、無遺產稅	V			1. 保險理賠併入遺產稅計算 2. 免遺產稅
			無信託	要保人死亡（等同被保人死亡）：理賠金有遺產稅			V	
		不同於要保人	使用信託	要保人有贈與稅（移入保單給信託）；要保人死亡：無稅務疑慮	V			
				要保人有贈與稅（移入保單給信託）；被保人死亡：信託受益分配無所得稅、無遺產稅	V			
			無信託	要保人死亡：有遺產稅為保單價值			V	
				被保人死亡 — 受益人為要保人：理賠金無稅務疑慮				
				被保人死亡 — 受益人為他人：理賠金有贈與稅	V			
	非美籍人士	同於要保人	使用信託	要保人贈與保單給信託：無贈與稅；要保人死亡（等同被保人死亡）；信託受益分配無所得稅、無遺產稅				
			無信託	要保人死亡（等同被保人死亡）：無贈與稅、無遺產稅問題				
		不同於要保人	使用信託	要保人贈與保單給信託：無贈與稅；要保人死亡：信託受益分配無所得稅、無遺產稅問題				
				要保人贈與保單給信託：無贈與稅；被保人死亡：理賠金無贈與稅、無遺產稅問題				
			無信託	要保人死亡：無遺產稅				
				被保人死亡：受益人為要保人或他人其理賠金皆無贈與稅、無遺產稅問題				

構建不可撤銷人壽保險信託（ILIT）

1. 設立信託：ILIT 合約必須經過適當的撰寫，通常是根據有利於信託創建的法律條款，如內華達州的法律。由於 ILIT 被視為一個獨立實體，需要為它申請一個獨立納稅人識別號（通常稱為 EIN 或 FEIN）。所有以 ILIT 的名義購買或轉移至 ILIT 的保單，都應在人壽保險政策的所有權和受益人表格上引用 ILIT 的納稅人識別號（而不是被保險人的社會安全號碼）。

2. 信託資金籌集：贈送現金或其他資產進 ILIT 是一種常見

ILIT free of U.S. gift tax.

3. Crummey Powers: To ensure that contributions to the trust qualify for the annual gift tax exclusion, the trust can include Crummey powers, allowing beneficiaries to withdraw contributions for a limited time. U.S. persons can generally make gifts of $18,000 to each beneficiary of the trust (in 2024) without using their lifetime gift exemptions.

Conclusion

ILITs can be a valuable tool for both U.S. and non-U.S. persons with significant assets. When purchasing a life insurance, always consult with your financial, legal and tax advisors to see if the policy is a good fit for your needs.

且簡單的注資方法，然而美國人經常需要考慮到他們的終身贈與免稅額（2024 年每人為 1,360 萬美元）。如果注資得當，非美國籍人士可以免除贈與給 ILIT 的美國贈與稅。

3. 有限領取權（Crummey Powers）：為確保對信託的注資可獲得年度贈與稅豁免，信託契約可以包括有限領取權，允許受益人在有限的時間內領取信託注資。美國人通常可以向信託的每位受益人贈與 18,000 美元（截至 2024 年），而無需使用他們的終身贈與豁免。

結語

ILIT 對於擁有大量資產的美國人和非美國人都是一種有價值的工具。在購買人壽保險時，請務必與您的財務、法律和稅務顧問進行諮詢，以確定該保單符合您的需求。

NOTE :

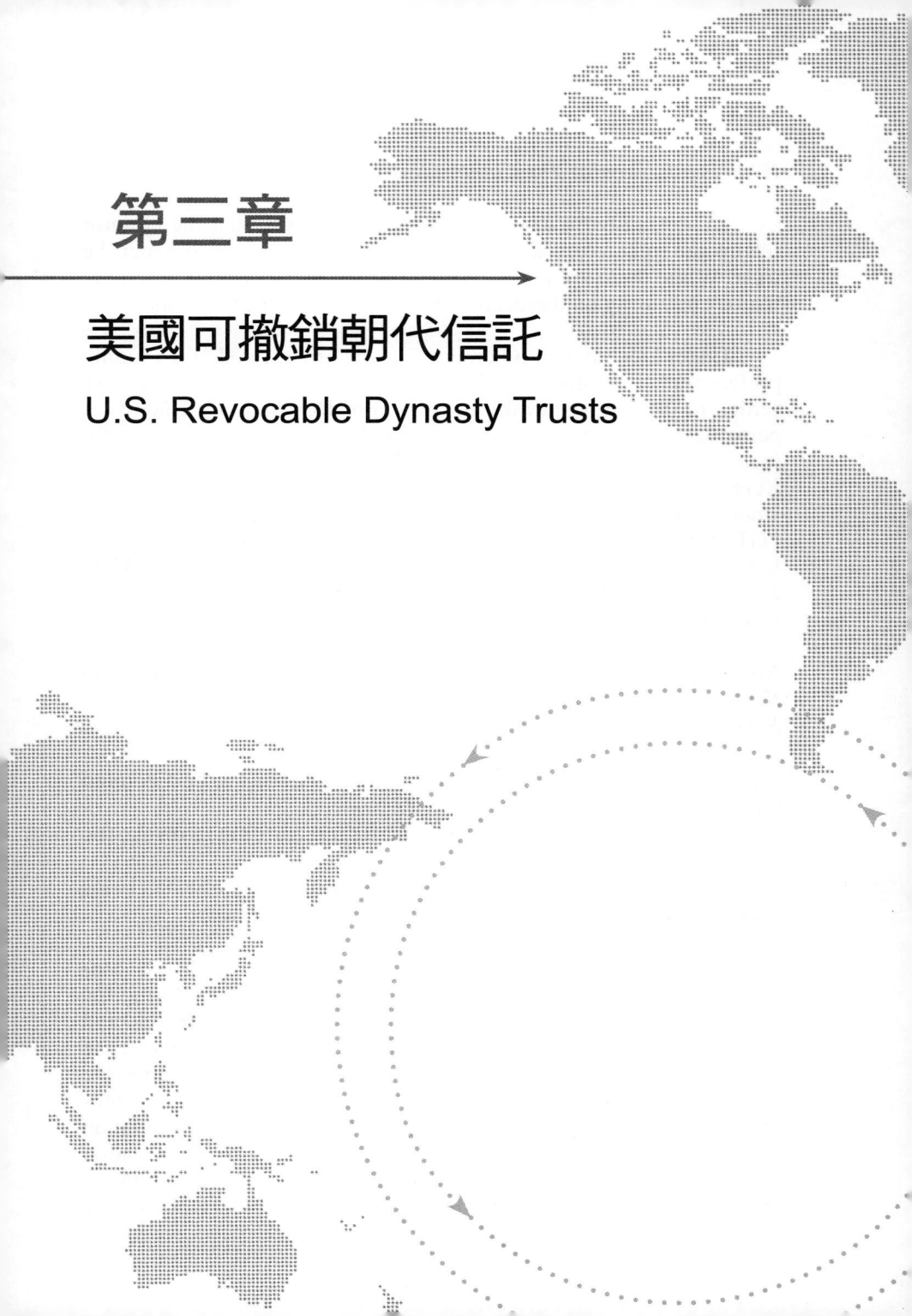

第三章

美國可撤銷朝代信託
U.S. Revocable Dynasty Trusts

What is a Revocable Trust and how is it relevant to me?

By definition, a Revocable Trust is set up so that the Grantor retains the right to revoke the trust and reclaim assets held under the trust. While there are many forms of Revocable Trusts, this chapter focuses primarily on Revocable Trusts with non-U.S. Grantors.

Under U.S. tax law, a Foreign Grantor Trust ("FGT") is a highly preferential trust structure for U.S. income tax purposes. A FGT settled in the U.S. (generally in Nevada or Delaware) by a non-U.S. person attributes income tax to the non-U.S. grantor of the trust for income tax purposes during the grantor's lifetime. Thus, if a FGT were to hold only non-U.S. assets (with no U.S.-sourced income), it would generally not be taxable in the U.S. Any distribution from an FGT, if properly structured, would be tax-free to both U.S. and non-U.S. beneficiaries. U.S. beneficiaries of a FGT must file Form 3520, as the distributions are deemed to be gifts from a non-U.S. person for U.S. tax purposes.

Note: For a detailed explanation of the Form 3520, please refer to the section of Chapter 4 that discusses the Form 1040 (including Form 3520).

There are two conditions that can qualify a trust to be a Foreign Grantor Trust:
1. During the non-U.S. Grantor's lifetime, his right to revoke the trust is unrestricted (a Revocable Trust).
2. During the non-US. Grantor's lifetime, the only beneficiaries must be the Grantor and his spouse (an Irrevocable Trust).

A FGT allows non-U.S. persons to place assets under U.S. protection without triggering U.S. income tax consequences during the grantor's lifetime. Furthermore, if assets in the FGT are selected carefully and the grantor only places non-U.S. situs assets in the FGT, the trust would also not be subject to U.S. estate taxes upon the grantor's death. Lastly, as the U.S. is not a participant in the Common Reporting Standards (CRS), as developed by the Organisation for Economic Co-operation and Development (OECD), information regarding assets held by a FGT established in the U.S. would not be shared with other countries, further protecting the privacy of the

甚麼是可撤銷信託，它與我有何相關？

根據定義，可撤銷信託是委託人保留撤銷信託並收回信託所持有資產權利的信託。雖然可撤銷信託有多種形式，本章主要關注在由非美國委託人設立的可撤銷信託。

外國委託人信託（Foreign Grantor Trust，或稱 FGT）是一種在美國所得稅法上相當有利的信託架構。由非美國人士在美國（通常在內華達州或德拉瓦州）設立的外國委託人信託，在委託人有生之年，信託的所得稅歸屬於非美國委託人。因此，如果外國委託人信託僅持有非美國資產（即非屬美國來源所得），該信託即無須在美國納稅。此外，若外國委託人信託的架構安排得當，當信託分配信託收益時，無論是美國或非美國受益人均為免稅，但美國受益人仍必須向美國國稅局提交 3520 表（境外信託及贈與申報表），因為此筆分配在美國稅法下被視為是來自非美國人的贈與。

注：有關 3520 表的詳細說明，請參閱第四章中有關 1040 表的段落。

不論信託被設計成可撤銷信託，亦或是不可撤銷信託，兩者均有機會被認定為外國委託人信託：

1. 設計成可撤銷信託的情況：如果非美國委託人在世時保有不受限制地撤銷信託的權利，則該信託即為外國委託人信託。

2. 設計成不可撤銷信託的情況：在非美國委託人在世時，若受益人僅為委託人及其配偶，則該信託即為外國委託人信託。

當非美國人士設立外國委託人信託時，委託人資產將得到美國的司法保護，且委託人生前無須繳納美國所得稅。此外，若委託人僅將非美國境內資產放入外國委託人信託中，則該信託於

Wealth Creator.

Aside from relevant tax considerations, Wealth Creators also often seek to establish a Revocable Trust to designate specific beneficiaries. Though most Wealth Creators establish trusts include their descendants as beneficiaries, some may choose to exclude certain descendants or others who may seek to claim their assets after their death.

What are the roles in a Foreign Grantor Trust?

The roles in a Foreign Grantor Trust (FGT) may be customized to the family's needs; however, the roles and responsibilities are similar in nature to those that are found in an U.S. Irrevocable Non-Grantor Trust with certain notable exceptions:

1. The Grantor retains the right to revoke the trust, which makes the trust a revocable trust rather than an irrevocable trust.
2. The Grantor retains the right to distribute all (and any) of the trust assets to whomever during the grantor's lifetime.
3. The trust agreement will have provisions that provide that the trust will remain a grantor trust unless the Grantor passes away or until the Grantor explicitly and unilaterally relinquish his right to revoke the trust. In either scenario, the trust will henceforth become an irrevocable trust.
4. The trust agreement would typically incorporate language that would facilitate the transition of the FGT to a U.S. irrevocable non-grantor trust. This would be especially important if the trust has current or future U.S.-based beneficiaries.

Note: For a detailed explanation of the remainder of the roles in a trust agreement, please refer to the section of Chapter 2 that discusses the roles and responsibilities of the trust's fiduciaries.

委託人過世時亦無須就信託資產繳納美國遺產稅。最後，由於美國未加入經濟合作與發展組織（OECD）所制定的共同申報準則（CRS），因此，在美國設立的外國委託人信託下所持有的資產相關資訊不會與其他國家共享，進而能保障創富者的隱私。

除了相關的稅務考量外，創富者通常希望藉由設立可撤銷信託來指定特定的受益人。儘管大多數創富者設立的信託會將其後代列為受益人，但有些創富者會選擇排除特定後代，或其他可能在創富者過世時對其資產進行主張之人。

外國委託人信託中的角色有哪些？

外國委託人信託中的角色得根據各個家庭的需求來客製化；然而，這些角色及職責在性質上與美國不可撤銷非委託人信託中的角色類似，唯有少數顯著的差別。在外國委託人信託中：

1. 委託人保留撤銷信託的權利，因而使該信託成為可撤銷信託，而非不可撤銷信託。

2. 委託人保留其在世時得將全部或一部分的信託資產分配給任何人的權利。

3. 信託合約規定信託將以委託人信託的狀態維持，除非委託人過世或直到委託人明確且單方面放棄其撤銷信託的權利。在任一情況發生時，該信託將從此成為不可撤銷信託。

4. 信託合約通常會包含便於將外國委託人信託轉變為美國不可撤銷非委託人信託的條款。如果該信託目前或未來有美國受益人，這一條款尤為重要。

注：有關信託合約其他角色之詳述說明，請參閱第二章「信託受託責任人的角色及職責」段落。

Which assets should I place in my Foreign Grantor Trust?

Assets held in a Foreign Grantor Trust (FGT) shift income tax liability from the trust to the Grantor (non-U.S. person) for U.S. income tax purposes. As such, for both U.S. and non-U.S. assets, the Grantor of the trust is viewed as the income taxpayer for U.S. income tax purposes.

When a foreigner (a non-U.S. person) holds non-U.S. assets, he is generally not liable for U.S. income tax (on income not "effectively connected" to the U.S.); however, when a foreigner holds U.S. assets, he is liable for U.S. income tax (often at a considerable higher tax rate than a U.S. person). As such, almost all assets placed in FGTs are non-U.S. assets.

It is often recommended that clients place interest in non-U.S. holding and / or operating companies into FGTs. These assets primarily consist of offshore companies established in offshore jurisdictions, including the British Virgin Islands (BVI), Cayman Islands, Samoa, or other countries.

哪些資產適合放入外國委託人信託（FGT）中？

依據美國所得稅法，當外國委託人信託持有信託資產而有信託收益時，就信託收益繳納所得稅的責任會從信託轉移至委託人本身（非美國人），因此，無論信託持有的是美國資產還是非美國資產，在美國所得稅法上，均以信託委託人為信託收益的納稅義務人。

當外國人（非美國人）持有非美國資產時，該外國人一般不須就其外國資產產生的所得繳納美國所得稅，因為該所得非屬與美國產生「有效連結」的所得；然而，當外國人持有美國資產時，則應就該美國資產產生的所得繳納美國所得稅，且稅率通常會比美國人高，也因此，實務上所有放入外國委託人信託中的資產幾乎都是非美國資產。

此外，通常會建議客戶將美國境外控股公司或在美國境外營運公司的股權移轉至外國委託人信託中；此類公司主要是以離岸公司的形式設立在離岸司法管轄區（如：英屬維京群島、開曼群島、薩摩亞或其他國家）。

Could you provide an example of a Foreign Grantor Trust structure?

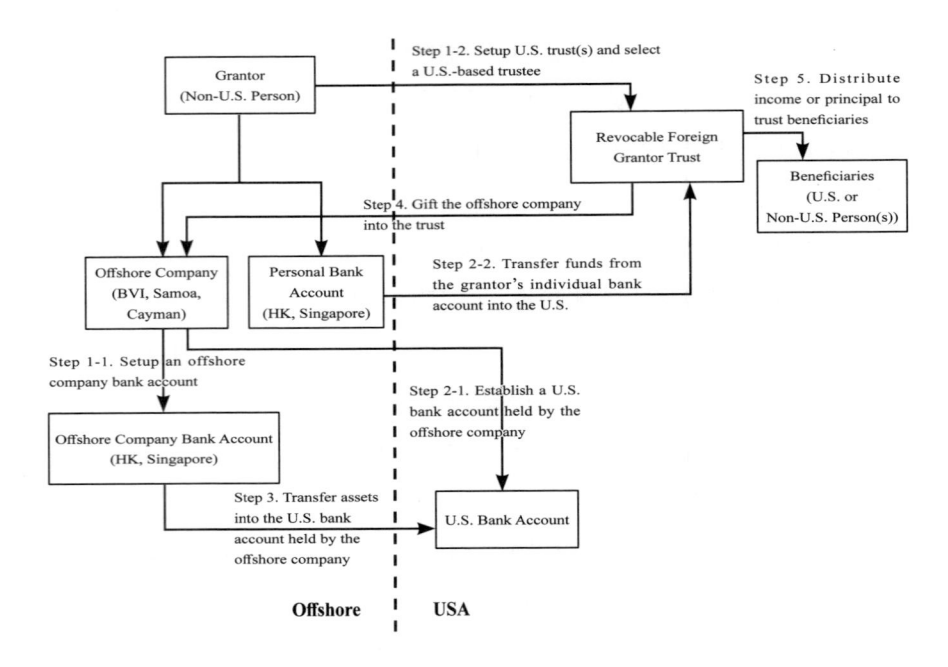

```
Grantor                    Step 1-2. Setup U.S. trust(s) and select
(Non-U.S. Person)          a U.S.-based trustee                          Step 5. Distribute
                                                                         income or principal to
                                            Revocable Foreign            trust beneficiaries
                                            Grantor Trust
                                                                         Beneficiaries
                      Step 4. Gift the offshore company                  (U.S. or
                      into the trust                                     Non-U.S. Person(s))

Offshore Company    Personal Bank     Step 2-2. Transfer funds from
(BVI, Samoa,        Account           the grantor's individual bank
Cayman)             (HK, Singapore)   account into the U.S.

Step 1-1. Setup an offshore
company bank account          Step 2-1. Establish a U.S.
                              bank account held by the
Offshore Company Bank Account offshore company
(HK, Singapore)

                    Step 3. Transfer assets
                    into the U.S. bank
                    account held by the     U.S. Bank Account
                    offshore company

            Offshore          USA
```

Are there assets I shouldn't put into my Foreign Grantor Trust?

An NRA is subject to gift and estate tax only on U.S. situs assets. However, domicile for U.S. gift and estate tax purposes is defined differently than that for U.S. income tax purposes. Unlike the substantial presence test for income tax purposes, which is generally based on the number of days one spends in the U.S., domicile for U.S. gift and estate tax purposes centers around being physically present in the U.S. and intending to permanently remain in the U.S. An individual can be deemed an income tax resident but not have a domicile in the U.S. and vice versa.

Whether an individual is deemed to remain permanently in the U.S. is a facts and circumstances test. The IRS characterizes the following as facts that may point to a U.S. domicile:

能舉一個外國委託人信託架構為例嗎？

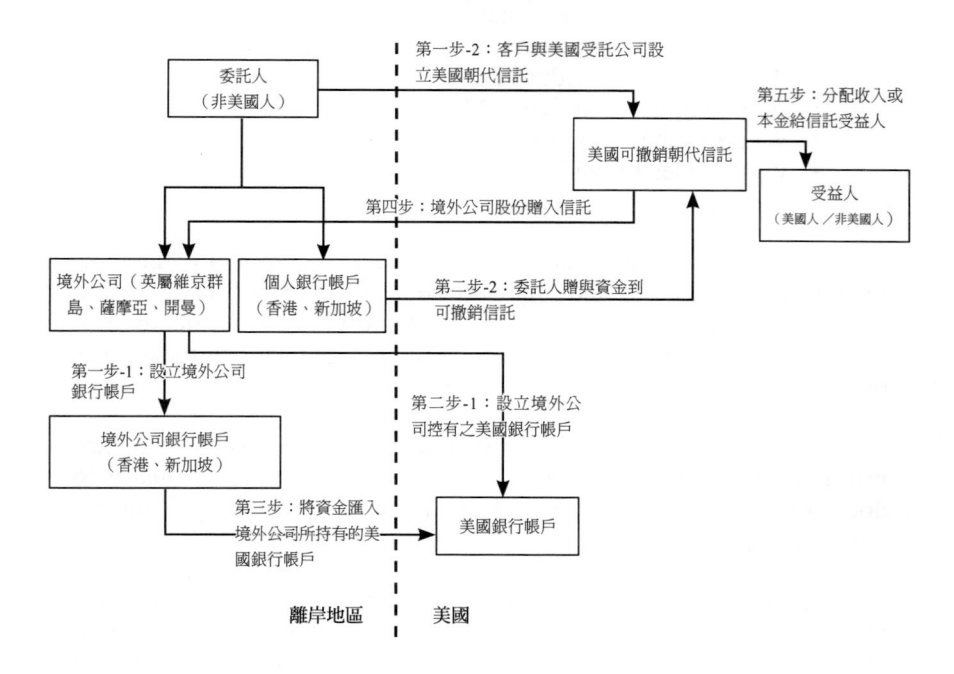

```
委託人                   第一步-2：客戶與美國受託公司設
(非美國人)                立美國朝代信託           第五步：分配收入或
                                                本金給信託受益人
                                  ┌─────────────┐
                                  │ 美國可撤銷朝代信託 │────┐
                                  └─────────────┘    │
                                                  ┌──────┐
                   第四步：境外公司股份贈入信託        │ 受益人 │
                                                  │(美國人/│
                                                  │非美國人)│
                                                  └──────┘
┌──────────┐  ┌──────────┐
│境外公司(英屬│  │個人銀行帳戶│   第二步-2：委託人贈與資金到
│維京群島、薩摩│  │(香港、新加坡)│  可撤銷信託
│亞、開曼)   │  └──────────┘
└──────────┘
第一步-1：設立境外公司
銀行帳戶           第二步-1：設立境外公
                  司控有之美國銀行帳戶
┌──────────┐
│境外公司銀行帳戶│
│(香港、新加坡) │        ┌──────────┐
└──────────┘        │ 美國銀行帳戶 │
      第三步：將資金匯入      └──────────┘
      境外公司所持有的美
      國銀行帳戶

         離岸地區    │   美國
```

哪些資產不應該放入外國委託人信託中？

美國對非美國居民（NRA）僅在其移轉美國資產（U.S. situs assets）時徵收贈與稅及遺產稅。然而，在判斷納稅人是否為美國贈與稅及遺產稅的稅務居民是以該個人是否在美國有「住所」（domicile）為要件，與所得稅採用的實質居留測試（substantial presence test）不同。所得稅的實質居留測試是以納稅人在美國停留的天數為準，而贈與稅及遺產稅的住所則關注納稅人是否在美國境內停留並打算永久居住在美國。納稅人可能被認定為所得稅上的稅務居民，但在美國沒有住所，反之亦然。

判斷個人是否被視為永久居留於美國境內必須依照事實情況

- Where does the individual pay state income tax?
- Where does the individual vote?
- Where does the individual own property?
- Where is the individual's citizenship?
- How long is the individual length of residence?
- Where is the individual's business based?
- Where does the individual have social ties to his or her community?

When an individual is deemed to have a U.S. domicile, the individual's worldwide gift and estate are subject to U.S. gift tax and U.S. estate tax, respectively. However, even individuals not deemed to have a U.S. domicile may be taxed by the U.S. when they make gifts or leave assets in their estate if their assets have a U.S. situs.

The IRS has defined assets that are and are not subject to U.S. gift and estate taxes when they are transferred by an individual who does not have a U.S. domicile. Assets that do trigger U.S. gift and estate taxes are generally termed assets with a U.S. situs.

The categorization of assets is different for U.S. estate and gift taxes. The following chart categorizes assets as those generally subject to U.S. gift tax, U.S. estate tax or both, when they are transferred from a person without a U.S. domicile.

Property Type	Gift Tax Yes	Gift Tax No	Estate Tax Yes	Estate Tax No
Tangible Personal Property in the U.S. (e.g. jewelry)	V		V	
Currency in U.S. Safe Deposit Box	V		V	
Cash Deposits in a U.S. Bank	Possibly			V
U.S. Real Property	V		V	
Non-U.S. Real Property		V		V
U.S. Stock		V	V	
Non-U.S. Stock		V		V
U.S. Government and Corporate Bonds		V		V
U.S. States/Muni Bonds		V		V
U.S. Partnership/LLC Interest		V	Possibly	
Life Insurance Cash Value		V	V	
Life Insurance Death Benefits		V		V

判斷。美國國稅局列舉以下可能被認定在美國境內有住所的事實：
- 個人支付哪一州的所得稅
- 個人在何處行使投票權
- 個人在何處擁有資產
- 個人的國籍
- 個人在特定地點居住時間長短
- 個人事業的座落地點
- 個人的主要社交地點

一旦個人被視為在美國境內有住所，該個人全球的贈與及遺產均會被納入美國贈與稅及遺產稅的課稅範圍。然而，即便個人未被認定有美國住所，如果其贈與或遺贈的資產屬於美國境內資產，仍會被課徵美國稅。

美國國稅局已明確界定，不具有美國住所的個人移轉哪些資產屬於美國贈與稅及遺產稅的課稅範圍。會觸發美國贈與稅及遺產稅的資產，通常被稱為美國境內資產。

美國稅法下，遺產稅及贈與稅對應稅資產有不同的分類。下表原則上列示在美國無住所的個人移轉資產時，該移轉是否需繳納美國贈與稅、美國遺產稅或兩者皆需繳納。

財產類型	贈與稅 是	贈與稅 否	遺產稅 是	遺產稅 否
在美國的有形個人財產（如珠寶）	V		V	
美國保險箱中的貨幣	V		V	
存放在美國銀行的現金存款	可能			V
美國不動產	V		V	
非美國不動產		V		V
美國股票		V	V	
非美國股票		V		V
美國政府和公司債券		V	V	
美國州債券/市政債券		V	V	
美國合夥/有限責任公司權益		V	可能	
壽險現金價值		V	V	
人壽保險死亡給付		V		V

Is Foreign Grantor Trust status relevant to me if I previously settled a non-U.S. (offshore) trust?

While we generally recommend that clients stray away from establishing offshore trusts (defined herein as trusts settled outside of the U.S.), particularly if they have U.S. descendants, Wealth Creators who previously established offshore trusts should familiarize themselves with Foreign Grantor Trust (FGT) rules. Offshore trusts include trusts settled in the British Virgin Islands (BVI), Cayman Islands, Bahamas, Bermuda, Switzerland, Cook Islands, Jersey, Nevis, or any other non-U.S. jurisdiction.

When a U.S. person is a beneficiary of a foreign trust, the tax consequences are generally quite punitive (often involving "throwback" taxes for distributions of undistributed net income ("UNI"). Oftentimes, when offshore trusts are established, the tax consequences of future distributions are not adequately analyzed by the recommending party (frequently non-U.S. financial advisors and bankers at non-U.S. financial institutions).

Offshore trusts are also frequently established prior to the grantor either having U.S. person beneficiaries or prior to the grantor disclosing their U.S. person beneficiaries. Wealth Creators should be extremely wary of this, as non-U.S. financial institutions tend to downplay the tax impact of trusts with U.S. beneficiaries or, in certain cases, choose to outright ignore the fact that the trust has U.S. persons.

Offshore trust companies typically retain many powers rather than stipulating that the family itself would control the trust. Sometimes, offshore trust agreements may also stipulate that the trustee would not be able to be removed barring certain exceptions. While this allows these trust companies to improve client retention, the Wealth Creator's family oftentimes lacks powers necessary to govern the trust.

Furthermore, the drafting of these trust agreements often leads to the Wealth Creator directing the offshore trustee to manage investments and distributions using Letters of Wish. While the Wealth Creator may feel like he or she is in charge of all functions of the trust,

如果我已經設立非美國（離岸）信託，我仍須關注外國委託人信託嗎？

我們通常不建議客戶設立離岸信託（在此定義為設立於美國境外的信託），特別是有美國籍後代的客戶，已設立離岸信託的創富者必須熟悉前述有關外國委託人可撤銷信託（FGT）的規定。離岸信託包括在英屬維京群島（BVI）、開曼群島、巴哈馬、百慕達、瑞士、庫克群島、澤西、尼維斯或任何其他非美國司法管轄區設立的信託。

離岸信託的受益人為美國人時，通常會導致相當嚴重的懲罰性稅務後果（因為當信託分配未分配所得（Undistributed Net Income）時，信託需要負擔高額的回溯稅）。然而在離岸信託設立時，推薦方（通常是非美國金融顧問及非美國金融機構的銀行人員）往往沒有對信託未來分配的稅負影響進行充分分析。

值得注意的是，通常在委託人尚未指定美國籍受益人，或是揭露信託有美國籍受益人之前，離岸信託已經設立完成。創富者對此應保持高度警覺，因為非美國金融機構會傾向淡化處理離岸信託有美國籍受益人的稅務影響，或在某些特定情形選擇完全忽略該信託涉有美國人的事實。

又離岸信託公司通常會保留多項權力，而非規定讓委託人家族控制信託。甚而有時離岸信託合約還可能規定除非有特定例外狀況，否則受託人無法被撤換。雖然這些限制條款讓離岸信託公司盡可能留住客戶，卻也同時使創富者家族缺乏管理信託的必要權力。

此外，在草擬離岸信託的信託合約時，通常會賦予創富者透過意願書（Letters of Wish）指示離岸信託的受託人進行信託資產

the trust could be deemed a sham trust if any lawsuit were to arise, leading to the trust's asset protection powers to be severely eroded.

In sharp contrast, Foreign Grantor Trusts established in the U.S. generally have explicitly defined powers for the trust's fiduciaries (trust protector, investment direction advisor, and distribution advisor), which allows the family to both stay in control of trust assets and swap out trustees if necessary. In addition, since the roles and responsibilities are generally set forth clearly in the trust agreement, it is extremely unlikely that the trust could be deemed a sham trust by outside creditors.

For Wealth Creators that had the foresight to adequately review and / or modify their offshore trusts, they often have them structured as Foreign Grantor Trusts (under certain circumstances, offshore trusts may qualify as FGTs as well). When doing so, Wealth Creators should undoubtedly seek U.S. tax advice from competent counsel.

Wealth Creators with offshore trusts should take steps to mitigate the risk of their trusts being deemed sham trusts by clearly delineating the powers assigned to each of the trust's fiduciaries in the trust agreement. If this cannot be done, the Wealth Creator should consider establishing a new trust and decanting (transferring) assets from the old trust to the new trust.

What do I do if I want to transfer assets held by my offshore trust to a U.S. trust?

Historically, many Asian Wealth Creators did not view the U.S. as a viable jurisdiction in which to establish trusts. As such, many families opted for offshore trusts (trusts established outside of the U.S.), perceiving the tax and disclosure requirements for those jurisdictions as less risky or stringent.

While establishing offshore trusts may satisfy certain Wealth Creators that have no U.S. ties (assets or descendants), the vast majority of Asian Wealth Creators have certain ties to the U.S. Specifically, if their descendants become U.S. persons or live in the U.S., offshore trusts are generally not as suitable as certain U.S.-based trusts.

投資及分配。雖然創富者可能覺得自己握有信託的所有管理權力，但如果發生訴訟，信託可能會被視為偽信託，從而嚴重削弱信託的資產保護功能。

與此截然不同的是，在美國設立的外國委託人信託一般會明確規範信託的受託責任人（信託保護人、投資指示顧問及分配顧問）的權力範圍，俾使創富者家族能持續地控制信託資產，又能在必要時更換受託人。此外，由於各別角色及責任通常會載明於信託合約中，因此外部債權人很難主張信託為偽信託。

具有遠見的創富者會充分審閱及／或修訂已設立的離岸信託，並通常會將其結構調整為外國委託人信託（在特定情況下，離岸信託也可能符合外國委託人信託的條件）。在進行此調整時，創富者無疑應該向專業的法律顧問諮詢美國稅務建議。

已設立離岸信託的創富者需採取步驟以降低其離岸信託被視為偽信託的風險，例如在信託合約中明確劃分各別信託受託責任人被賦予的權力。如果無法採行此步驟，創富者應考慮設立一個新的信託，並將資產從既有的離岸信託轉注（即移轉）到此新設立的信託中。

如果我想將離岸信託持有的資產轉移到一個美國信託，該如何進行？

歷史上，許多亞洲創富者並不認為美國是建立信託的可行地區，因此，許多家族著眼於離岸司法管轄區的稅負優勢以及相對寬鬆的資訊揭露要求，而選擇設立離岸信託（在美國境外所設立的信託）。

雖然設立離岸信託或許可以滿足一些與美國沒有關聯性（以

Aside from tax consequences, many offshore trust agreements also contain language that unnecessarily restrict the family's control over the trust's assets. Trustees of offshore trusts often have immense control over the trusts they administer. Furthermore, the trust agreement's language is often static, and Wealth Creators are frequently convinced to "just sign" instead of reviewing all the trust agreement's terms and suggesting changes. By doing so, Wealth Creators and their families may face considerable and unexpected obstacles when managing their offshore trusts.

Luckily, many Wealth Creators are able to transfer assets held in their offshore trust into a U.S.-based trust in a process typically called decanting. Decanting is especially important for families with investments in the U.S. or family members based in the U.S.

When initiating a decanting, Wealth Creators may face considerable resistance from their offshore trust's trustee (typically an offshore trust company) and the Wealth Creator's non-U.S. financial advisors (typically employed by a non-U.S. financial institution), both of whom could impose obstacles to such a transfer. The reluctance to transferring assets can typically be attributed to the loss of future revenues from the account, including both investment management fees and trust administration service fees. To facilitate a seamless transition and an efficient timeline, experienced advisors should be retained to negotiate on the family's behalf.

When decanting assets from an offshore trust to a U.S. trust, the Wealth Creator should prepare the following documents for original and new trustees, respectively:

其資產或後代而言）的創富者，但絕大多數亞洲創富者都與美國有一定的關聯性。具體而言，如果亞洲創富者的後代成為美國人或居住在美國境內，相較於特定的美國信託，離岸信託通常並非合適的選項。

除了潛在的稅負影響，許多離岸信託合約尚包含不必要地限制創富者家族控制信託資產的條款，致使離岸信託的受託人通常對其管理的信託擁有極大的控制權。此外，由於離岸信託合約條款之僵固性，創富者經常被說服「在此簽名即可」，而非審閱信託合約的所有條款並提出修改建議。如此一來，創富者及其家族在管理其離岸信託時可能會面臨許多意想不到的障礙。

幸運的是，許多創富者能夠將其離岸信託中持有的資產轉移至美國信託中；這個過程通常稱為「轉注」（decanting）。對於在美國進行投資或在美國有家庭成員的家族，轉注尤其重要。

在啟動轉注過程時，創富者可能會面臨來自離岸信託受託人（通常是離岸信託公司）及非美國財務顧問（通常受雇於非美國金融機構）相當大的阻力，這兩者都可能對移轉信託資產設下障礙。受託人及財務顧問反對移轉信託資產的理由通常是因為會導致其未來收入（包括投資管理費及信託管理服務費）的損失。為促進信託轉注的無縫接軌及有效率地完成，創富者應聘請有經驗的顧問代表家族進行談判。

當資產從離岸信託轉注到美國信託時，創富者應為原始受託人和新受託人準備以下文件：

Original Trustee(s)
1. Background information regarding the new trust (the trust assets will be decanted into):
   (1) the name of the new trust
   (2) the name and address of the new trustee
   (3) the date the new trust was established
   (4) the U.S. tax identification number (EIN) of the new trust

2. Background information regarding the new Trustee:
   (1) the name of the new Trustee
   (2) the contact information of the new Trustee
   (3) other background information required of the original Trustee

3. The structure of the new trust agreement:
   (1) a list of the new trust's fiduciaries
   (2) background information of the new trust's fiduciaries (including identification documents and background checks)
   (3) a list of authorized signers in the new trust
   (4) any consent to accept trust assets by the new trustee

4. Other required information:
   (1) the contact information of drafting attorneys in the new trust's jurisdiction
   (2) documents indemnifying the original trustee for legal responsibility over the decanting
   (3) a memo detailing the rationale for the creation of the new trust (this would generally state that decanting the trust assets is in the best interest of the trust's beneficiaries)
   (4) a memo discussing the tax ramifications of decanting the assets to the trust's new jurisdiction (often provided by a tax attorney)
   (5) an asset transfer agreement whereby assets to be transferred are listed

原始受託人

1. 有關新信託（信託資產將被轉注至此信託中）的背景資料：
(1) 新信託的名稱
(2) 新受託人的名稱及地址
(3) 新信託成立的日期
(4) 新信託的美國納稅人識別號碼（EIN）

2. 有關新受託人的背景資料：
(1) 新受託人的名稱
(2) 新受託人的聯繫資料
(3) 原始受託人所需的其他背景資料

3. 新信託合約架構：
(1) 新信託的受託責任人名單
(2) 新信託受託責任人的背景資料（包括身分證明文件及背景調查）
(3) 新信託的授權簽署人名單
(4) 新受託人表示接受信託資產的同意書

4. 其他所需資料：
(1) 新信託司法管轄區擬約律師的聯繫資訊
(2) 賠償原始受託人在轉注事務上之法律責任文件
(3) 關於設立新信託的理由的備忘錄（一般會說明將信託資產轉注是符合信託受益人的最佳利益）
(4) 討論將資產轉注到新信託司法管轄區之稅務影響的備忘錄（通常由稅務律師出具）
(5) 資產轉移協議，列明要轉移的資產

New Trustee(s)
1. The notarized version of the original trust agreement (electronic copies are often acceptable)

2. Information regarding the new trust agreement:
   (1) the new trust agreement, as drafted by a competent attorney in the new trust jurisdiction
   (2) background information regarding the new trusts' Grantor(s), fiduciaries and beneficiaries (including identification information)
   (3) information regarding the Grantor's sources of wealth
   (4) information regarding the assets being transferred to the new trust

3. A release and indemnity agreement signed by the beneficiaries (if required)

4. A Beneficiary Statement for the previous year prepared by the original Trustee detailing:
   (1) background information on the original trust
   (2) known information regarding the original trusts' beneficiaries
   (3) any trust income previously distributed to the original trusts' beneficiarie
   (4) the types of assets held by the original trust agreement
   (5) information regarding any funds held directly by the original trust

What happens to my Foreign Grantor Trust after I die?

When the grantor of a Foreign Grantor Trust (FGT) dies, the trust generally becomes irrevocable. Depending on the language of the trust agreement, the trust either becomes a U.S. irrevocable trust or a foreign irrevocable trust, as determined by the Control Test and Court Test (described in length in the previous chapter).

As the grantor is no longer alive, the trust typically becomes a non-grantor trust and becomes its own taxable entity for U.S. income tax purposes. Assets held by the FGT are generally only taxable for U.S. estate tax purposes to the extent that trust assets possess U.S. situs.

新受託人

1. 經公證的原始信託合約（通常可接受電子副本）
2. 有關新信託合約的資料：
   （1）由新信託司法管轄區內專業的律師起草的新信託合約
   （2）有關新信託的委託人、受託責任人及受益人的背景資料（包括身分識別資料）
   （3）關於委託人財富來源的資料
   （4）有關轉移到新信託的資產資料
3. 受益人簽署的免責與賠償協議（如果需要）
4. 由原始受託人準備的上一年度的受益人聲明，其中詳述：
   （1）原始信託的背景資料
   （2）有關原始信託受益人的已知資料
   （3）先前已分配給原始信託受益人的任何信託所得
   （4）原始信託合約持有的資產類型
   （5）有關原始信託直接持有的任何資金的資料

委託人去世後，外國委託人信託會發生甚麼變化？

當外國委託人信託的委託人去世時，該信託通常會變成不可撤銷。根據信託合約的條款，藉由控制測試及法院測試（已於前一章中詳細介紹）判定該信託將成為美國不可撤銷信託或外國不可撤銷信託。

由於委託人已不在人世，該信託一般會成為非委託人信託，並在美國所得稅上成為一個獨立的應稅實體。對於美國遺產稅而言，外國委託人信託持有的資產通常僅在該資產屬於美國境內資產時才會被課稅。

For Wealth Creators with U.S.-person beneficiaries, it is extremely important to note that these two types of trusts fall under vastly different U.S. income tax regimes. Clients should seek competent U.S. tax counsel in determining the most favorable form of taxation and have the FGT trust agreement drafted accordingly. Both the drafting attorney and the tax attorney should review and sign off on the final version of the trust agreement. This can ensure that the trust agreement is optimized for the client's specific needs, the trust jurisdiction's state laws, and U.S. tax consequences.

Generally speaking, it is advisable that Wealth Creators with U.S. beneficiaries consider language that would effectively convert a FGT into a U.S. irrevocable trust, rather than a foreign irrevocable trust, upon the grantor's death. Typically, if this is the grantor's intent, the trust agreement would incorporate language that would allow it to fulfill the Control Test and Court Test immediately upon the grantor's death.

Even if the trust does not immediately fulfill both the Control Test and the Court Test, thereby becoming a U.S. trust, it generally has one year to fulfill both and "cure" itself of foreign trust status. Thus, the trust would be treated as a U.S. trust from the day the grantor deceases, thereby relieving the trust of foreign trust status for U.S. tax purposes for the period between the grantor's death and the time it fulfills both the Control and Court Tests in accordance with Regs. Sec. 301.7701-7(d)(2).

After converting the trust to a U.S. irrevocable trust, all trust income is generally taxed on a current basis, which could avoid any "throwback" taxes that may arise for trusts treated as foreign trusts.

在此特別提醒有美國受益人的創富者，由於美國不可撤銷信託及外國不可撤銷信託在美國所得稅申報上有極大差異，創富者應該諮詢專業的美國稅務顧問，以確定最有利之稅務模式，並據以起草外國委託人信託合約。起草合約的律師及稅務律師均應審閱並核可最終版本的信託合約，以確保該信託合約得以滿足客戶的具體需求、符合信託準據法之規範、並降低潛在的美國稅務風險。

一般而言，會建議有美國受益人的創富者考慮在信託合約中設計適當的條款，以便在委託人去世時，能有效率地將外國委託人信託轉變成美國不可撤銷信託（而非外國不可撤銷信託）。如果委託人有意在自己過世後將信託轉變成美國不可撤銷信託，信託合約通常會包含能使該信託在委託人去世時能立即通過控制測試及法院測試的條款。

即便信託在委託人去世後未能立即通過控制測試及法院測試而成為美國信託，該信託仍有一年的時間來通過這兩項測試，以變更其外國信託的身分。如果該信託能在一年內順利通過控制測試及法院測試，根據《美國財政部法規》第 301.7701-7(d)(2) 條規定，該信託自委託人去世之日起取得美國信託的地位，從而在委託人去世至信託通過測試的期間內，該信託在美國稅法上不會以外國信託的身分被課稅。

在信託轉變為美國不可撤銷信託後，信託通常必須就全部的信託所得進行年度稅務申報，如此一來即可避免該信託被視為外國信託而可能產生的「回溯稅」。

Is there any way to reduce income taxes after an FGT converts to a U.S. irrevocable trust?

Form 8832 Election (step up basis)

Assets in the FGT ae includible in the grantor's estate for U.S. estate tax purposes. Any capital gains held in the trust may be "stepped up" to fair market value through a "deemed liquidation" immediately prior to the grantor's death by filing an entity classification election (Form 8832). This election may be activated retroactively, subject to certain limitations.

Note: For a detailed explanation of entity classification elections, please refer to the section of Chapter 4 that discusses the Form 8832

U.S. Tax Treatment for Foreign Estates

Under certain circumstances, assets held in a FGT may also be treated as being held by a foreign estate rather than a U.S. trust. When properly structured, this tax treatment may defer or alleviate U.S. income taxes for a period of time not exceeding two years. This could allow for the foreign estate to realize income without incurring U.S. income taxes.

外國委託人信託轉變為美國不可撤銷信託後，有辦法減少所得稅嗎？

8832 表 – 企業類型選擇（墊高資產稅基）

在美國遺產稅上，外國委託人信託中的資產會被納入委託人的遺產中。在委託人去世之前，信託可以藉由提交企業實體身分選擇表（8832 表）進行所謂「視同清算」，將信託中持有資產的稅基「墊高」到公允市場價值，這項機制可以追溯適用，但會受到一定限制。

注：關於企業實體身分選擇的詳細說明，請參閱第四章中有關 8832 表的段落。

美國對外國遺產的稅務處理

在特定情況下，外國委託人信託持有的資產也可能被視為由外國遺產持有而非美國信託持有。如果安排得當，可以在不超過兩年的時間內遞延或減輕美國所得稅，而使外國遺產在不產生美國所得稅稅負的情況下實現所得。

NOTE :

第四章

信託與個人之相關美國稅表

Relevant U.S. Tax Forms for
U.S. Trusts & Individuals

Summary

While the beginning of this book focused primarily on the utilization of U.S.-based dynasty trusts, this chapter focuses primarily on the various tax filing requirements for cross-border families and entities controlled by them. Specifically, this book briefly describes each of the tax forms we find relevant for cross-border families.

The U.S. imposes various obligations on many entities it has varying levels of jurisdiction over. These obligations are generally mandated by laws passed by the U.S. Congress and operationally carried out by U.S. Department of The Treasury ("USDT"). The Internal Revenue Service ("IRS") is one of the many agencies that report to the USDT.

The descriptions that follow are for purely education purposes and is not meant to be and should not be used as a guide for tax filing purposes. Clients that must complete one or more of the following forms should engage professional CPAs and licensed attorneys for their unique tax filing and estate planning needs.

In our experience, cross-border families often must file one or more of the following forms. The following charts illustrate which forms could potentially be relevant for which taxpayers; please note that this is not an exhaustive list of the disclosures required of each individual within but rather an illustration of how and when each form could be used.

第四章 信託與個人之相關美國稅表

引言

本書的前半章節主要關注如何使用美國朝代信託，本章則聚焦於跨境家族及在其控制下之實體的各種稅務申報義務，更具體來說，本書將簡要闡述筆者認為與跨境家族有關的各種稅務表格。

美國政府對不同主體課徵不同的申報與納稅義務。這些義務通常是由美國國會透過法律所制定，並由美國財政部（U.S. Department of The Treasury，USDT）負責執行。在諸多主管機關中，美國國稅局（Internal Revenue Service，IRS）是向美國財政部負責並報告的眾多機構之一。

本書以下內容僅供教育目的使用，不建議讀者將本書內容視為稅務申報指南。客戶若有義務填寫以下稅務表格，應聘請專業的註冊會計師及執業律師，以滿足其特定之稅務申報和財產規劃需求。

根據我們的經驗，跨境家族通常必須提交以下其中一份或多份稅務表格。以下圖示說明了哪些申報書可能與哪些納稅人相關；需要注意的是，以下圖示僅列示出每一種表格的使用時機及用途，並非每個人都需要就下圖所列舉之各份報表逐一揭露並向有關機構進行申報。

U.S. taxpayers generally report income from various sources on the Form 1040.

U.S. person owning domestic assets

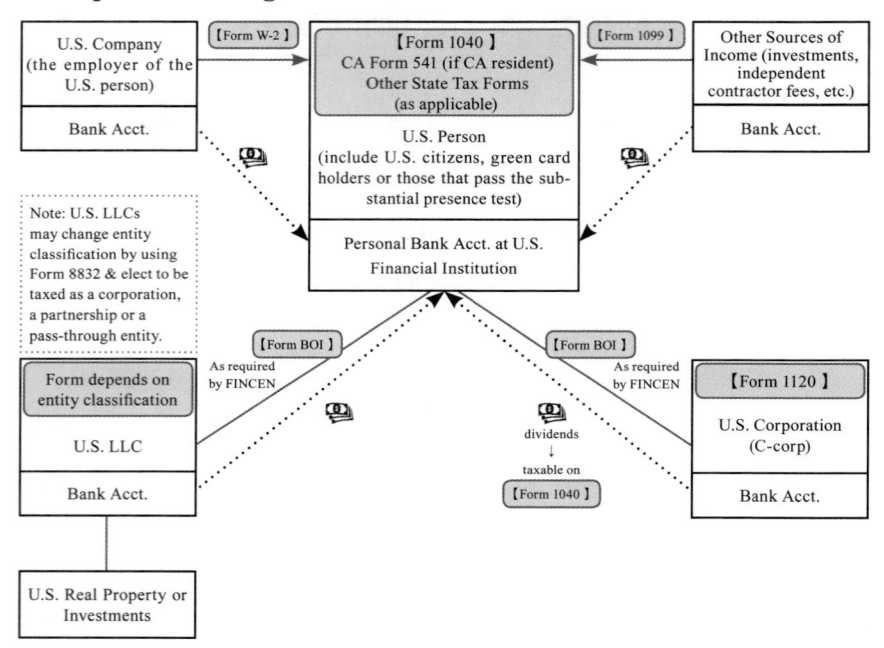

```
┌─────────────────────┐  [Form W-2]   ┌──────────────────────────┐  [Form 1099]  ┌──────────────────────┐
│ U.S. Company        │──────────────▶│ 【Form 1040】            │◀──────────────│ Other Sources of     │
│ (the employer of the│               │ CA Form 541 (if CA       │               │ Income (investments, │
│ U.S. person)        │               │ resident)                │               │ independent          │
│                     │               │ Other State Tax Forms    │               │ contractor fees, etc.)│
├─────────────────────┤               │ (as applicable)          │               ├──────────────────────┤
│ Bank Acct.          │               └──────────────────────────┘               │ Bank Acct.           │
└─────────────────────┘                    U.S. Person                           └──────────────────────┘
                                      (include U.S. citizens, green card
                                      holders or those that pass the sub-
                                      stantial presence test)

┌─────────────────────┐               ┌──────────────────────────┐
│ Note: U.S. LLCs     │               │ Personal Bank Acct. at U.S.│
│ may change entity   │               │ Financial Institution    │
│ classification by   │               └──────────────────────────┘
│ using Form 8832 &   │
│ elect to be taxed as│
│ a corporation, a    │
│ partnership or a    │
│ pass-through entity.│
└─────────────────────┘
┌─────────────────────┐  [Form BOI]                               [Form BOI]    ┌──────────────────────┐
│ Form depends on     │  As required                              As required   │ 【Form 1120】        │
│ entity classification│ by FINCEN                                 by FINCEN    │                      │
├─────────────────────┤                                                         │ U.S. Corporation     │
│ U.S. LLC            │              dividends                                  │ (C-corp)             │
├─────────────────────┤                 ↓                                       ├──────────────────────┤
│ Bank Acct.          │              taxable on                                 │ Bank Acct.           │
└─────────────────────┘              【Form 1040】                                └──────────────────────┘
┌─────────────────────┐
│ U.S. Real Property  │
│ or Investments      │
└─────────────────────┘
```

第四章 信託與個人之相關美國稅表

美國納稅人通常會在 1040 表上申報各種來源的所得。

持有國內資產的美國人

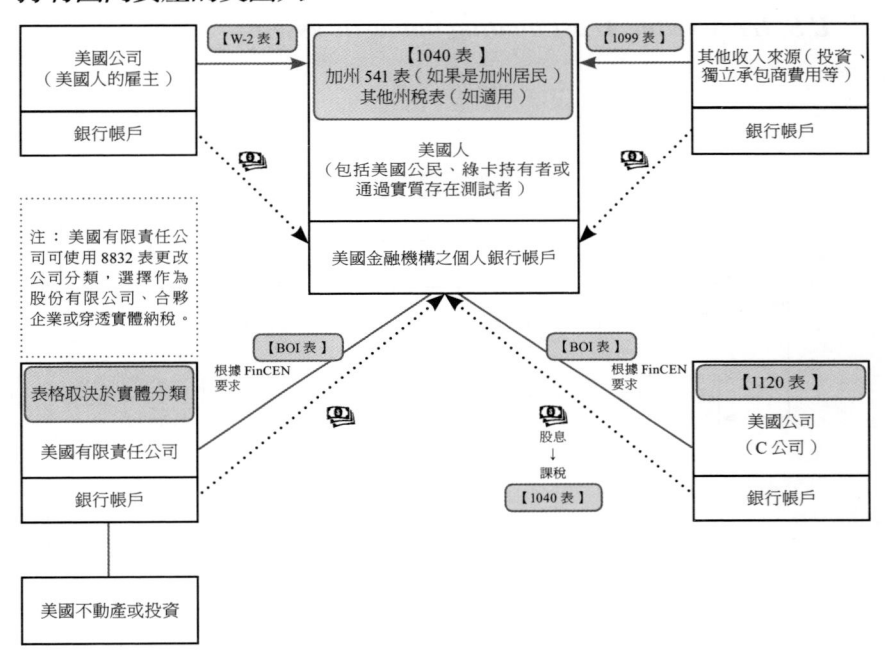

```
美國公司                【W-2表】      【1040表】          【1099表】    其他收入來源（投資、
（美國人的雇主）                      加州541表（如果是加州居民）              獨立承包商費用等）
                                其他州稅表（如適用）
銀行帳戶                                                                 銀行帳戶
                                    美國人
                              （包括美國公民、綠卡持有者或
                                通過實質存在測試者）

注：美國有限責任公                  美國金融機構之個人銀行帳戶
司可使用8832表更改
公司分類，選擇作為
股份有限公司、合夥            【BOI表】              【BOI表】
企業或穿透實體納稅。          根據FinCEN            根據FinCEN
                          要求                   要求          【1120表】

表格取決於實體分類                        股息                  美國公司
                                        ↓                   （C公司）
美國有限責任公司                          課稅
                                    【1040表】               銀行帳戶
銀行帳戶


美國不動產或投資
```

U.S. irrevocable trusts are generally subject to many of the same requirements as U.S. persons are subject to; however, trusts must complete a Form 1041 rather than a Form 1040.

U.S. Irrevocable Trust holding domestic assets

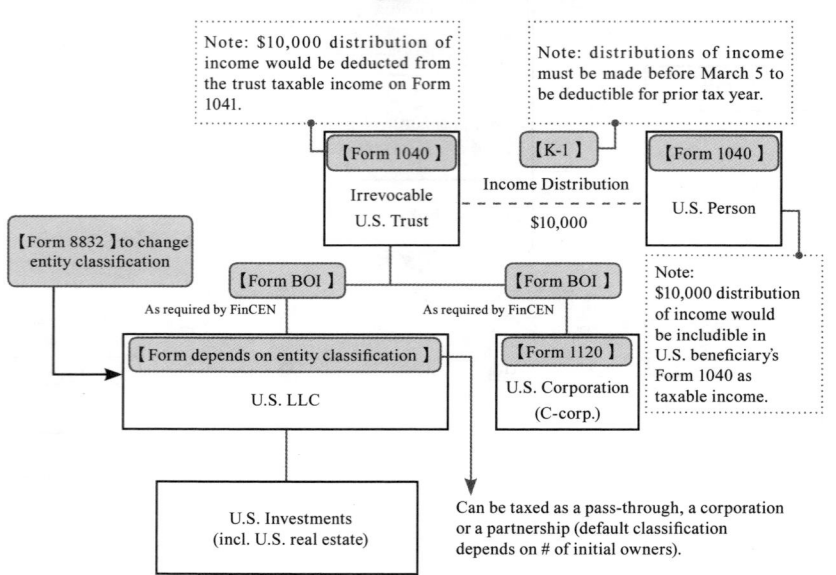

```
                    Note: $10,000 distribution of        Note: distributions of income
                    income would be deducted from        must be made before March 5 to
                    the trust taxable income on Form     be deductible for prior tax year.
                    1041.

                            【Form 1040】      【K-1】       【Form 1040】
                                          Income Distribution
                            Irrevocable   ----------------    U.S. Person
                            U.S. Trust         $10,000

【Form 8832】to change
entity classification
                            【Form BOI】              【Form BOI】         Note:
                        As required by FinCEN      As required by FinCEN   $10,000 distribution
                                                                           of income would
                                                                           be includible in
       【Form depends on entity classification】   【Form 1120】           U.S. beneficiary's
                                                                           Form 1040 as
                            U.S. LLC              U.S. Corporation         taxable income.
                                                     (C-corp.)


                            U.S. Investments     Can be taxed as a pass-through, a corporation
                           (incl. U.S. real estate)   or a partnership (default classification
                                                  depends on # of initial owners).
```

美國不可撤銷信託如同美國籍人士,通常會受相同要求的規範;但是,在申報所得稅方面,信託必須填寫的是 1041 表而不是 1040 表。

持有國內資產的美國不可撤銷信託

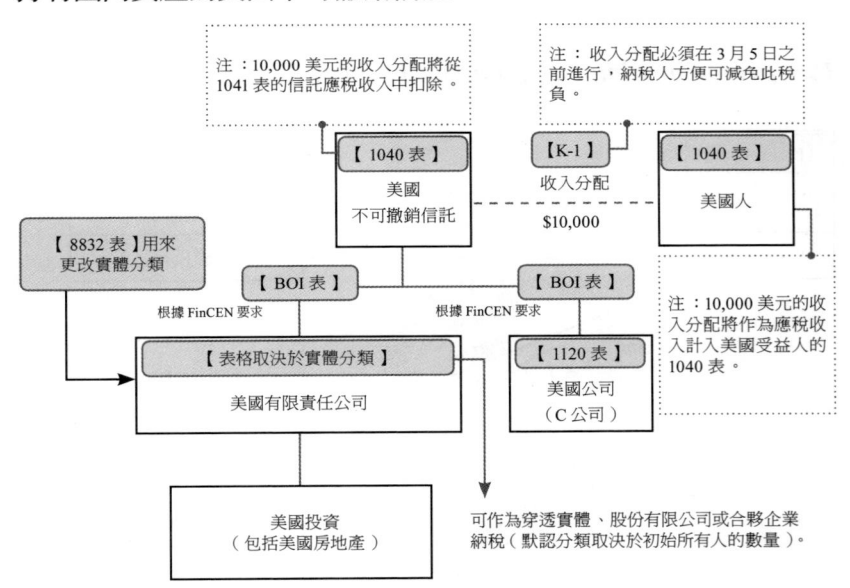

注:10,000 美元的收入分配將從 1041 表的信託應稅收入中扣除。

注:收入分配必須在 3 月 5 日之前進行,納稅人方便可減免此稅負。

【1040 表】
美國
不可撤銷信託

【K-1】
收入分配
$10,000

【1040 表】
美國人

【8832 表】用來更改實體分類

【BOI 表】
根據 FinCEN 要求

【BOI 表】
根據 FinCEN 要求

注:10,000 美元的收入分配將作為應稅收入計入美國受益人的 1040 表。

【表格取決於實體分類】
美國有限責任公司

【1120 表】
美國公司
(C 公司)

美國投資
(包括美國房地產)

可作為穿透實體、股份有限公司或合夥企業納稅(默認分類取決於初始所有人的數量)。

U.S. persons who own assets overseas are generally subject to U.S. taxation on their worldwide income. In addition, they may face certain disclosure requirements when receiving gifts from non-U.S. persons or trusts.

The following two charts include certain forms that may be required of U.S. persons when they directly or indirectly own or receive assets outside of the U.S:

U.S. person owning foreign assets (Part I)

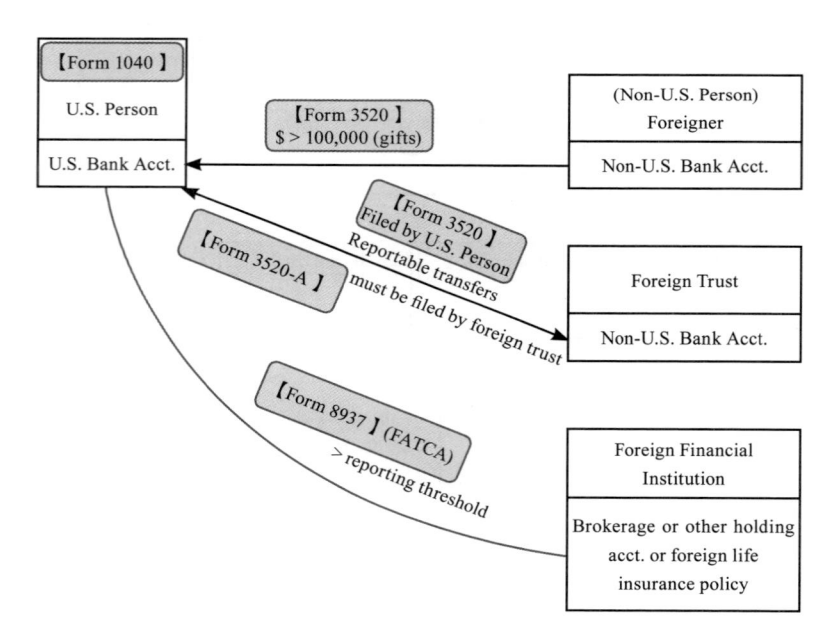

【Form 1040】
U.S. Person
U.S. Bank Acct.

【Form 3520】 $ > 100,000 (gifts)

(Non-U.S. Person) Foreigner
Non-U.S. Bank Acct.

【Form 3520】 Filed by U.S. Person Reportable transfers

【Form 3520-A】 must be filed by foreign trust

Foreign Trust
Non-U.S. Bank Acct.

【Form 8937】 (FATCA) ≥ reporting threshold

Foreign Financial Institution

Brokerage or other holding acct. or foreign life insurance policy

第四章　信託與個人之相關美國稅表

　　擁有海外資產的美國籍人士通常要就其全球所得繳納美國稅。此外，他們在收到來自非美國籍個人或信託的贈與時可能會需要盡特定揭露義務。

　　以下兩張圖表是美國人在美國境外直接或間接擁有或接收境外資產時，可能需要填寫的表格：

持有外國資產的美國人（第一部分）

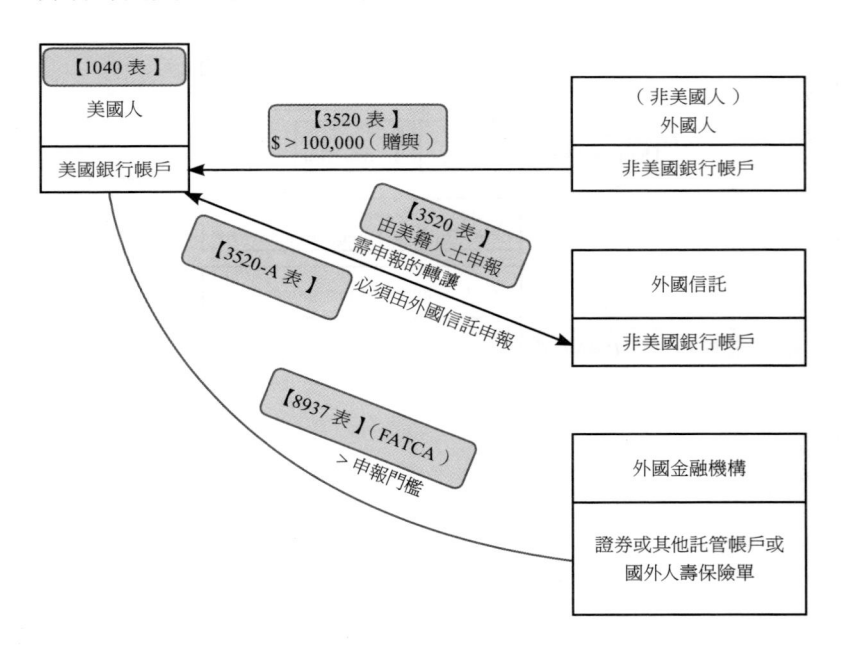

```
┌─────────────┐                              ┌─────────────┐
│ 【1040 表】  │      【3520 表】             │ （非美國人） │
│  美國人      │   $ > 100,000（贈與）        │   外國人     │
│  美國銀行帳戶│◄─────────────────────────── │ 非美國銀行帳戶│
└─────────────┘                              └─────────────┘

                      【3520 表】
                    由美籍人士申報
         【3520-A 表】 需申報的轉讓          ┌─────────────┐
                    必須由外國信託申報       │  外國信託    │
                                             │ 非美國銀行帳戶│
                                             └─────────────┘

              【8937 表】（FATCA）           ┌─────────────┐
                > 申報門檻                   │ 外國金融機構 │
                                             │ 證券或其他託管帳戶或│
                                             │ 國外人壽保險單│
                                             └─────────────┘
```

U.S. person owning foreign assets (Part II)

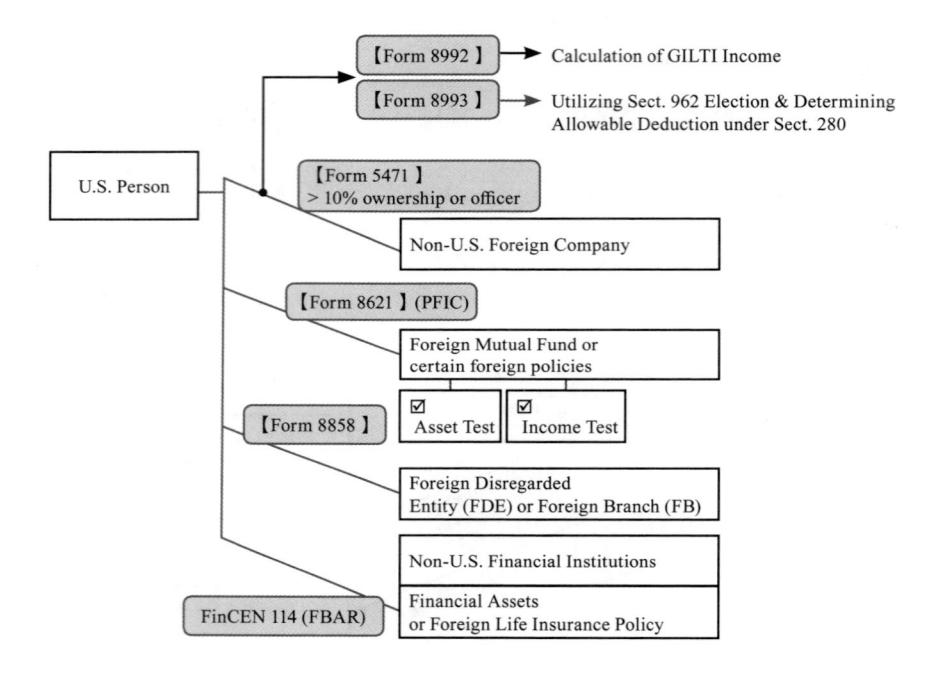

- 【Form 8992】 → Calculation of GILTI Income
- 【Form 8993】 → Utilizing Sect. 962 Election & Determining Allowable Deduction under Sect. 280
- 【Form 5471】 > 10% ownership or officer — Non-U.S. Foreign Company
- 【Form 8621】(PFIC) — Foreign Mutual Fund or certain foreign policies
  - ☑ Asset Test
  - ☑ Income Test
- 【Form 8858】 — Foreign Disregarded Entity (FDE) or Foreign Branch (FB)
- FinCEN 114 (FBAR) — Non-U.S. Financial Institutions; Financial Assets or Foreign Life Insurance Policy

持有外國資產的美國人（第二部分）

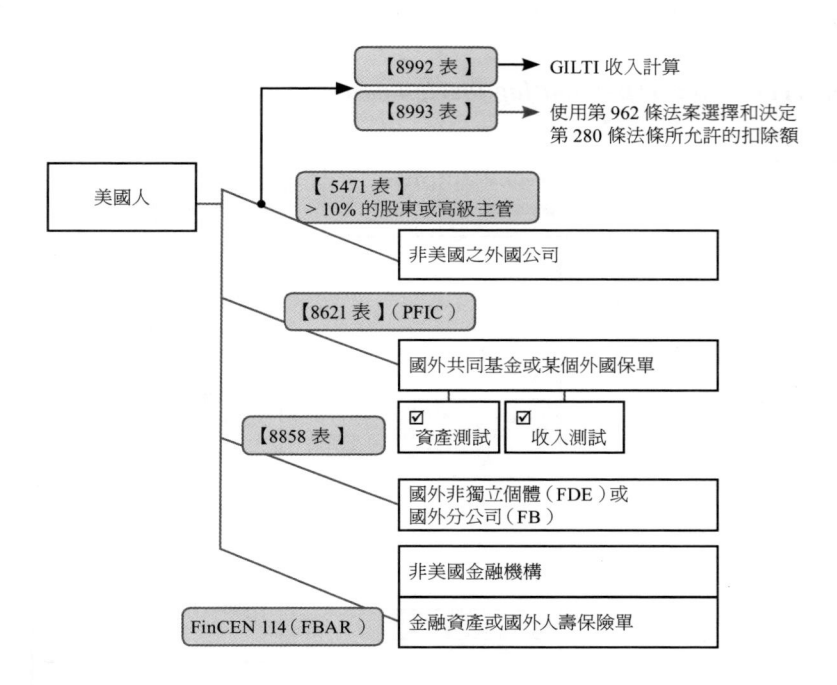

```
美國人 ─┬─ 【8992 表】 → GILTI 收入計算
        │
        ├─ 【8993 表】 → 使用第 962 條法案選擇和決定
        │              第 280 條法條所允許的扣除額
        │
        ├─ 【5471 表】
        │  > 10% 的股東或高級主管
        │  └─ 非美國之外國公司
        │
        ├─ 【8621 表】（PFIC）
        │  └─ 國外共同基金或某個外國保單
        │     ☑ 資產測試    ☑ 收入測試
        │
        ├─ 【8858 表】
        │  └─ 國外非獨立個體（FDE）或
        │     國外分公司（FB）
        │
        └─ FinCEN 114（FBAR）
           ├─ 非美國金融機構
           └─ 金融資產或國外人壽保險單
```

A U.S. irrevocable trust that owns assets overseas are also subject to a variety of requirements.

U.S. Irrevocable Trust holding foreign assets

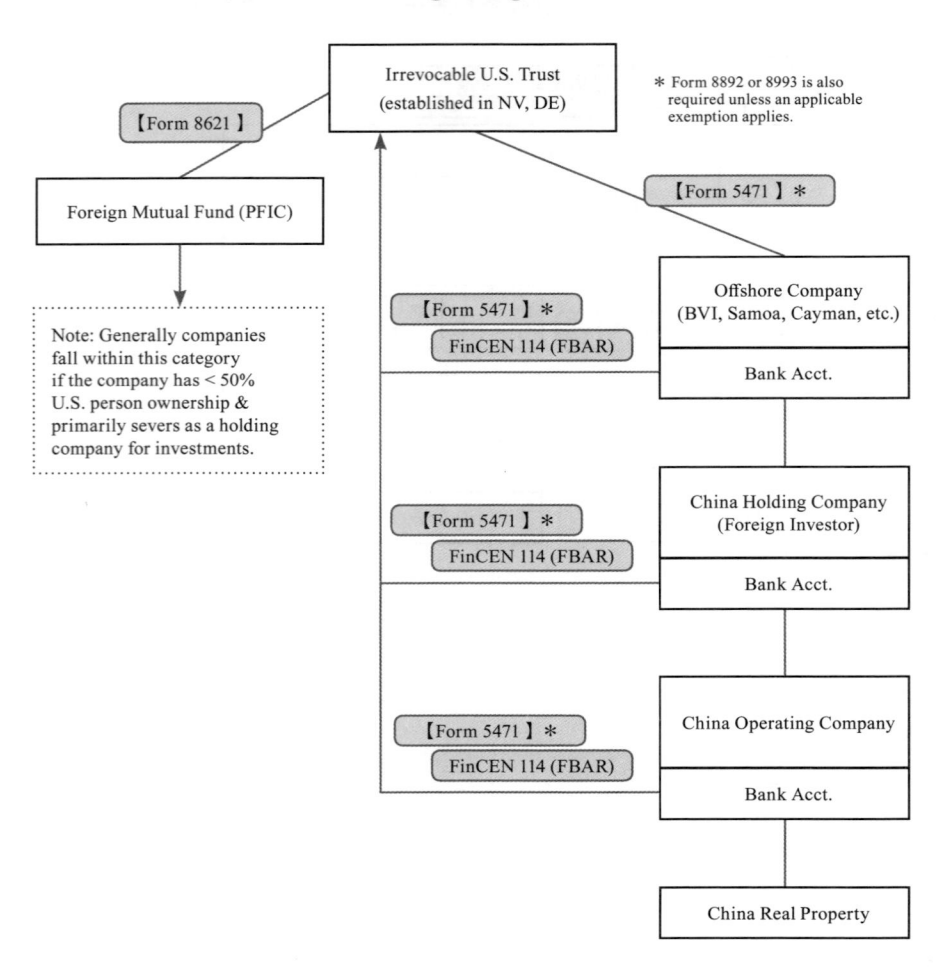

```
                    ┌─────────────────────────┐
                    │  Irrevocable U.S. Trust │      * Form 8892 or 8993 is also
                    │  (established in NV, DE)│        required unless an applicable
                    └─────────────────────────┘        exemption applies.
     【Form 8621】
                              【Form 5471】 *

   Foreign Mutual Fund (PFIC)           ┌─────────────────────────┐
                                        │    Offshore Company     │
                                        │ (BVI, Samoa, Cayman, etc.)│
         【Form 5471】 *                 ├─────────────────────────┤
         FinCEN 114 (FBAR)               │       Bank Acct.        │
                                        └─────────────────────────┘

   Note: Generally companies
   fall within this category              ┌─────────────────────────┐
   if the company has < 50%               │  China Holding Company  │
   U.S. person ownership &                │   (Foreign Investor)    │
   primarily severs as a holding          ├─────────────────────────┤
   company for investments.               │       Bank Acct.        │
                                         └─────────────────────────┘
         【Form 5471】 *
         FinCEN 114 (FBAR)

                                        ┌─────────────────────────┐
         【Form 5471】 *                 │  China Operating Company│
         FinCEN 114 (FBAR)               ├─────────────────────────┤
                                        │       Bank Acct.        │
                                        └─────────────────────────┘

                                        ┌─────────────────────────┐
                                        │   China Real Property   │
                                        └─────────────────────────┘
```

第四章 信託與個人之相關美國稅表

擁有海外資產的美國不可撤銷信託也需要遵守各種要求。

持有外國資產的美國不可撤銷信託

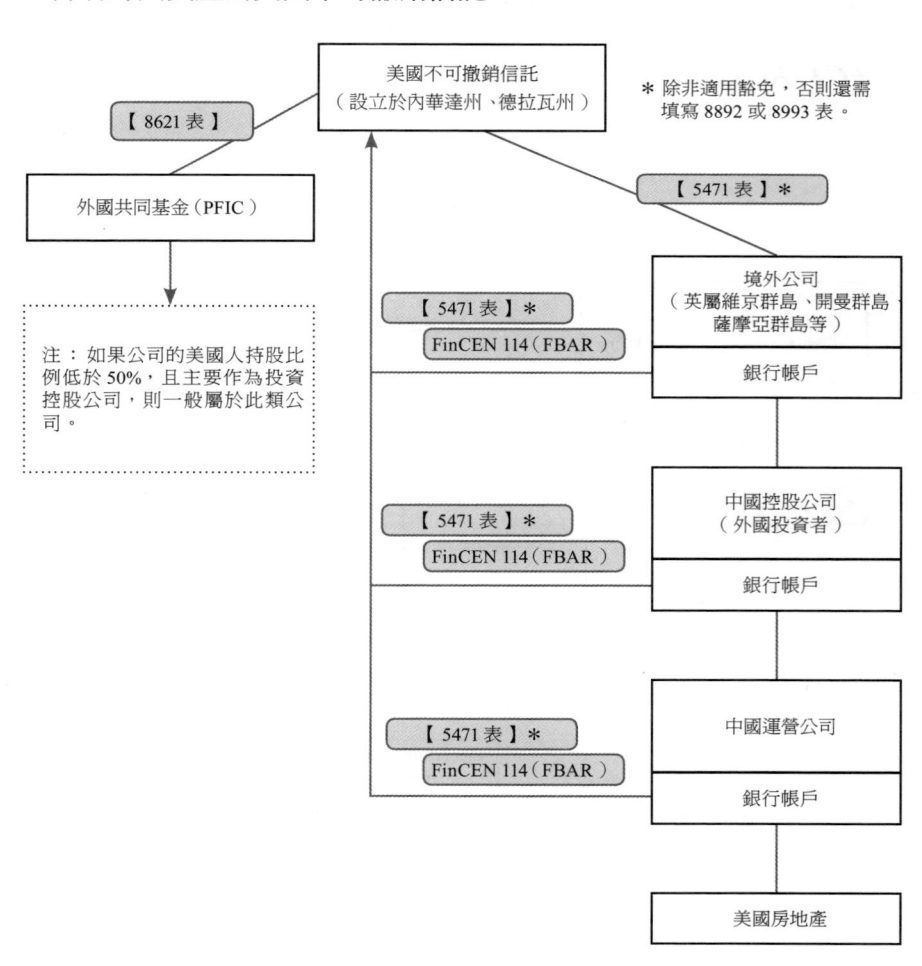

```
                    ┌─────────────────────────┐
                    │    美國不可撤銷信託      │      ＊除非適用豁免，否則還需
                    │（設立於內華達州、德拉瓦州）│       填寫 8892 或 8993 表。
                    └─────────────────────────┘
   【8621 表】
                                            【5471 表】＊
   ┌──────────────┐
   │ 外國共同基金（PFIC）│              ┌─────────────────┐
   └──────────────┘              │     境外公司      │
                                    │（英屬維京群島、開曼群島、│
           ↓            【5471 表】＊   │   薩摩亞群島等）   │
   ┌──────────────┐   FinCEN 114（FBAR）├─────────────────┤
   │ 注：如果公司的美國人持股比│              │     銀行帳戶      │
   │ 例低於 50%，且主要作為投資│              └─────────────────┘
   │ 控股公司，則一般屬於此類公│
   │ 司。                    │              ┌─────────────────┐
   └──────────────┘              │    中國控股公司    │
                       【5471 表】＊   │   （外國投資者）   │
                       FinCEN 114（FBAR）├─────────────────┤
                                    │     銀行帳戶      │
                                    └─────────────────┘

                       【5471 表】＊   ┌─────────────────┐
                       FinCEN 114（FBAR）│    中國運營公司    │
                                    ├─────────────────┤
                                    │     銀行帳戶      │
                                    └─────────────────┘

                                    ┌─────────────────┐
                                    │     美國房地產    │
                                    └─────────────────┘
```

While foreign trusts (including foreign grantor trusts) that do not generate U.S.-sourced income generally does not file an income tax return, it is subject to FBAR requirements, which requires the completion of FINCEN Form 114.

FGT (Revocable Trust)

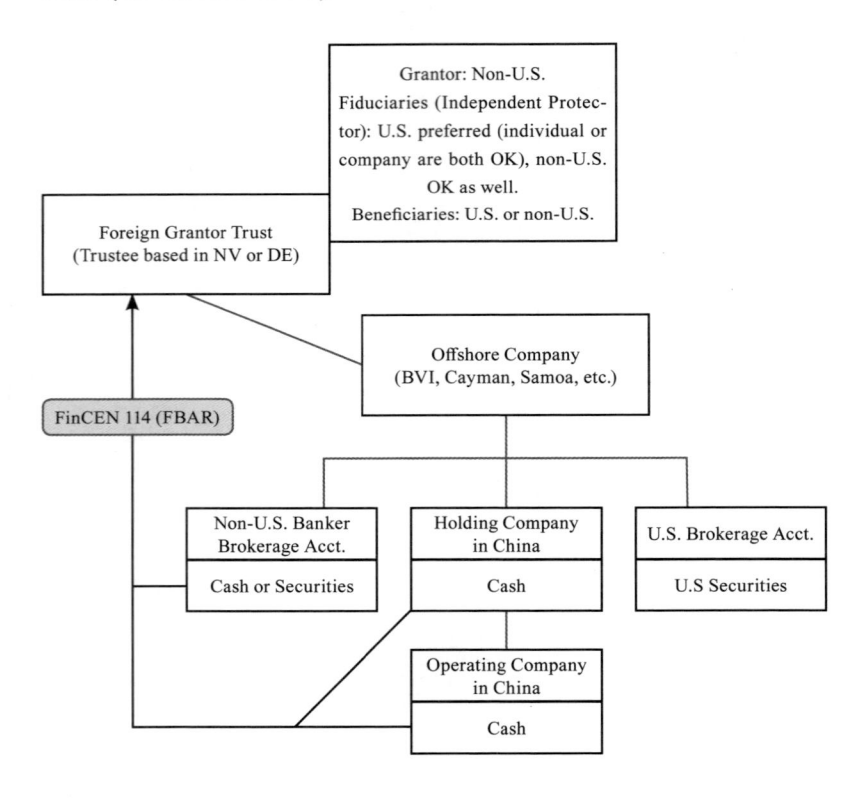

```
Foreign Grantor Trust
(Trustee based in NV or DE)

Grantor: Non-U.S.
Fiduciaries (Independent Protector): U.S. preferred (individual or company are both OK), non-U.S. OK as well.
Beneficiaries: U.S. or non-U.S.

Offshore Company
(BVI, Cayman, Samoa, etc.)

FinCEN 114 (FBAR)

Non-U.S. Banker Brokerage Acct.    Holding Company in China    U.S. Brokerage Acct.
Cash or Securities                  Cash                        U.S Securities

                                    Operating Company in China
                                    Cash
```

雖然沒有美國來源所得的外國信託（包括外國授予人信託）通常不用提交所得稅申報書，但這些信託仍須按照 FBAR 要求完成 FinCEN 114 表。

外國委託人信託

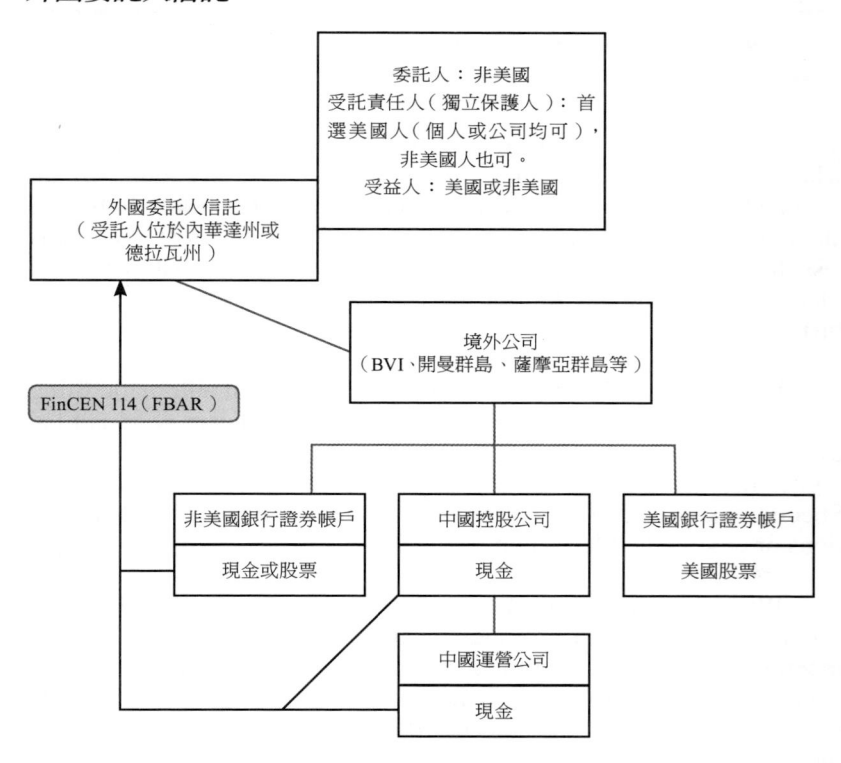

```
                    ┌─────────────────────────┐
                    │  委託人：非美國          │
                    │  受託責任人（獨立保護人）：首│
                    │  選美國人（個人或公司均可），│
                    │  非美國人也可。          │
                    │  受益人：美國或非美國    │
                    └─────────────────────────┘
┌──────────────────┐           │
│  外國委託人信託  │───────────┘
│ （受託人位於內華達州或│
│    德拉瓦州）    │
└──────────────────┘
        ▲              ┌──────────────────┐
        │              │  境外公司        │
FinCEN 114（FBAR）     │（BVI、開曼群島、薩摩亞群島等）│
        │              └──────────────────┘
        │                       │
   ┌────┴────┬──────────────────┼──────────────────┐
┌──────────────┐  ┌──────────────┐  ┌──────────────┐
│非美國銀行證券帳戶│  │中國控股公司  │  │美國銀行證券帳戶│
├──────────────┤  ├──────────────┤  ├──────────────┤
│  現金或股票  │  │    現金      │  │   美國股票   │
└──────────────┘  └──────────────┘  └──────────────┘
                         │
                  ┌──────────────┐
                  │ 中國運營公司 │
                  ├──────────────┤
                  │     現金     │
                  └──────────────┘
```

1. Form 1040

[Form 1040 — Department of the Treasury – Internal Revenue Service, U.S. Individual Income Tax Return, 2023, OMB No. 1545-0074]

Individuals who are U.S. citizens or resident aliens (non-Citizens who are residents for income tax purposes) generally must file an income tax return in their individual capacity (Form 1040). Individuals may be exempt from filing a Form 1040 if their gross income is less than certain thresholds as set forth by the IRS ($13,850 for single filers under 65 and $27,700 for married filers under 65 filing joint returns in 2023).

Form 1040 is due on April 15 of each year. An automatic filing extension to October 15 is generally applicable if Form 4868 is filed by April 15. The U.S. imposes higher income taxes on those with higher incomes up to a maximum Federal income tax rate of 37%. Specific tax rates depend on the status of the filer and any tax deductions or credits the filer is applicable for.

When preparing your Form 1040 filing, your tax preparer will often request that you provide certain information regarding your income including but not limited to any Form 1099s or W-2s that you have received. When a U.S. beneficiary receives a distribution, the income from the K-1 needs to be filled on Form 1040 and attached Schedule E. These forms inform the tax preparer of income you've received over the course of the previous calendar year.

1. 1040 表

美國公民或居民外國人（非美國公民，但屬於聯邦所得稅法上的稅務居民）通常必須以個人身分提交所得稅申報書（1040表）。如果個人的總所得低於美國國稅局規定的特定門檻（例如，在 2023 年，未滿 65 歲的單身納稅人其年度總所得低於 13,850 美元，或是未滿 65 歲的已婚納稅人其與配偶合併申報的年度總所得低於 27,700 美元），或許得以免除申報 1040 表之義務。

每年申報 1040 表之截止日為 4 月 15 日，若納稅義務人在 4 月 15 日前先行提交 4868 表，則申報截止日可自動延期至 10 月 15 日。在美國，所得較高者適用較高的所得稅稅率，當前聯邦所得稅稅率最高為 37%。實際稅率取決於納稅義務人的身分以及納稅義務人是否有可供使用之扣除額或稅額抵減。

在準備您的 1040 表時，您的稅務代理人通常會要求您提供有關您所得的特定資訊，這些資訊包括但不限於您收到的任何 1099 表或 W-2 表。當美國受益人從信託收到分配時，受益人需要將 K-1 表中的所得填寫在 1040 表和附表 E 上，這些表會讓稅務代理人知悉您在上一年度中收到的所得總額。

2. Form 3520

Form 3520 (Rev. December 2023)
Department of the Treasury
Internal Revenue Service

Annual Return To Report Transactions With Foreign Trusts and Receipt of Certain Foreign Gifts

Go to www.irs.gov/Form3520 for instructions and the latest information.

OMB No. 1545-0159

Note: All information must be in English. Show all amounts in U.S. dollars. File a **separate** Form 3520 for **each** foreign trust.

For calendar year 20___, or tax year beginning ___, 20___, ending ___, 20___

A Check appropriate boxes: ☐ Initial return ☐ Final return ☐ Amended return

B Check box that applies to person filing return: ☐ Individual ☐ Partnership ☐ Corporation ☐ Trust ☐ Executor

C Check if any excepted specified foreign financial assets are reported on this form. See instructions . . . . ☐

Part I — Transfers by U.S. Persons to a Foreign Trust During the Current Tax Year (see instructions)

5a Name of trust creator | **b** Address | **c** TIN, if any

6a Country code of country where trust was created | **b** Country code of country whose law governs the trust | **c** Date trust was created

7a Will any person (other than the foreign trust) be treated as the owner of the transferred assets after the transfer? . . . ☐ Yes ☐ No

b
(i) Name of foreign trust owner	(ii) Address	(iii) Country of residence	(iv) TIN, if any	(v) Relevant Code section

---

Part II — U.S. Owner of a Foreign Trust (see instructions)

20
(a) Name of foreign trust owner	(b) Address	(c) Country of tax residence	(d) TIN, if any	(e) Relevant Code section

21a Country code of country where foreign trust was created | **b** Country code of country whose law governs the trust | **c** Date foreign trust was created

22 Did the foreign trust file Form 3520-A for the current tax year? . . . . ☐ Yes ☐ No

If "Yes," attach the Foreign Grantor Trust Owner Statement you received from the foreign trust.
If "No," to the best of your ability, complete and attach a substitute Form 3520-A for the foreign trust.
See instructions for information on penalties for failing to complete and attach a substitute Form 3520-A.

23 Enter the gross value of the portion of the foreign trust that you are treated as owning at the end of your tax year . . $ ___

Part III — Distributions to a U.S. Person From a Foreign Trust During the Current Tax Year (see instructions)

Note: If you received an amount from a portion of a foreign trust of which you are treated as the owner, only complete lines 24 and 27.

24 Enter cash amounts or FMV of property received, directly or indirectly, during your current tax year, from the foreign trust (exclude loans and uncompensated use of trust property included on line 25).

(a) Date of distribution	(b) Description of property received	(c) FMV of property received (determined on date of distribution)	(d) Description of property transferred, if any	(e) FMV of property transferred	(f) Excess of column (c) over column (e)

Part IV — U.S. Recipients of Gifts or Bequests Received During the Current Tax Year From Foreign Persons (see instructions)

54 During your current tax year, did you receive more than $100,000 that you treated as gifts or bequests from a nonresident alien (including a distribution received from a domestic trust treated as owned by a foreign person) or a foreign estate? See instructions for special rules regarding related donors . . . . ☐ Yes ☐ No

If "Yes," complete columns (a) through (c) with respect to each such gift or bequest in excess of $5,000. If more space is needed, attach a statement.

(a) Date of gift or bequest	(b) Description of property received	(c) FMV of property received

---

A gift is subject to U.S. gift tax when made by a foreign donor (who would pay the tax) only if it is a gift of tangible personal property physically situated in the United States. However, even if a gift

2. 3520表

| Form **3520** (Rev. December 2023) Department of the Treasury Internal Revenue Service | **Annual Return To Report Transactions With Foreign Trusts and Receipt of Certain Foreign Gifts** Go to *www.irs.gov/Form3520* for instructions and the latest information. | OMB No. 1545-0159 |

Note: All information must be in English. Show all amounts in U.S. dollars. File a **separate** Form 3520 for **each** foreign trust.

For calendar year 20_____ , or tax year beginning _____ , 20 _____ , ending _____ , 20 _____

- **A** Check appropriate boxes: ☐ Initial return ☐ Final return ☐ Amended return
- **B** Check box that applies to person filing return: ☐ Individual ☐ Partnership ☐ Corporation ☐ Trust ☐ Executor
- **C** Check if any excepted specified foreign financial assets are reported on this form. See instructions . . . . ☐

Form 3520 (Rev. 12-2023) — Page **2**

Part I Transfers by U.S. Persons to a Foreign Trust During the Current Tax Year (see instructions)

- **5a** Name of trust creator
- **b** Address
- **c** TIN, if any

- **6a** Country code of country where trust was created
- **b** Country code of country whose law governs the trust
- **c** Date trust was created

- **7a** Will any person (other than the foreign trust) be treated as the owner of the transferred assets after the transfer? . . . ☐ Yes ☐ No

- **b**

(i) Name of foreign trust owner	(ii) Address	(iii) Country of residence	(iv) TIN, if any	(v) Relevant Code section

Form 3520 (Rev. 12-2023) — Page **4**

Part II U.S. Owner of a Foreign Trust (see instructions)

- **20**

(a) Name of foreign trust owner	(b) Address	(c) Country of tax residence	(d) TIN, if any	(e) Relevant Code section

- **21a** Country code of country where foreign trust was created
- **b** Country code of country whose law governs the trust
- **c** Date foreign trust was created

- **22** Did the foreign trust file Form 3520-A for the current tax year? . . . . ☐ Yes ☐ No
  - If "Yes," attach the Foreign Grantor Trust Owner Statement you received from the foreign trust.
  - If "No," to the best of your ability, complete and attach a substitute Form 3520-A for the foreign trust.
  - See instructions for information on penalties for failing to complete and attach a substitute Form 3520-A.
- **23** Enter the gross value of the portion of the foreign trust that you are treated as owning at the end of your tax year . . $ _____

Part III Distributions to a U.S. Person From a Foreign Trust During the Current Tax Year (see instructions)

Note: If you received an amount from a portion of a foreign trust of which you are treated as the owner, only complete lines 24 and 27.

- **24** Enter cash amounts or FMV of property received, directly or indirectly, during your current tax year, from the foreign trust (exclude loans and uncompensated use of trust property included on line 25).

(a) Date of distribution	(b) Description of property received	(c) FMV of property received (determined on date of distribution)	(d) Description of property transferred, if any	(e) FMV of property transferred	(f) Excess of column (c) over column (e)

Form 3520 (Rev. 12-2023) — Page **6**

Part IV U.S. Recipients of Gifts or Bequests Received During the Current Tax Year From Foreign Persons (see instructions)

- **54** During your current tax year, did you receive more than $100,000 that you treated as gifts or bequests from a nonresident alien (including a distribution received from a domestic trust treated as owned by a foreign person) or a foreign estate? See instructions for special rules regarding related donors . . . . ☐ Yes ☐ No
  - If "Yes," complete columns (a) through (c) with respect to each such gift or bequest in excess of $5,000. If more space is needed, attach a statement.

(a) Date of gift or bequest	(b) Description of property received	(c) FMV of property received

　　當外國贈與人行使的贈與為美國境內的有形個人財產時，美國國稅局會對該贈與課徵贈與稅（由外國贈與人支付稅款）。然

does not give rise to U.S. federal income tax or gift tax liability, if a U.S. person receives gifts from a foreign person, the U.S. person may be required to report such gifts.

More specifically, if the value of the aggregate foreign gifts received by a U.S. person during any tax year exceeds a certain threshold, the U.S. person is required to report certain information on such foreign gifts on Form 3520. For this purpose, a "foreign gift" is any amount received from a foreign person that the recipient treats as a gift or bequest. Thus, foreign gifts could include gifts of cash or personal property (such as cars, art, or furniture), as well as gifts of residential real property. In addition, foreign gifts could include payments made by the foreign person on behalf of the U.S. person.

With respect to the threshold, a U.S. person must report the receipt of gifts from a foreign individual or foreign estate if the aggregate amount of gifts from that foreign individual or foreign estate exceeds $100,000 during the tax year. Form 3520 further requires that the U.S. person separately identify each gift in excess of $5,000 by providing the date of the gift, a description of the property received, and the fair market value (FMV) of the property received.

For individuals receiving gifts from non-U.S. persons totaling more than $100,000 or Foreign Trusts, Form 3520 is required. Certain trusts may also be required to file Form 3520 upon receiving gifts from non-U.S. persons.

Since the penalties for failing to file Form 3520 are especially heavy, you should pay special attention to ensure that the form is filed both timely and accurately. Those who fail to report foreign gifts may be liable for up to 25% of the amounts received. Penalties for individuals who received distributions from Foreign Trusts may be liable for 35% of the amounts received.

而,即便贈與行為不在美國聯邦所得稅或贈與稅課稅範圍,當美國個人收到外國人贈與時,也可能需要申報。

更具體地說,如果美國人在任何稅務年度內收到的外國贈與總額超過一定門檻,那麼該美國人就必須在 3520 表上報告有關這些外國贈與的特定資訊。所謂的「外國贈與」,是指接收者將來自外國人的任何財產移轉視作「贈與」或「遺贈」的總額。因此,外國贈與可能包括現金或個人財產(如汽車、藝術品或傢俱),以及可供居住之房地產。此外,外國贈與也可能是外國人代美國人所支付的款項。

至於初始申報門檻,倘若美國人在稅務年度內從外國個人或外國遺產收到的贈與總額超過 10 萬美元,則該美國人必須申報這些贈與。同時,3520 表要求美國人需就單筆超過 5,000 美元的贈與填報贈與日期、描述收到的財產以及財產的公允市場價值。

如果個人收到來自非美國人或外國信託之贈與總額超過 10 萬美元,則該個人需要提交此表。某些信託如果從非美國人處收到贈與時,可能也需要提交此表。

當申報義務人未能及時和正確地申報此表時,該申報義務人將面臨嚴峻的處罰,因此應確保及時和準確地申報 3520 表。未能申報外國贈與的申報義務人可能會被追究責任,未報或漏報贈與之罰鍰金額可能高達收到贈與金額的 25%;若受贈人從外國信託收到分配而未及時、如實申報,罰鍰金額可能高達所收到贈與金額的 35%。

3. Form 1041 (including Form 7004)

Fiduciaries of U.S. trusts and estates which meet the following criteria must file Form 1041 to report income:

(1) Any taxable income for the tax year;
(2) Gross income of $600 or more (regardless of taxable income);
(3) A beneficiary who is a nonresident alien.

The form is due on April 15 of each year. An automatic filing extension to September 30 is generally applicable if Form 7004 is filed by April 15. You must provide Schedule K-1 (Form 1041), on or before the day you are required to file Form 1041, to each beneficiary who receives a distribution of property or an allocation of an item of the estate.

Irrevocable trusts established by non-U.S. persons are generally treated as non-grantor trusts, with certain exceptions. Non-grantor trusts generally pay income tax on any income generated by income not distributed to the trust's beneficiaries. Income distributed to trust beneficiaries is typically recorded on a Form K-1 and provided to the beneficiaries' tax preparers. Beneficiaries who receive income generally must include income received from the trust on their Form 1040. Distributions within the first 65 days of the year are generally treated as distributions for the previous calendar year. As such, qualified tax professionals often give clients' an estimate of income taxes owed at the beginning of the year to give the clients' a chance to decide if they would like to distribute to the trusts' beneficiaries.

3. 1041表（含7004表）

符合以下條件的美國信託和遺產之受託責任人必須提交1041表來申報信託所得：

（1）在稅務會計年度內有應稅所得；

（2）總所得達到或超過600美元（無論是否為應稅所得）；

（3）有非美籍受益人。

1041表的申報截止日為每年的4月15日。通常，如果申報義務人在4月15日之前提交了7004表，則可將申報期限自動延期至9月30日。您必須在提交1041表的截止日前向每位接收財產分配或遺產分配的受益人提供K-1表（1041表）。

非美國人設立的不可撤銷信託常被視為非委託人信託，但也有特定的例外情況。非委託人信託通常需要就未分配給信託受益人的信託收益支付所得稅。分配給信託受益人的信託收益一般會記錄於K-1表上，並提供給受益人的稅務代理人。收到信託收益的受益人必須在他們的1040表上申報來自信託的收入。正常情況下，信託在新一年度開始後的65天內所進行的分配會被視為前一年度的分配。因此，合格的稅務專業人士多會在年初為客戶估算信託的應納稅額，以便客戶決定是否將信託收益分配給信託的

A trust is a grantor trust if the grantor retains certain powers or ownership benefits. Generally, a revocable trust settled by a non-U.S. person is treated as a foreign grantor trust. In general, a grantor trust is ignored for income tax purposes and all of the income, deductions, etc., are treated as belonging directly to the grantor. This also applies to any portion of a trust that is treated as a grantor trust. If the entire trust is a grantor trust, fill in only the entity information of Form 1041. Don't show any dollar amounts on the form itself; show dollar amounts only on an attachment to the form. Don't use Schedule K-1 (Form 1041) as the attachment.

Note: For a detailed explanation of the Form 3520, please refer to the previous section, which discusses the Form 1040. A Form 3520 may be required to be filed with the Form 1041 if a trust receives a gift from a non-U.S. donor (certain exceptions apply).

Late Filing Penalty: The law provides a penalty of 5% of the tax due for each month, or part of a month, for which a return isn't filed up to a maximum of 25% of the tax due (15% for each month, or part of a month, up to a maximum of 75% if the failure to file is fraudulent). The penalty won't be imposed if you can show that the failure to file on time was due to reasonable cause. If you receive a notice about penalty and interest after you file this return, send us an explanation and we will determine if you meet reasonable-cause criteria.

Late Payment Penalty: Generally, the penalty for not paying tax when due is 1/2 of 1% of the unpaid amount for each month or part of a month it remains unpaid. The maximum penalty is 25% of the unpaid amount. The penalty applies to any unpaid tax on the return. Any penalty is in addition to interest charges on late payments.

受益人。

　　當信託委託人保留了某些權力或所有權利益，則信託被視作委託人信託。通常情況下，由非美國人設立的可撤銷信託會被視為外國委託人信託。一般來說，委託人信託在所得稅上是一個虛擬的個體，並非所得稅上的納稅人，所有的信託所得、扣除額等都將直接歸屬於委託人。當信託僅有部分屬於委託人信託時，上述操作也同樣適用於被視為委託人信託的任何部分。如果整個信託都是委託人信託，只須填寫 1041 表上關於信託的基本資料即可，切勿在表上顯示任何金額；所有金額只能顯示於表格的附件上。最後，請不要使用 K-1 表（1041 表）作為附件。

注：有關 3520 表的詳細介紹，請參閱前一節 1040 表的討論。如果信託從非美籍捐贈人那裡收到贈與，則申報 1041 表的同時可能須同時提交 3520 表（僅特定情況除外）。

　　遲延申報罰款：美國稅法規定，若申報義務人未按時申報，美國國稅局將以每月（或不足一個月）為期間單位，以未繳稅款的 5% 計算款罰金額，該罰款最高不超過未繳稅款的 25%；但如果是納稅義務人故意未按時申報，款罰金額將以每月（或不足一個月）為期間單位，以未繳稅款的 15% 計算款罰金額，該罰款金額最高不超過未繳稅款的 75%。如果納稅人能證明基於合理原因未能按時申報，則不會被處以罰款。如果您在提交此表後收到罰款和利息的裁罰通知，請您告知我們遲延申報的理由，我們將為您確認該理由是否符合合理原因的標準。

　　遲延繳納罰款：通常情況下，未在稅款繳款截止日時支付稅款，美國國稅局將以每月（或不足一個月）為期間單位，以未繳稅款的 0.5% 計算款罰金額，該罰款最高不超過未繳稅款的 25%。該罰款適用於申報表中的任何未支付稅款。任何罰款均不包含逾期支付稅款的利息費用。

4. Form 1065, Form 1120, and Form 8832

Form 1065 — U.S. Return of Partnership Income (2023)

Form 1120 — U.S. Corporation Income Tax Return (2023)

Form 8832 — Entity Classification Election (Rev. December 2013)

Form 8832 categorizes an **eligible entity** (typically, a U.S. LLC) as either a corporation, a partnership, or a disregarded entity for federal tax purposes.

- When an LLC is categorized as a partnership, it generally must file Form 1065. This is the "default" state for U.S. LLCs with more than one owner when it was formed under state law.
- When an LLC is categorized as a disregarded entity, its income is includible in the income tax form filed by the company's owner. This is the "default" state for U.S. LLCs with a single owner when it was formed under state law.
- When an LLC is categorized as a corporation, it generally

4. 1065 表、1120 表以及 8832 表

[Form 1065 — U.S. Return of Partnership Income, 2023]

[Form 1120 — U.S. Corporation Income Tax Return, 2023]

[Form 8832 — Entity Classification Election (Rev. December 2013)]

　　某些符合條件的**企業實體**（通常是指美國的有限責任公司，亦即 LLC），可以透過提交 8832 表，選擇按公司、合夥企業或非獨立個體的形式進行聯邦所得稅的稅務申報：

- 當 LLC 選擇按合夥企業的形式申報納稅時，通常必須申報 1065 表。LLC 按州法成立時如果擁有多位組成成員（members），則 LLC 的「預設」申報形式就是比照合夥企業的形式進行。
- 當 LLC 選擇按非獨立個體的形式申報納稅時，則 LLC 之

must file Form 1120. This tax treatment is generally only eligible if a LLC has filed Form 8832 to elect to be treated as an association taxable as a corporation.

Under Form 8832, **eligible entities** include LLCs, partnerships, disregarded entities, foreign entities, and business entities that are not considered a per se corporation. Form 8832 lists the business entities that must be recognized as "Per Se Corporations" (PSCs). For U.S. federal tax purposes, a per se corporation should be treated as a "corporation" at all times and cannot be changed (Treasury Regulation § 301.7701-2(b)).

An eligible entity uses Form 8832 to elect how it will be classified for federal tax purposes, as a corporation, a partnership, or an entity disregarded as separate from its owner. An eligible entity is classified for federal tax purposes under the default rules described below unless it files Form 8832 or Form 2553. The IRS will use the information entered on this form to establish the entity's filing and reporting requirements for federal tax purposes.

An LLC is an entity formed under state law by filing articles of organization as an LLC. Unlike a partnership, none of the members of an LLC are personally liable for its debts. An LLC may be classified for federal income tax purposes as a partnership, a corporation, or an entity disregarded as an entity separate from its owner by applying the rules in Regulations section 301.7701-3.

Form 1065 is an information return used to report the income, gains, losses, deductions, credits, and other information from the operation of a partnership. Generally, a partnership doesn't pay tax on its income but passes through any profits or losses to its partners. Partners must include partnership items on their tax or information returns.

所有者應在其個人之申報書中納入 LLC 之所得。這是當 LLC 按州法形成當下僅有一位組成成員（member）時的「預設」申報形式。
- 當 LLC 選擇按公司的形式申報納稅時，一般必須提交 1120 表。通常只有在 LLC 提交了 8832 表選擇以公司作為納稅主體時，才有資格以公司的形式申報納稅。

在 8832 表下，所謂「**符合條件的企業實體**」（eligible entities）包括有限責任公司（LLC）、合夥企業（Partnership）、非獨立個體（Disregarded Entities）、外國實體（Foreign Entities）以及不被視為實質公司（Per Se Corporations，PSCs）的企業實體。《財政部法規》第 301.7701-2(b) 條規定，實質公司在其存續期間均應被視為稅法上的「公司」，無法更改其稅法上企業型態。實質公司的態樣在 8832 表中有具體列示。

「符合條件的企業實體」可使用 8832 表選擇其在聯邦稅法上的身分，該實體可選擇按公司、合夥企業或是非獨立個體的身分申報納稅。除非「符合條件的企業實體」提交了 8832 表或 2553 表，否則該企業實體將根據以下的預設規則進行分類。美國國稅局將使用在該表格上輸入的資訊來確定企業實體在聯邦稅的申報義務。

有限責任公司（LLC）是根據州法成立，藉由提交有限責任公司組織章程而成立的企業實體。與合夥企業不同，LLC 的成員並不會就 LLC 之債務負無限責任。LLC 可以根據《財政部法規》第 301.7701-3 條的規定，在聯邦所得稅法上，選擇按合夥企業、公司或非獨立個體之形式進行稅務申報及納稅。

1065 表是一種資訊申報表，用於報告合夥企業的經營活動所產生的所得、利得、損失、扣除額、稅額扣抵及其他資訊。一般來說，合夥企業不須為其所得申報繳納所得稅，而是應將合夥

Form 1120 is the U.S. Corporation Income Tax Return used to report the income, gains, losses, deductions, credits, and to figure the income tax liability of a corporation. Unless exempt under section 501, all domestic corporations (including corporations in bankruptcy) must file an income tax return whether or not they have taxable income. Domestic corporations must file Form 1120.

Note: When owners of a foreign corporation agree to file an entity classification election (Form 8832) to treat the foreign company as a partnership for U.S. tax purposes, the election would trigger a deemed liquidation of the corporation for U.S. federal tax purposes on the day immediately preceding the effective date of the election. In a foreign grantor trust structure, a timely filed Form 8832 could increase the outside cost basis of an offshore company held by the trust prior to the grantor's death without triggering U.S. income taxes. A subsequent sale of those assets (shares in the offshore company) could be fully taxable outside the U.S.; however, within the U.S., it would be taxable only for appreciation of the offshore company that materializes after the grantor's death. Proper application and use of the "check the box" election (Form 8832) for eligible taxpayers could effectively reduce U.S. income tax.

之利潤或虧損移轉給其合夥人，合夥人必須在其稅務或資訊申報表上將合夥企業的所得納入其個人稅表中進行申報。

　　1120 表是美國公司所得稅申報表，用於報告公司的所得、利得、損失、扣除額、稅額扣抵，並計算公司的應納稅額。除非按稅法第 501 條取得豁免申報之待遇，否則所有美國境內公司（包括破產的公司），無論是否有應稅所得都必須提交所得稅申報表。國內公司必須提交 1120 表。

注： 當外國公司的所有者同意提交企業實體身分選擇表（8832 表），並將外國公司視為美國稅務目的上之合夥企業時，該選擇將在選擇生效日前一天觸發美國聯邦稅法上對外國公司的「視為清算」機制。而在外國委託人信託結構中，準時申報的 8832 表可以墊高委託人去世前，信託持有的海外公司的外部成本基礎，當成本基礎上升，就不會觸發美國所得稅。儘管日後出售這些資產（海外公司的股份）可能須在美國以外地區繳納所得稅，然而，在美國境內，只有在委託人去世後所實現的海外公司的增值才會變成美國應稅所得。對於符合條件的納稅人，正確運用 8832 表的「企業實體身分選擇」機制可以有效降低美國所得稅。

5. Form 5471

Form **5471** (Rev. December 2023) Department of the Treasury Internal Revenue Service	**Information Return of U.S. Persons With Respect to Certain Foreign Corporations** Go to www.irs.gov/Form5471 for instructions and the latest information. Information furnished for the foreign corporation's annual accounting period (tax year required by section 898) (see instructions) beginning _____ , 20 ___ , and ending _____ , 20 ___	OMB No. 1545-0123 Attachment Sequence No. **121**

Form 5471 is used by certain U.S. persons who are officers, directors, or shareholders in certain foreign corporations. The form and schedules are used to satisfy the reporting requirements of sections 6038 and 6046, and the related regulations. Generally, if you own or control a foreign company, directly or indirectly, you may be required to file Form 5471 and should consult with your U.S. accountant to determine how to appropriately satisfy your tax and disclosure obligations.

A U.S. shareholder for these purposes is a U.S. person that owns (directly, indirectly, or constructively) 10% or more of the total combined voting power or value of shares of all classes of a foreign corporation's stock. A CFC is any foreign corporation if more than 50% of the total combined voting power or value of shares of all classes of stock of the corporation is owned by U.S. shareholders on any day during the foreign corporation's tax year. A U.S. shareholder of a CFC is required to include in gross income on a current basis their pro rata share of certain income earned by the CFC, regardless of whether they receive a distribution. An SFC is a CFC or any foreign corporation whose shares (at least 10%) are held by a U.S. person, unless it is otherwise categorized as a PFIC.

A controlled foreign corporation (CFC) that is not a foreign insurance company generally must satisfy the following requirements:

(1) A foreign company formed in a foreign country that is classified as a foreign corporation for U.S. purposes:
- Mandatory per se foreign corporation on the IRS list. See Form 8832 instructions.
- By default if all owners have limited liability
- By election on Form 8832 entity classification election for certain foreign eligible entities

(2) More than 50% of the vote or value is owned by U.S. share-

5. 5471 表

Form **5471** (Rev. December 2023)	**Information Return of U.S. Persons With Respect to Certain Foreign Corporations** Go to *www.irs.gov/Form5471* for instructions and the latest information.	OMB No. 1545-0123
Department of the Treasury Internal Revenue Service	Information furnished for the foreign corporation's annual accounting period (tax year required by section 898) (see instructions) beginning _____ , 20 ___ , and ending _____ , 20 ___	Attachment Sequence No. **121**

5471 表是由在特定外國公司擔任高階管理人員、董事或股東的美國人或美國股東（U.S. Shareholder）申報。該表格和附表是用於達成《美國聯邦稅法》第 6038 條、第 6046 條及相關法規的申報要求。一般來說，如果您直接或間接擁有或控制外國公司，您可能須提交 5471 表。建議您應諮詢美國會計師，以確定如何適當地滿足您的稅務和揭露義務。

所謂美國股東（U.S. Shareholder），是指一個美國個人，直接、間接或實質地控制一家外國公司 10% 以上的投票權，或是其所持有之股權價值佔該外國公司的所有類別股票價值總和的 10% 以上。而受控外國公司（Foreign Controlled Corporation，CFC）是指任何外國公司，如果在該外國公司的稅務年度中的任何一天，美國股東擁有該外國公司全部類型股票 50% 以上之投票權或 50% 以上的股權價值，則該外國公司就會被認定為受控外國公司。無論該美國股東是否收到 CFC 之股利分配，CFC 的美國股東需要在當前基礎上將 CFC 賺取的特定所得，按其持股比例包含在個人之年度總所得中。特定外國公司（Specified Foreign Corporations，SFC）是指非屬被動海外投資公司（PFIC）的 CFC 或任何外國公司，其股票（至少 10%）由美國個人持有的公司。

通常，一家非屬外國保險公司的 CFC 必須滿足以下要求：

（1）在外國成立並根據美國規定被分類為外國公司的外國公司：

holder who each own at least 10% of the vote or value.

(3) Direct, indirect, and constructive ownership percentages are taken into account under I.R.C. §§ 958(a) and (b) attribution rules to determine if a foreign corporation is a CFC.

Generally, all U.S. persons described in Categories of Filers below must complete the schedules, statements, and/or other information. The word "generally" is used, as there are many rules, interpretations and exceptions that may apply to the Wealth Creator's specific situation; thus, Wealth Creators and their families should defer to their professional legal and tax advisors.

Category 1: A person who was a U.S. shareholder of an SFC at any time during the SFC's tax year ending with or within the U.S. shareholder's tax year and who owned stock on the last day in that year in which the foreign corporation was an SFC.

Category 2: A U.S. person who is an officer or director of a foreign corporation in which a U.S. person has acquired (in one or more transactions): (1) 10% stock ownership (by vote or value) with respect to the foreign corporation, or (2) an additional 10% or more of the outstanding stock (by vote or value) of the foreign corporation.

Category 3: This category includes:
- A U.S. person who acquires stock in a foreign corporation that, when added to any stock owned on the date of acquisition, meets the 10% ownership threshold (by vote or value) with respect to the foreign corporation.
- A U.S. person who acquires stock that, without regard to stock already owned on the date of acquisition, meets the 10% ownership threshold (by vote or value) with respect to the foreign corporation.
- A person who is treated as a U.S. shareholder of a captive insurance company under Sec. 953(c) with respect to a foreign corporation.
- A person who becomes a U.S. person while meeting the 10% ownership threshold (by vote or value) with respect to the foreign corporation.
- A U.S. person who disposes of sufficient stock in the foreign corporation to reduce their interest to less than the 10%

- 該公司在美國國稅局列表上的屬於不可變更身分的外國實質公司（Mandatory per se foreign corporation），請參見 8832 表說明。
- 該公司如果全部所有者都具有有限責任，則預設分類為外國公司。
- 該公司藉由提交 8832 表對某些外國合格實體之稅務上身分進行選擇。

（2）超過 50% 的投票權或股權價值由一位或多位（每位至少擁有 10% 投票權或股權價值）的美國股東擁有。

（3）根據《美國聯邦稅法》第 958(a) 條和第 958(b) 條的歸屬規則，考慮直接、間接和實質的所有權百分比，以確定外國公司是否為 CFC。

通常，下文所列舉之各類美國個人申報者都必須完成所列示之附表、聲明和／或其他資訊。這裡使用了「通常」一詞是因為有許多規則、解釋和例外情況可能適用於財富創造者的具體情況；因此，財富創造者及其家人應該聽從他們專業的法律和稅務顧問的建議。

類別一：任何在特定外國公司（SFC）的稅務年度內（該年度結束時或在該課稅年度內），曾是該外國公司的美國股東，並在該外國公司被視為 SFC 年度的最後一天仍持有該公司股票。

類別二：美國人擔任外國公司的管理階層或董事，且該美國人透過（一項或多項交易）獲得：(1) 該外國公司的 10% 股權（按投票權或價值計算），或(2) 該外國公司已發行股份的另外 10% 或以上的股權（按投票權或價值計算）。

類別三：該類別包括：

ownership threshold.
- A U.S person who owns at least 10% of the corporation (by vote or value) when the corporation is reorganized.

Category 4: A U.S. person who had control (i.e., ownership of stock possessing either more than 50% of the total combined voting power or value of shares of all classes of stock) of a foreign corporation during the annual accounting period of the foreign corporation.

Category 5: A U.S. person who was a U.S. shareholder that owned stock in a foreign corporation that was a CFC at any time during the foreign corporation's tax year ending with or within the U.S. shareholder's tax year, and who owned that stock on the last day in that year in which the foreign corporation was a CFC.

- 美國人在當年度取得了外國公司股票，若取得日期取得之股票與之前持有的任何股票相加後，達到了10%的所有權門檻（按投票權或價值計算）。
- 美國人在不考慮取得前已擁有外國公司股票的情況下，在購買日期取得的股票數量達到了10%的所有權門檻（按投票權或價值計算）的美國人。
- 美國人成為美國保險公司之專屬保險公司的股東（依據《美國聯邦稅法》第953(c)條中有關外國公司的規定）。
- 非美國人成為美國人的當下對外國公司之持股達到10%所有權門檻（按投票權或價值計算）。
- 美國人出售了足夠數量的外國公司股票，使其持股比例降至低於10%。
- 美國人在公司重組時，成為擁有公司至少10%股權（按投票權或價值計算）之股東。

類別四： 在外國公司的會計年度內，對該外國公司擁有控制權（即擁有該公司50%以上總投票權或股份價值）的美國人。

類別五： 美國人在外國公司的稅務會計年度結束時，或在美國股東的稅務會計年度內的任何時間，被視為受控外國公司（CFC）的美國股東，並且該美國人在該年度最後一天仍持有該外國公司的股票。

6. Form 8621

Form **8621** (Rev. December 2018) Department of the Treasury Internal Revenue Service	**Information Return by a Shareholder of a Passive Foreign Investment Company or Qualified Electing Fund** ▶ Go to *www.irs.gov/Form8621* for instructions and the latest information.	OMB No. 1545-1002 Attachment Sequence No. **69**

A U.S. person with a direct or indirect interest in a Passive Foreign Investment Company ("PFIC") may be required to file Form 8621. A foreign corporation is a PFIC if it meets either a passive income test or a passive asset test.

Under the income test, a foreign corporation is treated as a PFIC if 75 percent or more of its gross income fits within the definition of "passive income", which generally includes dividends, interest, royalties, rents, and annuities; there are many other special rules for determining what income is included.

Under the asset test, a foreign corporation is treated as a PFIC if the average percentage of assets held by such corporation during the taxable year which produces passive income, or which are held for the production of passive income, is at least 50 percent.

A foreign mutual fund is a common example of a PFIC. U. S. persons that own PFIC interests may be subject to additional tax and interest charges with respect to PFIC earnings and distributions. There is no threshold ownership requirement with respect to the PFIC rules, and thus a U. S. person can be subject to the PFIC rules even if their ownership interest in the PFIC is very small. However, to the extent that a foreign corporation is both a PFIC and a CFC, a U.S. investor that is a U.S. shareholder of the foreign corporation is generally only subject to the CFC rules with respect to their interest in the foreign corporation.

A U.S. investor in a PFIC is subject to one of three alternative taxing regimes generally at the investor's election:
 (1) the excess distribution regime (the default regime);
 (2) the "qualified electing fund"(QEF) regime; or
 (3) the "mark-to-market" regime.

6. 8621 表

Form 8621 (Rev. December 2018) Department of the Treasury Internal Revenue Service

Information Return by a Shareholder of a Passive Foreign Investment Company or Qualified Electing Fund

▶ Go to *www.irs.gov/Form8621* for instructions and the latest information.

OMB No. 1545-1002
Attachment Sequence No. **69**

　　如果美國人直接或間接持有被動外國投資公司（PFIC）的利益，可能需要提交 8621 表。PFIC 是指一間符合「被動所得測試」（passive income test）或「被動資產測試」（passive asset test）任一測試的外國公司。

　　所謂所得測試是指，如果外國公司 75% 以上的總所得符合「被動所得」的定義，則該外國公司即被視為 PFIC。被動所得通常包括股息、利息、權利金、租金和年金，此外，還有許多其他特殊規定來決定哪些所得應包括在內。

　　所謂資產測試是指，如果一家公司在產生被動所得的稅務會計年度內，產生被動所得的資產的百分比達到 50% 以上或為了產生被動所得而持有的資產佔全公司總資產的百分比達到 50% 以上，則該外國公司即被視為 PFIC。

　　外國共同基金是一種常見的 PFIC。擁有 PFIC 利益的美國個人可能會因為 PFIC 的收益和分配而需要繳納額外的稅負和利息費用。由於 PFIC 規則並未設計股權持有門檻，因此，即使美國個人在 PFIC 中的所有權利益非常小，他們也可能受到 PFIC 規則的影響。然而，如果外國公司既是 PFIC 又是 CFC，一名美國投資者（亦即外國公司的美國股東）通常只須遵循適用 CFC 規則。

　　在一般情況下，美國投資者在 PFIC 中可從三種課稅方法中選擇其中一種來完成稅上申報，投資者可以選擇：

　　（1）超額分配法（the excess distribution regime）（此為預設

The specific information required on Form 8621 varies depending upon which PFIC taxing regime applies. Generally, a U.S. investor is required to file a Form 8621 if they:

(1) receive certain direct or indirect distributions from a PFIC;

(2) recognize a gain on a direct or indirect disposition of PFIC stock;

(3) are making certain elections with respect to the PFIC, including a QEF or mark-to-market election;

(4) are reporting information with respect to a QEF or mark-to market election; or

(5) are required to file an annual report with respect to a PFIC.

制度）；

（2）合格的選擇資金法（Qualified Electing Fund，QEF）；或

（3）市價法（Mark-to-Market）。

美國投資者選用的 PFIC 不同的課稅方法，8621 表上需要提交的資訊也會有所不同。一般來說，美國投資者如果符合下述情形，即須提交 8621 表：

（1）從 PFIC 接收了特定之直接或間接分配；

（2）在直接或間接處分 PFIC 股票的過程中實現了資本利得；

（3）就 PFIC 的課稅方法作出選擇，包括「合格的選擇資金法」或是「市價法」；

（4）提交關於採用「合格的選擇資金法」或按「市價法」的選擇資訊；或者

（5）須就 PFIC 提交年度報告。

7. Form 8858

Form **8858** (Rev. September 2021) Department of the Treasury Internal Revenue Service	**Information Return of U.S. Persons With Respect to Foreign Disregarded Entities (FDEs) and Foreign Branches (FBs)** ▶ Go to www.irs.gov/Form8858 for instructions and the latest information. Information furnished for the FDE's or FB's annual accounting period (see instructions) beginning , 20 , and ending , 20	OMB No. 1545-1910 Attachment Sequence No. **140**

Form 8858 is used by certain U.S. persons that operate a Foreign Branch ("FB") or own a Foreign Disregarded Entity ("FDE") directly or, in certain circumstances, indirectly or constructively. The form and schedules are used to satisfy the reporting requirements of sections 6011, 6012, 6031, and 6038, and related regulations. Form 8858 reports certain information about the foreign disregarded entity, including information regarding the entity's income, losses, earnings and profits, and income taxes paid.

An FB is defined in Regulations section 1.367(a)-6T(g). For purposes of filing a Form 8858, an FB also includes a qualified business unit (QBU) (as defined in Regulations section 1.989-1(b)(2)(ii)) that is foreign.

An FDE is an entity that is not created or organized in the United States and that is disregarded as an entity separate from its owner for U.S. income tax purposes under Regulations sections 301.7701-2 and 301.7701-3. An eligible entity uses Form 8832 to elect how it will be classified for federal tax purposes. A copy of Form 8832 is generally attached to the entity's federal tax return for the tax year of the election. The tax owner of the FDE is the person that is treated as owning the assets and liabilities of the FDE for purposes of U.S. income tax law.

The following U.S. persons that are tax owners of FDEs, operate an FB, or that own certain interests in tax owners of FDEs or FBs must file Form 8858 and Schedule M (Form 8858):

Category 1: A U.S. person that is a tax owner of an FDE or operates an FB at any time during the U.S. person's tax year or annual accounting period. Complete the entire Form 8858, including the separate Schedule M (Form 8858) and other schedules as required.

Category 2: A U.S. person that directly (or indirectly through

7. 8858 表

Form **8858** (Rev. September 2021) Department of the Treasury Internal Revenue Service	**Information Return of U.S. Persons With Respect to Foreign Disregarded Entities (FDEs) and Foreign Branches (FBs)** ▶ Go to www.irs.gov/Form8858 for instructions and the latest information. Information furnished for the FDE's or FB's annual accounting period (see instructions) beginning _____, 20 ____, and ending _____, 20 ____	OMB No. 1545-1910 Attachment Sequence No. **140**

　　8858 表是由經營國外分公司（Foreign Branch，FB）或直接擁有（在某些情況下，間接或結構性地擁有）海外非獨立個體（Foreign Disregarded Entity，FDE）的特定美國個人填報。該表格和附表是用於滿足《美國聯邦稅法》第 6011、6012、6031 和 6038 條及相關《財政部法規》的報告要求。8858 表會反映海外非獨立個體的特定資訊，包括該個體的所得、損失、收益和利潤以及已繳納之所得稅等資訊。

　　國外分公司之定義規範在《財政部法規》第 1.367(a)-6T(g) 條。在 8858 表中，國外分公司尚包括位於境外的合格業務單位（Qualified Business Unit，QBU）（QBU 之定義規範在《財政部法規》第 1.989(a)-1(b)(2)(ii) 條）。

　　按《財政部法規》第 301.7701-2 條和第 301.7701-3 條，海外非獨立個體是指在美國境外創建或成立的企業實體，該企業實體在美國所得稅法上與其所有者視為同一個體。符合條件的企業實體可透過 8832 表選擇其稅務申報身分。8832 表的副本通常會附隨於該海外非獨立個體進行身分選擇年度的所得稅申報書中。在所得稅法上，所謂稅法上所有人（tax owner）被視作擁有海外非獨立個體資產和負債的人。

　　若美國人（U.S. Persons）屬於海外非獨立個體的所有人（tax owner），國外分公司的經營人，或是對於海外非獨立個體或國外分公司的所有者具有特定利益之人，該美國人必須提交 8858 表和 M 表（8858 表）：

a tier of FDEs) is a tax owner of an FDE or operates an FB. Complete the entire Form 8858, including the separate Schedule M (Form 8858).

Category 3: Certain U.S. persons that are required to file Form 5471 with respect to a CFC that is a tax owner of an FDE or operates an FB at any time during the CFC's annual accounting period.

Category 4: Certain U.S. persons that are required to file Form 8865 with respect to a controlled foreign partnership ("CFP") that is a tax owner of an FDE or operates an FB at any time during the CFP's annual accounting period.

Category 5: Certain U.S. person that is a partner in a partnership that owns an FDE or operates an FB and applies section 987 to the activities of the FDE or FB. The U.S. person must complete the first page of the Form 8858 and Schedule C-1 for each FDE and FB of the partnership.

Category 6: Certain U.S. corporations (other than a RIC, a REIT, or an S corporation) that is a partner in a U.S. partnership, which checked box 11 on Schedules K-2 and K-3 (Form 1065). Even though the U.S. corporation is not the tax owner of the FDE and/or the FB, the U.S. corporation must complete lines 1 through 5 of the Form 8858, line 3 of Schedule G, and report its distributive share of the items on lines 10 through 13 of Schedule G for each FDE and FB of the U.S. partnership.

類別一：若美國人在其納稅年度或年度會計期間的任何時候，是海外非獨立個體的稅收所有者或國外分公司的經營人，該美國人必須完成整份 8858 表，包括單獨的 M 表（8858 表）和其他附表。

類別二：若美國人直接（或通過一層海外非獨立個體）擁有海外非獨立個體或經營國外分公司，該美國人必須完成整份 8858 表，包括單獨的 M 表（8858 表）和其他附表。

類別三：若美國人在受控外國公司的年度會計期間內，該受控外國公司是海外非獨立個體的所有者或國外分公司之經營者，則該美國人必須要申報 5471 表。

類別四：若特定美國人在受控外國合夥（Controlled Foreign Partnership，CFP）的年度會計期間內，該受控外國合夥是海外非獨立個體的所有者或國外分公司之經營者，則該美國人必須申報 5471 表。

類別五：若特定美國人為合夥企業的合夥人，而合夥企業又擁有海外非獨立個體或經營國外分公司，並按《美國聯邦稅法》第 987 條計算海外非獨立個體或國外分公司的活動，則該美國人必須為合夥企業的每個海外非獨立個體和國外分公司完成 8858 表及 C-1 表的第一頁。

類別六：若一間非 RIC、REIT 或 S 公司的美國公司是美國合夥企業的合夥人，並在 1065 表的 K-2 和 K-3 上勾選了 11 號框（dual consolidated loss），則即使該美國公司不是海外非獨立個體和／或國外分公司的所有者，該美國公司也必須完成 8858 表的第 1 至第 5 行，以及 G 表的第 3 行，並報告其對於美國合夥企業的每個海外非獨立個體和國外分公司的 10 至 13 行的分配份額。

What are the penalties for the failure to file Form 8858 and Schedule M (Form 8858)?

A $10,000 penalty is imposed for each annual accounting period of each CFC or CFP for failure to furnish the required information within the time prescribed. If the information is not filed within 90 days after the IRS has mailed a notice of the failure to the U.S. person, an additional $10,000 penalty (per CFC or CFP) is charged for each 30-day period, or fraction thereof, during which the failure continues after the 90-day period has expired. The additional penalty is limited to a maximum of $50,000 for each failure.

Any person who fails to file or report all of the information required within the time prescribed will be subject to a reduction of 10% of the foreign taxes available for credit under sections 901 and 960. If the failure continues 90 days or more after the date the IRS mails notice of the failure to the U.S. person, an additional 5% reduction is made for each 3-month period during which the failure continues after the 90-day period has expired.

Criminal penalties. Criminal penalties under sections 7203, 7206, and 7207 may apply for failure to file the information required by section 6038.

未按時申報 8858 表以及 M 表之裁罰

　　未能在規定時間內完成年度申報的每個受控外國公司或受控外國合夥,將被裁處 10,000 美元的罰款。如果 IRS 向您發送通知,要求您提交 8858 表,您將有 90 天的寬限期進行補交。90 天寬限期後,IRS 將以 30 天為一期,就每一間 CFC、CFP,每期加徵申報義務人 10,000 美元的未繳納罰款。每次違規的附加罰款以 50,000 美元為限。

　　根據《美國聯邦稅法》第 901 和 960 條,未能在規定時間內申報或報告所有資訊的人不得使用 10% 的外國稅額扣抵。在 IRS 郵寄遲延申報通知後的 90 天後,如果申報義務人仍未補交,則在 90 天期限過後,IRS 將以 3 個月為一期,每期額外減少申報義務人 5% 的外國稅額扣抵。

　　刑事處罰。申報義務人未提交《美國聯邦稅法》第 6038 條所要求之資訊可能會被處以《美國聯邦稅法》第 7203、7206 和 7207 條之刑事處罰。

8. Form 8938

Form 8938 (Rev. November 2021)
Department of the Treasury
Internal Revenue Service

Statement of Specified Foreign Financial Assets
► Go to www.irs.gov/Form8938 for instructions and the latest information.
► Attach to your tax return.
For calendar year 20___ or tax year beginning ___, 20___, and ending ___, 20___

OMB No. 1545-2195
Attachment Sequence No. 938

Unless an exception applies, you must file Form 8938 if you are a **specified person (specified individual or a specified domestic entity)** that has an interest in specified foreign financial assets and the value of those assets is more than the **applicable reporting threshold**. If you are required to file Form 8938, you must report the specified foreign financial assets in which you have an interest even if none of the assets affects your tax liability for the year. Typically, filed with the Form 1040 (for individuals) or Form 1041 (for domestic trusts).

You are a **specified individual** if you are one of the following.
(1) A U.S. citizen.
(2) A resident alien of the United States for any part of the tax year (green card or substantial presence).
(3) A nonresident alien who makes an election to be treated as a resident alien for purposes of filing a joint income tax return.
(4) A nonresident alien who is a bona fide resident of American Samoa or Puerto Rico.

You are a **specified domestic entity** if you are one of the following.
(1) A closely held domestic corporation that has at least 50% of its gross income from passive income.
(2) A closely held domestic corporation if at least 50% of its assets produce or are held for the production of passive income.
(3) A closely held domestic partnership that has at least 50% of its gross income from passive income.
(4) A closely held domestic partnership if at least 50% of its assets produce or are held for the production of passive income (see Passive income and Percentage of passive assets held by a corporation or partnership, later).
(5) A domestic trust described in section 7701(a)(30)(E) that has one or more specified persons (a specified individual or a specified domestic entity) as a current beneficiary.

8. 8938 表

Form 8938 (Rev. November 2021)
Department of the Treasury
Internal Revenue Service

Statement of Specified Foreign Financial Assets
▶ Go to *www.irs.gov/Form8938* for instructions and the latest information.
▶ Attach to your tax return.

For calendar year 20___ or tax year beginning ___, 20___, and ending ___, 20___

OMB No. 1545-2195
Attachment Sequence No. 938

除非有例外情況，否則，如果您是擁有特定外國金融資產權益的**特定個人**（**specified person／specified individual**）或**特定國內企業實體**（**specified domestic entity**），且這些外國金融資產的價值超過了**規定的報告門檻**，則您有義務提交 8938 表。如果您必須提交 8938 表，您必須報告那些您所擁有利益的特定外國金融資產（即便這些資產對您當年的稅務責任沒有影響）。通常 8938 表與 1040 表（針對個人）或 1041 表（針對國內信託）須一起申報。

如果您是以下之一，則屬**特定個人**（**specified individual**）：

（1）美國公民。

（2）在任何稅收年度的某個時段內屬於美國居民之外國人（持有綠卡或通過實質居留測試）。

（3）為了提交合併所得稅申報書而選擇被視為居民外國人的非居民外國人。

（4）雖被歸類為非居民外國人但通過真實住所測試的美屬薩摩亞或波多黎各居民。

如果您是以下之一，則屬**特定國內企業實體**（**specified domestic entity**）：

（1）非公開持有的國內公司（閉鎖型公司）有 50% 以上的總所得屬於被動所得，則該公司屬於特定國內實體。

（2）非公開持有的國內公司（閉鎖型公司）有 50% 以上的資產用於生產被動所得，則該公司屬於特定國內實體（請參見後文有關被動所得以及公司或合夥企業持有產生被動所得資產百分

A domestic corporation is closely held if, on the last day of the corporation's tax year, a specified individual directly, indirectly, or constructively owns at least 80% of the total combined voting power of all classes of stock of the corporation entitled to vote or at least 80% of the total value of the stock of the corporation.

Applicable Reporting Threshold

If you are a specified individual, your applicable reporting threshold depends upon whether you are married, file a joint federal income tax return, and live inside (or outside) the United States.

	Single		Married Filing Joint		Married Filing Separate	
	Last Day	Anytime	Last Day	Anytime	Last Day	Anytime
Inside U.S.	50,000	75,000	100,000	150,000	50,000	75,000
Outside U.S.	200,000	300,000	400,000	600,000	200,000	300,000

	Specified Domestic Entities (as defined above)	
	Last Day	Anytime
Inside U.S.	50,000	75,000

You satisfy the reporting threshold only if:

(1) the total value of your specified foreign financial assets exceeds the amount specified under "Last Day" on the last day of the tax year; or

(2) the total value of your specified foreign financial assets exceeds the amount specified under "Anytime" at any time during the tax year.

比之說明）。

（3）非公開持有的國內合夥企業有 50% 以上的總所得來自被動所得，則該合夥屬於特定國內實體。

（4）非公開持有的國內合夥有 50% 以上的資產用於生產被動所得，則該合夥屬於特定國內實體（請參見後文有關被動所得以及公司或合夥企業持有產生被動所得資產百分比之說明）。

（5）有一個或多個特定個人或特定國內實體作為受益人的國內信託（《美國聯邦稅法》第 7701(a)(30)(E) 條）。

所謂非公開持有的國內公司（閉鎖型公司）是指如果在公司稅務年度的最後一天，一個特定個人直接、間接或實質地擁有公司所有類股票中至少 80% 的總投票權或至少 80% 的公司股票總價值，則該國內公司是非公開持有的公司（閉鎖型公司）。

申報門檻

如果您是特定個人，您所適用申報門檻取決於您的婚姻狀態，是否提交合併聯邦所得稅申報書，以及您是否居住在美國境內。

	單身		結婚且共同申報		結婚但分開申報	
	最後一天	任何一天	最後一天	任何一天	最後一天	任何一天
居住於美國境內	50,000	75,000	100,000	150,000	50,000	75,000
居住於美國境外	200,000	300,000	400,000	600,000	200,000	300,000

	特定國內企業實體（如前述定義）	
	最後一天	任何一天
於美國境內	50,000	75,000

您只有在滿足以下條件才會跨過申報門檻：

（1）您所擁有之特定外國金融資產的總價值在稅務會計年度的最後一天超過規定金額門檻；或者

（2）您擁有之特定外國金融資產的總價值在稅務會計年度的任何時候超過規定金額門檻。

What are the penalties for the failure to file Form 8938?

If you are required to file Form 8938 but do not file a complete and correct Form 8938 by the due date (including extensions), you may be subject to a penalty of $10,000. If you do not file a correct and complete Form 8938 within 90 days after the IRS mails you a notice of the failure to file, you may be subject to an additional penalty of $10,000 for each 30-day period (or part of a period) during which you continue to fail to file Form 8938 after the 90-day period has expired. The maximum additional penalty for a continuing failure to file Form 8938 is $50,000.

Reasonable Cause Exception

No penalty will be imposed if you fail to file Form 8938 or to disclose one or more specified foreign financial assets on Form 8938 and the failure is due to reasonable cause and not to willful neglect. You must affirmatively show the facts that support a reasonable cause claim. The determination of whether a failure to disclose a specified foreign financial asset on Form 8938 was due to reasonable cause and not due to willful neglect will be determined on a case-by-case basis, taking into account all pertinent facts and circumstances.

未申報 8938 表之裁罰為何？

如果您有義務提交 8938 表但未能在截止日（包括延期）前申報完整且正確的 8938 表，您可能會面臨 10,000 美元的罰款。如果您在 IRS 郵寄遲延申報之通知日起 90 天之寬限內，未能申報正確和完整的 8938 表，則在 90 天寬限期結束後，IRS 可能會以 30 天（或不足 30 天）為一期，就您未完成申報 8938 表每一期處以 10,000 美元的額外罰款。持續未申報 8938 表的最高額外罰款為 50,000 美元。

合理原因例外

如果您未能申報 8938 表或未在 8938 表上揭露一個或多個特定外國金融資產，但這種漏未申報是基於合理原因而非故意忽略，則您不會被處以罰款。為了支持您有合理原因而漏未申報之主張，您必須積極提出相關事實。IRS 將在考慮所有相關事實和情況後，依個案認定標準，判斷您不是出於故意忽略，而是基於合理原因而未在 8938 表上揭露特定外國金融資產。

9. Form 8992 and Form 8993 (including Section 962 Election)

Form 8992 (Rev. December 2022) — U.S. Shareholder Calculation of Global Intangible Low-Taxed Income (GILTI)

Form 8993 (Rev. December 2021) — Section 250 Deduction for Foreign-Derived Intangible Income (FDII) and Global Intangible Low-Taxed Income (GILTI)

Generally, a person who is a U.S. shareholder of at least one foreign corporation (ownership of at least 10%) that is considered a CFC must file Form 8992.

All domestic corporations (and U.S. individual shareholders of controlled foreign corporations (CFCs) making a section 962 election (962 electing individual)) must use Form 8993 to determine the allowable deduction under section 250. A section 962 election, when properly elected, can:
- allow individual CFC shareholders the ability to offset their subpart F liability with foreign tax credits for taxes paid by the CFC.
- reduce the income tax consequence of a GILTI inclusion to only 10.5 percent.
- generate a second layer of tax as if the CFC shareholder received a dividend from a C corporation (which could potentially be beneficial for income tax purposes).

Note: For a detailed explanation of the definition of a Controlled Foreign Corporation ("CFC"), please refer to the section of this chapter that discusses the Form 5471.

When an individual U.S. shareholder of a CFC has an income inclusion under either Subpart F or GILTI and makes an election pursuant to Sec. 962 to be taxed at corporate rates, the amount of income itself is not reported on Form 1040. Instead, taxpayers must track that information separately, attach a statement to the tax return, and report any tax directly on Form 1040, line 12a.

A 10% U.S. shareholder of a CFC is required to report inclusions of GILT and Subpart F income on the U.S. federal income tax

9. 8992 表以及 8993 表（包含《聯邦所得稅法》第 962 選擇）

Form 8992 (Rev. December 2022) Department of the Treasury Internal Revenue Service — U.S. Shareholder Calculation of Global Intangible Low-Taxed Income (GILTI). OMB No. 1545-0123. Go to www.irs.gov/Form8992 for instructions and the latest information. Attachment Sequence No. 992

Form 8993 (Rev. December 2021) Department of the Treasury Internal Revenue Service — Section 250 Deduction for Foreign-Derived Intangible Income (FDII) and Global Intangible Low-Taxed Income (GILTI). OMB No. 1545-0123. ▶ Go to www.irs.gov/Form8993 for instructions and the latest information. Attachment Sequence No. 993

通常情況下，若美國股東對一間以上之受控外國公司持股達 10% 以上，則該美國股東必須申報 8992 表。

所有美國境內公司（以及依《美國聯邦稅法》第 962 條進行選擇的受控外國公司的美國個人股東）必須使用 8993 表來確定《美國聯邦稅法》第 250 條的可允許扣除額。藉由《美國聯邦稅法》第 962 條的選擇，可以讓個人：

- 允許個人受控外國公司股東使用受控外國公司取得的外國稅額扣抵，降低其 Subpart F 所得。
- 將 GILTI（境外無形資產所得）適用的有效稅率降低至 10.5%。
- 產生第二層稅收，就如同受控外國公司股東收到了 C 公司的股息（從稅收角度來看，這可能是有益的）。

注：有關受控外國公司（CFC）的定義的詳細解釋，請參閱本章討論 5471 表的部分。

當美國受控外國公司的個人股東依《美國聯邦稅法》第 962 條選擇按公司稅率納稅並有 Subpart F 或 GILTI 所得時，該所得金額本身不會在美國個人股東之 1040 表上申報。相反地，納稅人必須單獨列出該資訊，將一份聲明附加到納稅申報表上，並在 1040 表的第 12a 行直接報告任何應納稅額。

持有受控外國公司 10% 以上股份之美國股東必須在美國聯邦

return. A U.S. shareholder's direct and indirect ownership percentages of a CFC under I.R.C. § 958(a) determine the allocable share of GILTI.

In the chart below, you can find a simplified version of the GILTI tax computations. It is generally advisable for you to seek professional advice regarding these calculations to ensure that the forms and eligible elections are properly filed.

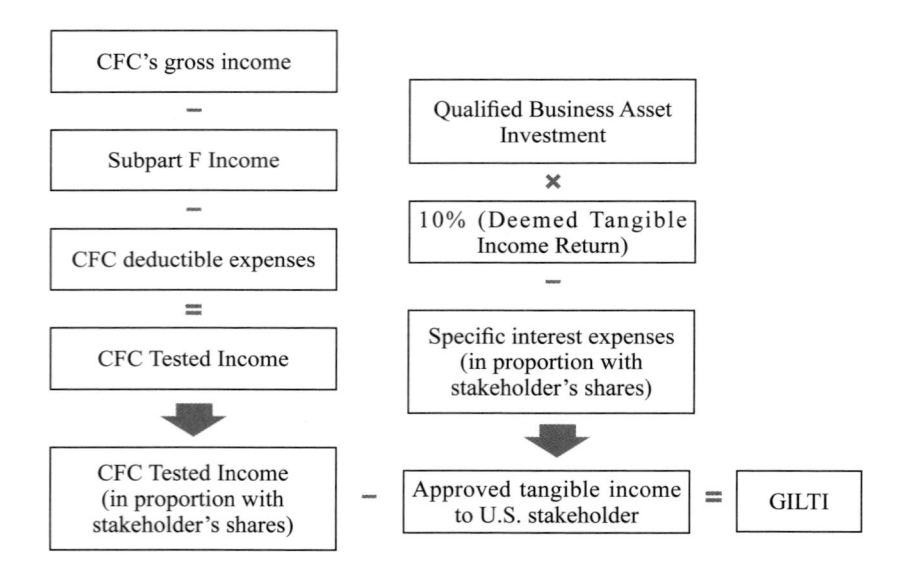

```
CFC's gross income
         −
   Subpart F Income
         −
 CFC deductible expenses
         =
   CFC Tested Income
         ↓
   CFC Tested Income
   (in proportion with
   stakeholder's shares)
```

```
Qualified Business Asset
      Investment
         ×
10% (Deemed Tangible
   Income Return)
         −
Specific interest expenses
   (in proportion with
   stakeholder's shares)
         ↓
```

CFC Tested Income (in proportion with stakeholder's shares) − Approved tangible income to U.S. stakeholder = GILTI

所得稅申報書上報告 GILTI 所得和 Subpart F 所得。根據《美國聯邦稅法》第 958(a) 條，美國股東對受控外國公司之直接及間接持股百分比會決定應申報的 GILTI。

下圖為如何計算 GILTI 稅的簡化示意圖。通常我們會建議您尋求專業意見，以確保表格之正確申報及勾選。

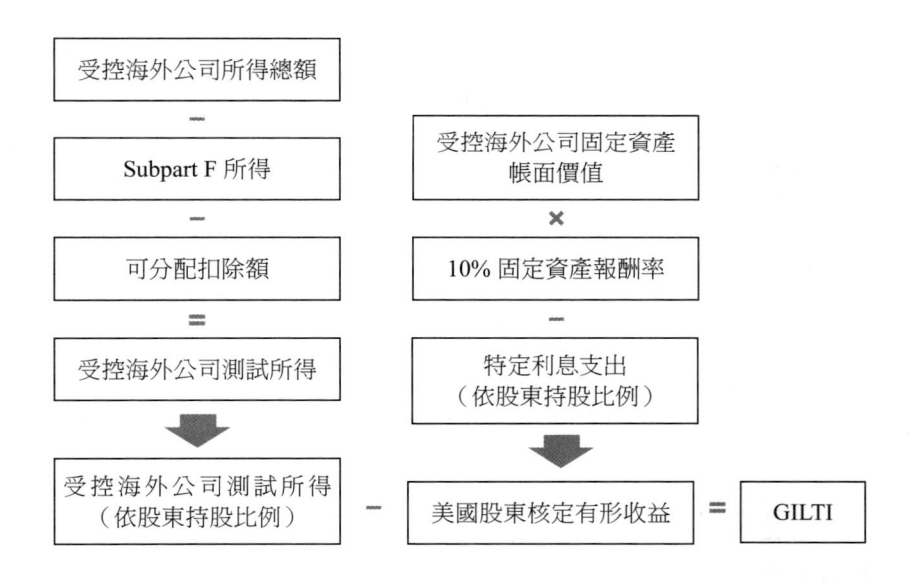

```
受控海外公司所得總額
        −
   Subpart F 所得                受控海外公司固定資產
                                    帳面價值
        −                            ×
    可分配扣除額                10% 固定資產報酬率
        =                            −
 受控海外公司測試所得              特定利息支出
        ↓                        （依股東持股比例）
 受控海外公司測試所得                  ↓
  （依股東持股比例）    −    美國股東核定有形收益    =    GILTI
```

10. Form SS-4

Form SS-4 (Rev. December 2023)
Department of the Treasury
Internal Revenue Service

Application for Employer Identification Number
(For use by employers, corporations, partnerships, trusts, estates, churches, government agencies, Indian tribal entities, certain individuals, and others.)
See separate instructions for each line. Keep a copy for your records.
Go to *www.irs.gov/FormSS4* for instructions and the latest information.

OMB No. 1545-0003
EIN

Form SS-4 is used when applying for an Employer Identification Number (EIN). An EIN is a nine-digit number the Internal Revenue Service (IRS) assigns to employers, sole proprietors, corporations, partnerships, estates, trusts, and other entities for tax filing and reporting purposes. When starting a new U.S. business, you will generally need to apply for an EIN using Form SS-4.

Before you complete your Form SS-4, you should prepare by doing the following:
- Determine the legal name of your business.
- Determine if the business has a trade name (i.e., doing business as, or DBA) that is different from its legal name.
- Know whether the business is a corporation, partnership or LLC.
- Determine the mailing address of your business.
- Gather information about the individual responsible for the business, including their tax ID number.
- Know the business start date and closing month of the accounting year.

If you don't know this information or your business hasn't yet been established, you should wait until this information is known to file your Form SS-4.

You can submit your Form SS-4 on the IRS's online application, via fax or by mail. If you use the online application, you will receive your EIN immediately. Phone applications are only available for international applicants. If you have no legal residence, principal place of business, or principal office or agency in the U.S. or U.S. territories, you can't use the online application to obtain an EIN. In certain cases, the online application for an EIN may be rejected, in which case, you may be required to call, mail, or fax the information to the IRS instead.

10. SS-4 表

Form SS-4 (Rev. December 2023)
Department of the Treasury
Internal Revenue Service

Application for Employer Identification Number
(For use by employers, corporations, partnerships, trusts, estates, churches, government agencies, Indian tribal entities, certain individuals, and others.)
See separate instructions for each line. Keep a copy for your records.
Go to www.irs.gov/FormSS4 for instructions and the latest information.

OMB No. 1545-0003
EIN

SS-4 表係用於申請雇主識別號碼（EIN）。EIN 是 IRS 分配給雇主、個體經營者、公司、合夥、遺產、信託和其他企業實體用於報稅和申報目的的九位號碼。在美國成立新企業時，通常需要使用 SS-4 表申請 EIN。

在填寫表格 SS-4 表之前，您應該做好以下準備：
- 確認您的企業法定名稱。
- 確認企業是否有與法定名稱不同的商業名稱（例如，Doing Business As 或 DBA）。
- 瞭解企業為公司、合夥企業還是有限責任公司（LLC）。
- 確認企業的收信地址。
- 收集有關負責人的資訊，包括他們的個人稅籍編碼。
- 瞭解企業的成立日期和會計年度的結束月份。

如果您不瞭解這些資訊或者您的企業尚未成立，應等到瞭解這些資訊後再提交表格 SS-4。

您可以通過 IRS 的線上申請、傳真或郵寄方式提交表格 SS-4。如果使用線上申請，將可立即收到您的 EIN。電話申請僅適用於國際申請者。如果您在美國或美國領土內沒有合法居所、主要營業地點或主要辦事處或代理機構，則不能使用線上申請獲得 EIN。在某些情況下，EIN 的線上申請可能會被拒絕，這種情況下，可能需要通過電話、郵寄或傳真方式將資訊發送給 IRS。

11. FinCEN Form 114

Report of Foreign Bank and Financial Accounts					
Home	Filer Information	Financial Account Owned Separately/Jointly	No Financial Interest Account Information	Consolidated Report	Signature Information

1 This report is for calendar year ended 12/31 [ ]   Amended ☐   Prior Report BSA Identifier [ ]

The Bank Secrecy Act (BSA) gives the Department of Treasury the authority to collect information from United States persons, including expats, who **have financial interests in** or **signature authority over** financial accounts maintained with financial institutions located outside of the United States.

The BSA requires that a Financial Crimes Enforcement Network ("FinCEN") Report 114, Report of Foreign Bank and Financial Accounts (FBAR), be filed if the maximum values of the foreign financial accounts exceed $10,000 in the aggregate at any time during the calendar year.

Essentially, any U.S. person who owns a financial account outside of the U.S. generally must file FinCEN Form 114. These "accounts" include:
- Bank accounts (savings accounts, checking accounts and fixed deposit accounts)
- Securities accounts (stocks, bonds, and derivatives)
- Insurance (any policy that has a cash value)

Examples of FBAR delinquency penalties include the following:
- FBAR Civil Penalties:
  - Negligent or "non-willful" delinquency can result in a penalty of $10,000 per account per year unless there is reasonable cause for failing to file.
  - A "willful" failure to file could be subject to civil penalties equal to the greater of $100,000 or 50% of the balance in each unreported account.
- FBAR Criminal Penalties: A willful violation can result in fines of up to $250,000 and 5 years of jail time.

11. 金融犯罪執法網路 FinCEN 114 表

銀行保密法（Bank Secrecy Act，BSA）賦予財政部收集美國人（包括海外居民）在美國境外金融機構開設的金融帳戶資訊。若美國人對海外金融帳戶有財務利益或簽署許可權，該美國人就必須申報海外帳戶的資訊。

銀行保密法要求當外國金融帳戶的最高價值在一個日曆年度內超過 10,000 美元時，帳戶持有人必須提交金融犯罪執法網路（FinCEN）114 表，以及外國銀行和金融帳戶報告。

基本上，當美國人在美國境外擁有金融帳戶時，都必須向 FinCEN 提交 114 表。這些「帳戶」包括：

- 銀行帳戶（儲蓄帳戶、支票帳戶和定期存款帳戶）
- 證券帳戶（股票、債券和衍生性金融商品）
- 保險（任何具有現金價值的保單）

遲延申報外國銀行和金融帳戶報告之罰款包括以下情況：

- 民事處罰：
  - 申報義務人疏忽或「非故意」遲延可能會導致每個帳戶每年 10,000 美元的罰款，除非申報義務人有合理理由未能提交。
  - 「故意」不提交可能會面臨民事處罰，金額為 100,000 美元或未申報帳戶餘額的 50% 兩者中之較大者。
- 刑事處罰：申報義務人故意違反申報規定可能會導致高

Generally, if the trust has a U.S.-based trustee and the trust has ownership over a financial account, the trust must report the account on its FBAR. Even if the trust is a foreign grantor trust for U.S. income tax purposes, the trust is deemed a United States person because it is organized in the United States and thus is required to report financial accounts it owns.

The FBAR is an annual report, due April 15 following the calendar year reported. You're allowed an automatic extension to October 15 if you fail to meet the FBAR annual due date of April 15. You don't need to request an extension to file the FBAR.

達 25 萬美元的罰款和 5 年的刑事監禁。

通常情況下,如果信託有一個美國受託人,並且該信託擁有財務帳戶所有權,則信託必須在其外國銀行和金融帳戶報告上報告該帳戶。即使信託在美國所得稅上是一個外國委託人信託,但因為該信託是在美國設立的,因此該信託會被視為美國人,從而必須報告其擁有的財務帳戶並提交 FBAR。

FBAR 是一份年度報告,該報告應於報告年度後的 4 月 15 日前進行申報。如果未能在 FBAR 年度申報截止日 4 月 15 日前完成報告,該申報期限會自動延至 10 月 15 日,帳戶所有人無須申請延期以提交 FBAR。

12. FinCEN Beneficial Ownership Filing (Corporate Transparency Act)

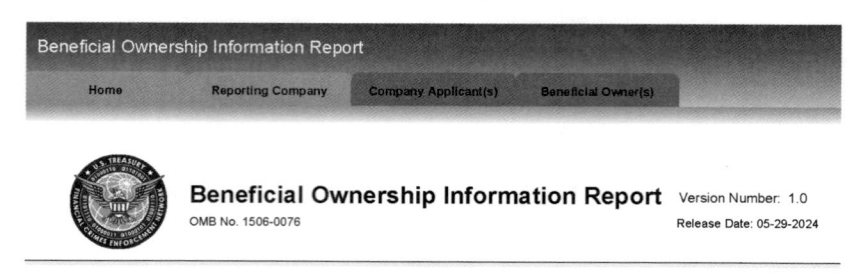

Beneficial Ownership Information Report			
Home	Reporting Company	Company Applicant(s)	Beneficial Owner(s)

Beneficial Ownership Information Report　　Version Number: 1.0
OMB No. 1506-0076　　Release Date: 05-29-2024

The Corporate Transparency Act ("CTA") enacted by Congress requires that existing and newly formed or registered corporations, limited liability companies, and other business entities operating in the United States report beneficial ownership information in the form of a Beneficial Ownership Information Report ("BOIR").

(1) The Corporate Transparency Act and FinCEN

The Corporate Transparency Act aims to combat illicit financial activities by requiring entities subject to its regulations to submit BOIR to the Financial Crimes Enforcement Network ("FinCEN") of the U.S. Department of the Treasury within specified deadlines (detailed below).

(2) Requirements for Beneficial Ownership Information Reports (BOIR)

Entities subject to the regulations ("Reporting Companies") must submit their initial reports by the following deadlines:

Existing companies (reporting companies established or registered to do business in the United States before January 1, 2024)	January 1, 2025.
New companies established or registered to do business in 2024.	Within 90 calendar days.
New companies established or registered to do business on or after January 1, 2025.	Within 30 calendar days.

The BOIR is not an annual requirement. A reporting company is required to file a BOIR upon formation within a certain allotted timeframe and after there is a change in the company's beneficial ownership. Generally, reporting companies must provide the follow-

12. 金融犯罪執法網路 FinCEN 受益所有權申報（企業透明法）

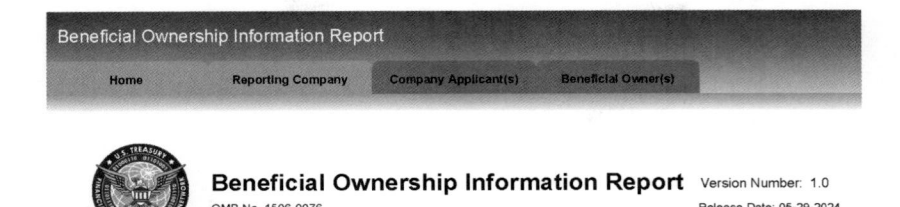

![Beneficial Ownership Information Report 介面截圖，顯示 Home, Reporting Company, Company Applicant(s), Beneficial Owner(s) 等標籤，以及 U.S. Treasury 標誌、OMB No. 1506-0076、Version Number: 1.0、Release Date: 05-29-2024]

美國國會通過的《企業透明法》（Corporate Transparency Act，CTA）要求現有和新成立或註冊的公司、有限責任公司以及其他在美國運營的商業實體，以「受益所有權訊息報告」（Beneficial Ownership Information Report，BOIR）的形式報告受益所有權訊息。

（1）企業透明法案以及 FinCEN

《企業透明法》旨在通過要求受其監管的實體在規定的截止日期內向美國財政部下屬的金融犯罪執法網路（FinCEN）提交 BOIR 來打擊非法金融活動。

（2）受益所有權訊息報告之內容要求

受法規規範的實體（報告公司）必須在以下截止日提供申報：

在 2024 年 1 月 1 日之前成立或註冊在美國開展業務的既存公司（報告公司）。	於 2025 年 1 月 1 日申報
2024 年成立或註冊營業的新公司。	於每日曆年後 90 日內申報
2025 年 1 月 1 日或之後成立或註冊以開展業務的新公司。	於每日曆年後 30 日內申報

BOIR 並非年度要求的申報項目。在某一特定規定時間內，報告公司成立後需要提交 BOIR，並在公司受益所有權發生變化後再次提交。一般來說，報告公司必須提供以下資訊：

ing information:
- Name of each beneficial owner ("BO"), as defined by FinCEN.
- Date of birth of each BO.
- Address of each BO.
- Personal identification of each BO (valid passport, driver's license, or ID).
- Information about the Reporting Company itself, including its name and address.
- Companies established on or after January 1, 2024, must also submit information about the individuals establishing the company ("Company Applicant").

(3) Penalties for non-compliance with the Beneficial Ownership Information Report (BOIR) requirements may include:

Potential violations include intentionally failing to submit BOIR, intentionally submitting incorrect BOIR, or intentionally failing to correct or update previously submitted BOIR. Violators may face civil penalties of up to $592 per day for the duration of the violation and criminal penalties of up to $10,000 and up to two years of imprisonment.

- 每個受益所有人（根據 FinCEN 定義）的姓名。
- 每個受益所有人的出生日期。
- 每個受益所有人的位址。
- 每個受益所有人的個人身分證明（有效護照、駕駛執照或身分證）。
- 關於報告公司本身的資訊，包括其名稱和地址。
- 從 2024 年 1 月 1 日起成立的公司還必須提交有關公司創辦人（或是公司申請人）的資訊。

（3）不遵守受益所有權資訊報告要求的懲罰可能包括：

可能的違規行為包括故意不提交 BOIR、故意提交不正確的 BOIR，或故意不更正或更新先前提交的 BOIR。違規者可能會在違規期間面臨每天最高 592 美元的民事罰款，以及最高 10,000 美元和最高兩年監禁的刑事處罰。

13. Streamlined Procedures (Form 14653 and 14654)

Form **14653** (August 2014)	Department of the Treasury - Internal Revenue Service **Certification by U.S. Person Residing Outside of the United States for Streamlined Foreign Offshore Procedures**	OMB Number 1545-2241

Form **14654** (August 2014)	Department of the Treasury - Internal Revenue Service **Certification by U.S. Person Residing in the United States for Streamlined Domestic Offshore Procedures**	OMB Number 1545-2241

Effective July 1, 2014, the IRS began to offer two types of Streamlined Procedures, herein referred to as "Streamline":
(1) Streamlined Foreign Offshore Procedures ("SFOP")
    -For U.S. taxpayers residing outside the United States
(2) Streamlined Domestic Offshore Procedures ("SDOP")
    -For U.S. taxpayers residing within the United States

Taxpayers who are U.S. citizens or lawful permanent residents (e.g., Green Card Holders) are considered to reside outside the United States if:
For at least one of the three Streamline years, the individual:
(1) did not have a U.S. "abode" (generally, one's home, habitation, residence, domicile, or place of dwelling); and
(2) was physically outside the United States for at least 330 full days (meaning, the taxpayer did not spend more than 35 days in the United States).

Under Streamline, the taxpayer is generally required to submit:
- 3 years of tax returns and information returns
- 6 years of Report of Foreign Bank and Financial Accounts ("FBARs") on Financial Crimes Enforcement Network ("FinCEN") Form 114
- Non-willful certification (U.S. Resident: Form 14654, Non-US: Form 14653)

13. 簡易自首申報計劃（14653 表及 14654 表）

Form **14653** (August 2014)	Department of the Treasury - Internal Revenue Service **Certification by U.S. Person Residing Outside of the United States for Streamlined Foreign Offshore Procedures**	OMB Number 1545-2241

Form **14654** (August 2014)	Department of the Treasury - Internal Revenue Service **Certification by U.S. Person Residing in the United States for Streamlined Domestic Offshore Procedures**	OMB Number 1545-2241

自 2014 年 7 月 1 日起，IRS 開始提供兩種類型的簡易型自首申報計劃，以下稱為「簡易自首申報計劃」：

（1）國外簡易自首申報計劃（SFOP）─適用於居住在美國境外的美國納稅人

（2）國內簡易自首申報計劃（SDOP）─適用於居住在美國境內的美國納稅人

如果納稅人是美國公民或合法永久居民（例如，綠卡持有者），且在最近 3 年中至少有 1 年符合下述情形，將被視為居住在美國境外：

（1）沒有在美國擁有「住所」（通常是指一個人的家、住所、住宅、居所或居住地）；

（2）在美國境外至少滿足了 330 天（即納稅人在美國沒有超過 35 天）。

在簡易自首申報計劃下，納稅人通常需要提交以下資料：

- 最近 3 年的納稅申報表和資訊申報表
- 最近 6 年的《金融犯罪執法網路》FinCEN 114 表，以及「海外銀行和金融帳戶報告」（FBAR）
- 境外所得／資產之漏報行為非出於故意之證明（美國居民：14654 表，非美國居民：14653 表）

Note: A taxpayer cannot participate if the IRS has already initiated a civil examination. Under this program, the taxpayer avoids all penalties normally associated with delinquency (e.g., failure-to-file and failure-to-pay penalties, accuracy-related penalty, information return penalties, FBAR penalties). The Streamline participant is required to pay only unpaid taxes and interest.

Domestic Streamline differs from Foreign Streamline in two main ways:

(1) A domestic resident taxpayer that has failed to file a U.S. income tax return in any of the three most recent tax years cannot participate in Domestic Streamline (while a foreign resident taxpayer that has been similarly delinquent can participate in the Foreign Streamline).

(2) Further, even if the taxpayer qualifies, Domestic Streamline bear a 5% miscellaneous penalty on the highest aggregate balance/value of one's foreign financial assets (i.e., assets reportable on the FBAR or Form 8938) during the FBAR period. Foreign Streamline does not have this penalty.

Non-Willful Standard

The language of the certification forms seems to offer a broader range of conduct that will be considered non-willful for purposes of Streamline.

In the form, the taxpayer must certify the following:

"My failure to report all income, pay all tax, and submit all required information returns, including FBARs, was due to non-willful conduct. I understand that non-willful conduct is conduct that is due to negligence, inadvertence, or mistake or conduct that is the result of a good faith misunderstanding of the requirements of the law."

The IRS does not send successful applicants an acceptance or closing letter. In this sense, "no news is good news." If the IRS does not receive adequate information in the Streamline submission, it will often follow up with the taxpayer and ask for that information.

注：如果 IRS 已經啟動了民事審查，納稅義務人就無法參與簡易自首申報計劃。在這個計劃下，納稅人通常可以免除與漏未申報有關的所有罰款（例如，未申報罰款和未支付稅額之罰款、申報不正確之罰款、未提交應申報資訊之罰款、未提交 FBAR 之罰款）。參與簡易自首申報計劃之納稅義務人只須支付未繳納的稅款和利息。

國內簡易自首申報計劃與國外簡易自首申報計劃有兩個主要的區別：

（1）在最近的三個納稅年度中，未能申報美國所得稅的國內居民納稅人不能參與國內簡易自首申報計劃（然而，未申報美國所得稅之外國居民納稅人可以參與國外簡易自首申報計劃）。

（2）此外，即使納稅人符合參與國內簡易自首申報計劃之資格，國內簡易自首申報計劃還是會對漏報 FBAR 之納稅義務人進行裁罰，裁罰金額為 FBAR 上申報年度的最高總資產／價值（即需在 FBAR 或 8938 表上申報的資產）的 5%；而國外簡易自首申報計劃沒有這項罰款。

非故意標準

目前，官方在適用簡易自首申報計劃之「非故意證明表」上，對「非故意」似乎採取了較為寬鬆之認定標準。

在表格中，納稅義務人必須對以下聲明提出證明：「我未能報告所有所得、支付所有稅款，並提交所有所需的資訊申報表，包括 FBAR，是由於非故意行為造成的。我明白，非故意行為是指由於疏忽、疏忽大意或錯誤所導致的行為，或是對法律要求存在善意誤解所造成的行為。」

It may ask for:
- More detailed account information
- More detailed foreign entity information
- More information about the professional whose advice you relied upon
- A further explanation to support your claim of non-willful conduct

The IRS will also compare the information given in the Certification form to the tax returns and FBARs filed. The IRS can compare the information you provide to account data received from foreign financial institutions under the FATCA regime.

If the IRS receives or discovers evidence of willfulness or criminal conduct on the part of the taxpayer (e.g., information received from foreign governments or financial institutions), the IRS could open an examination or investigation that could lead to civil fraud penalties, FBAR penalties, information return penalties, or even a referral to Criminal Investigation. Entrance to the Streamlined program does not guarantee immunity from criminal prosecution.

若 IRS 接受納稅義務人之補報，納稅義務人通常不會收到 IRS 寄送之接受遵從或結案的信函，換句話說，對納稅義務人而言「沒有 IRS 的消息就是好消息」。如果 IRS 沒有辦法藉由簡易自首申報計劃蒐集到足夠的資訊，通常會再聯繫納稅義務人，並要求納稅義務人提供所需的資訊。

IRS 可能會再向納稅義務人要求提供：

- 更為詳盡之帳戶資訊
- 更為詳盡之外國企業實體資訊
- 更多有關您所依賴的專業人士的相關資訊
- 有關您提出之「非故意聲明」的進一步說明

IRS 會將您在「非故意證明表」中提供的資訊與您過去提交之納稅申報表和 FBAR 進行交叉比對。IRS 也會將您提供的資訊與您在外國之金融機構帳戶（透過 FATCA 機制獲取）的資料進行比對。

如果 IRS 收到或發現納稅義務人存在故意或犯罪行為的證據（例如，透過外國政府或金融機構取得的資訊），IRS 可能會展開審查或調查，納稅義務人可能將因此面臨民事詐欺罰款、FBAR 罰款、資訊報告罰款，甚至可能被轉交給刑事調查部門。納稅義務人應知曉加入簡易自首申報計劃並不保證免於刑事起訴。

14. California Form 541

TAXABLE YEAR			FORM
2022	**California Fiduciary Income Tax Return**		**541**

For calendar year 2022 or fiscal year beginning (mm/dd/yyyy) _____, and ending (mm/dd/yyyy) _____

| Type of entity. Check all that apply. | Name of estate or trust | FEIN | A |
| (1) ☐ Decedent's estate (2) ☐ Simple trust | Name and title of all fiduciaries, see instructions | | B |

When it comes to taxes, oftentimes clients focus almost exclusively on completing their federal tax obligations; however, state law and state taxation should play a part in the clients' trust and estate planning as well. In addition to taxing trusts that are administered in California, the Franchise Tax Board of California (FTB) also imposes taxes on trusts that have fiduciaries and beneficiaries based in California. Below you can find a map of the U.S., with how various states impose income taxes on trusts.

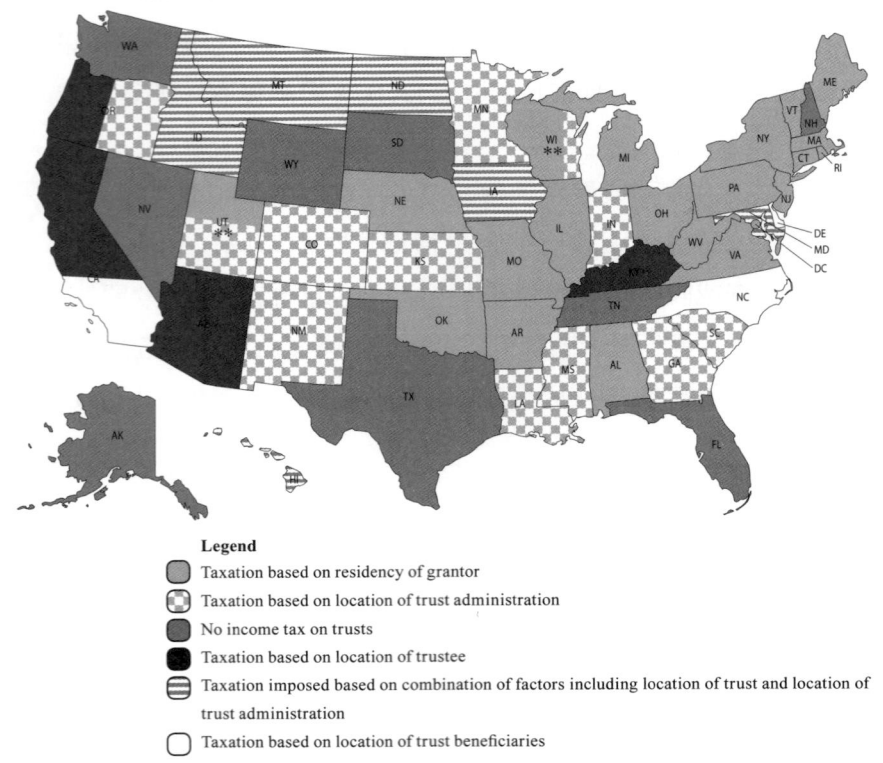

SUMMARY OF STATE TAXATION OF TRUSTS

Legend

- Taxation based on residency of grantor
- Taxation based on location of trust administration
- No income tax on trusts
- Taxation based on location of trustee
- Taxation imposed based on combination of factors including location of trust and location of trust administration
- Taxation based on location of trust beneficiaries

14. 加州 541 表格

```
TAXABLE YEAR                                              FORM
  2022      California Fiduciary Income Tax Return        541
For calendar year 2022 or fiscal year beginning (mm/dd/yyyy) _____, and ending (mm/dd/yyyy) _____
● Type of entity.    Name of estate or trust                          FEIN        A
  Check all that apply.
(1) ☐ Decedent's estate  Name and title of all fiduciaries, see instructions     B
(2) ☐ Simple trust
```

在涉及稅收問題時，客戶通常幾乎只專注於完成他們的聯邦稅務義務；然而，客戶也應該考慮州法律和州稅對信託和遺產規劃的影響。加州稅務局（Franchise Tax Board of California，FTB）除了對在加州管理的信託徵稅外，也對受託人和受益人為加州居民的信託課稅。下圖顯示了各州如何對信託徵收所得稅。

美國各州信託徵稅概況

說明
- 根據委託人居住地徵稅
- 根據信託管理地點徵稅
- 不徵收信託所得稅
- 根據受託人所在地徵稅
- 根據信託所在地和信託管理所在地等綜合因素徵稅
- 根據信託受益人所在地徵稅

If an irrevocable non-grantor trust has one the following characteristics, it will be deemed a California trust (for California income tax purposes):

(1) One or more California trustee(s)

(2) One or more California fiduciaries (including the Trust Protector, Trust Distribution Advisor or Trust Investment Direction Advisor)

(3) One or more California beneficiaries receiving a distribution in that tax year

A California trust is required to file an income tax return in California if the trust: (i) has net income from all sources in excess of $100; or (ii) has gross income from all sources in excess of $10,000, regardless of the amount of net income. Taxes due in connection with a Form 541 along with the form are due on April 15; however, taxpayers are generally allotted a filing extension (without filing an extension) until October 15.

While state taxes often come as an afterthought when it comes to estate planning, Wealth Creators should be mindful when it comes to the jurisdiction(s) of the trusts' fiduciaries when settling a trust. In addition, special attention should be paid to those with California residency. This is especially the case when a trust makes distributions of income to California tax residents, as doing so may trigger both high California state income taxes and California "throwback" taxes.

如果一個不可撤銷的非委託人信託具有一個以下特徵，在加州稅法下，該信託可能需要在加州申報繳納州所得稅：

（1）該信託有一個或多個加州受託人

（2）該信託有一個或多個加州受益人（包括信託保護人、信託分配顧問或信託投資顧問）

（3）在同一稅務會計年度中，有一個或多個加州受益人收到分配

信託如果滿足以下條件，就需要在加州申報州所得稅：

（i）信託之全部淨所得超過 100 美元；或（ii）無論淨所得金額多寡，信託之總所得超過 10,000 美元。其他與 541 表相關的稅款以及表格應在 4 月 15 日前申報繳納；然而，納稅人通常可以獲得延期至 10 月 15 日再行申報（無需提交延期申請）。

雖然州稅在進行財產規劃時往往被忽視，但財富創造者在設立信託時應注意受託人所處之司法管轄區的州稅法規。此外，特別需要注意受託人是否為加州的居民。這種情況尤其適用於信託向加州稅務居民分配所得時，因為這樣做可能會產生高額的加州「州所得稅」和加州的「回溯稅」。

NOTE :

第五章

全球家族辦公室的崛起與家族信託

The Rise of the Global Family Office

What is a Family Office? How does a Family Office typically add value?

A Family Office is a private wealth advisory entity established by an individual or family to manage wealth and provide a variety of personal and financial services. Family Offices serve high-net-worth individuals and families, offering a comprehensive approach to managing their financial affairs and providing services beyond traditional wealth management. Family Offices typically provide some, if not all, of the following services:

1. Wealth Management:
   - Investment management, asset allocation, and risk management.
   - Property management, rent collection and lease renewals.
   - Developing and implementing investment strategies aligned with the family's goals and risk tolerance.

2. Tax Services:
   - Tax planning and compliance.
   - Tax risk mitigation and analysis.
   - Strategies to minimize tax liabilities and maximize tax efficiency.

3. Legal Services:
   - Estate planning, including the creation of wills and trusts.
   - Legal advice on establishing and managing closely held family businesses.

4. Succession Planning:
   - Developing plans for the transition of wealth and business to the next generation.
   - Ensuring the continuity of family values and objectives.

5. Risk Management:
   - Evaluating and managing risks associated with the family's assets and activities.
   - Managing the family's risk exposure to various incidents and investments.

家族辦公室是甚麼？家族辦公室如何提供加值服務？

家族辦公室是由個人或家族所設立的私人財富管理顧問公司。有別於傳統的財富管理，家族辦公室為高淨值的個人或家族提供全面性的資產管理規劃及多種私人及財務服務。

家族辦公室通常提供下列服務：

1. 資產管理：
   - 規劃並執行投資管理、資產配置及風險管理。
   - 規劃並執行物業管理、租金收取及租約續簽。
   - 評估家族目標及風險承受能力，以制定及執行與之一致的投資策略。
2. 稅務服務：
   - 稅務規劃及並執行相關法令遵循。
   - 稅務風險的降低及相關分析。
   - 制定並執行減少稅務負擔及最大化稅務效率的策略。
3. 法律服務：
   - 遺產規劃，包括協助草擬遺囑及設立信託。
   - 就閉鎖性家族企業之設立及管理提供法律諮詢服務。
4. 世代傳承計劃：
   - 制定財富及事業傳承予下一代的計劃。
   - 確保家族價值及目標的延續。
5. 風險管理：
   - 評估並管理與家族資產及活動相關的風險。
   - 管理家族就各種事件及投資的風險暴露。

6. Insurance Management
   - Comparing, procuring and managing insurance policies.
   - Planning for liquidity to pay estate taxes and other expenses, ensuring that the estate can pass to heirs without being diminished.

7. Administrative Services:
   - Handling day-to-day administrative tasks, such as bill payments, financial reporting, bookkeeping, and record-keeping.
   - Managing household staff and personal affairs.

8. Lifestyle Management:
   - Personal services such as travel arrangements and luxury purchases.
   - Assistance with health and wellness, education, and other personal needs.

9. Philanthropy
   - Providing advice on philanthropy, charitable giving, and legacy planning.

Family Offices can provide the family with the following benefits:
   (A) Customization: Tailored solutions that align with the family's specific needs and goals.
   (B) Control and Privacy: Greater control over investments and decision-making, with a high level of privacy.
   (C) Holistic Approach: Integration of various aspects of wealth management, from investments to lifestyle services, under one roof.
   (D) Long-Term Planning: Focus on long-term wealth preservation and intergenerational transfer.

In essence, a Family Office acts as a centralized entity that coordinates and manages all aspects of a family's wealth, aiming to preserve and grow their wealth while providing a suite of bespoke services to meet their unique needs.

6. 保險管理：
   - 保單的比較、採購及管理。
   - 規劃資產流動性以支付遺產稅及其他費用，確保遺產能在不減損的狀況下傳承予繼承人。
7. 行政性服務：
   - 處理日常行政事務，如帳單支付、財務報告、記帳及資料保存。
   - 管理家事服務人員及個人事務。
8. 生活管理：
   - 規劃個人休閒服務，如安排旅行及購買奢侈品。
   - 規劃健康保健、教育及其他個人需求。
9. 慈善事業：
   - 提供慈善事業、慈善捐贈及遺產捐贈的規劃建議。

對家族而言，選擇家族辦公室有以下優點：
 (A) 客製化：家族辦公室會量身制定解決方案以符合家族的各別需求及目標。
 (B) 控制及隱私性：家族能更大程度地控制其投資及決策，並具有高度隱私性。
 (C) 全面性方案：就財富管理的各個面向，從投資到生活服務，提供整合性的一站式服務。
 (D) 長遠性規劃：專注於長期財富保值及跨世代傳承規劃。

綜上所述，家族辦公室作為家族資產的統籌管理機構，協調並管理家族資產的各面向，旨在保護及增長家族資產，同時提供一系列定製化服務以滿足家族的各別需求。

When establishing a U.S. family trust, are there additional professional staffing requirements?

Wealth Creators with considerable net worth should also consider establishing a U.S. family trust (the types and steps have been described at length in previous chapters). When establishing a familial trust, the family's Family Office is particularly important. A properly staffed Family Office, for the purposes of establishing a trust, should include:
1. A U.S. Trust Attorney, who typically drafts the trust agreement.
2. A U.S. Tax Attorney, who typically analyzes the tax effect of the family trust.
3. A U.S. Certified Public Accountant (CPA), who can complete and submit applicable and required U.S. tax forms and disclosures.
4. A Local Certified Public Accountant (CPA), who resides in the Grantor's resident country and can analyze the local tax effects of establishing a U.S. trust.
5. A Local Attorney, who can analyze the legal ramifications of transferring certain assets into a U.S. trust in the Grantor's resident country.
6. A Compliance Secretary, who can manage the transfer of funds from Asia to the U.S. along with any required Know-Your-Client (KYC) paperwork.
7. A Specialized Secretary, who can manage offshore companies (typically established in the British Virgin Islands (BVI) or the Cayman Islands).
8. One or more Financial Advisors, who can manage investments in Asia and in the U.S.
9. A United States trust company that is able and willing to act as trustee of a family trust. United States Trust Company, which mainly serves Chinese, should preferably have Chinese communication skills; All trust establishment documents (including trust contracts) can be provided in both English and Chinese; The trust professionals are also bilingual in English and Chinese, so as not to misunderstand the meaning of family trust.

Since the process of establishing a family trust typically can take anywhere from 6 months to several years, it is extremely important that all parties maintain open communication and are synced to

設立美國家族信託時，家族辦公室是否需配置專業人員？

具有可觀規模淨資產的創富者亦應考慮設立家族信託（信託類型及設立步驟請參閱第二章及第三章）。設立家族信託時，家族辦公室的角色尤為重要。以設立美國家族信託為例，家族辦公室應配置以下專業人士：

1. 美國信託律師：通常負責撰擬信託合約。

2. 美國稅務律師：通常分析家族信託所涉的稅務影響。

3. 美國註冊會計師：能完成並提交相關之必要稅表及資訊揭露。

4. 信託委託人居住國家的當地註冊會計師：能分析於美國設立信託在委託人居住國家可能的稅務影響。

5. 信託委託人居住國家的當地律師：能分析為信託目的移轉特定資產在委託人居住國家可能造成的法律後果。

6. 合規秘書：能管理資金從亞洲移轉至美國以及其所涉及的驗證客戶身分（KYC）之必要書面文件。

7. 專業秘書：能管理與家族辦公室業務相關的離岸公司（通常設立在英屬維京群島(BVI)或開曼群島）。

8. 財務顧問：能管理在美國及亞洲的投資。

9. 能夠且願意擔任家族信託受託人的美國信託公司，尤其在設立以華人為主要服務對象之美國信託公司，最好能有華語之溝通能力，甚至須將所有的信託文件（含信託合約）均能提供英中雙語文件，所配備的信託專業服務人員亦具備英中雙語之能力，如此才不會誤解家族信託的相關含意。

由於成立家族信託通常歷時 6 個月至數年不等，所有當事人保持開放溝通並按家族的特定需求及狀況調整行動方案至關重要。

the client's particular needs and circumstances.

How is a Family Office different from a Multi-Family Office?

A Single-Family Office (SFO) and a Multi-Family Office (MFO) are both entities designed to manage the wealth and financial affairs of families, but they differ in structure, clientele, and the range of services offered. Here are the key differences:

Item	Single-Family Office (SFO)	Multi-Family Office (MFO)
Clientele	One family.	Multiple families.
Customization	Tailored specifically to the needs and preferences of that single family.	Typically provides more professional advice than customized personal services.
Control	Possesses a high degree of control over the operations and decisions.	Less direct control by any single family; MFOs typically assign a primary contact, which can assist with any of the client's needs at the client's convenience.
Privacy	Depends on the experience and capability individuals hired.	Still a priority, but shared resources mean slightly less exclusivity.
Qualifications of Professionals	Professionals are often searching for solutions that the family is more inclined to accept, rather than finding innovative solutions.	Subject matter experts are able to find customized and efficient solutions to address a family's individual requirements.
Professional Licenses	Typically only includes one or two individuals with qualified U.S. or Asia-based license(s).	Includes licensed U.S. and Asia-based CPAs and attorneys that have worked on a broad spectrum of cases.
Areas of Expertise and Experience	Typically confined to only cases that the family has faced; most situations are being dealt with by individuals without relevant experience.	Experience across a broad range of challenges (especially from legal and tax authorities) and leverages standardized solutions that can be adapted and customized for different families.
Staff Members	Two thirds of SFOs employ 10 or less employees.	Typically 100+ employees (~30% of which are positioned in direct client-facing roles).
Professional Expenditures	Fixed personnel salaries, bonuses and fees for outsourced advisors often exceeding US$400,000 per annum and US$100,000 per em-ployee. Administrative expenses typically grow at 5% ~ 10% per annum.	Annual consulting fees are typically fixed, ranging from US$25,000 ~ US$100,000; additional expenditures include legal and accounting fees for specific investments and one-time projects.
Frequency and Nature of Payments	Payments are constantly made and need to be actively managed. A performance review of employees is typically conducted at least annually.	Payments are only made at the beginning of the engagement and upon the completion of certain preset goals.

單一家族辦公室（SFO）與聯合家族辦公室（MFO）有何區別？

單一家族辦公室（SFO）和聯合家族辦公室（MFO）都是為管理家族財富及財務事務而設立的私人管理顧問公司，但它們在結構、客群及提供的服務範圍皆有所不同，主要的特色區別如下：

項目	單一家族辦公室（SFO）	聯合家族辦公室（MFO）
客群	單一家族	多個家族
客製化	專為單一家族的需求及偏好量身定制。	通常提供更多專業建議，而非僅有客製化的私人服務。
控制	擁有高度的控制權，掌控運營及決策。	任一家族的直接控制權較少；MFO通常指派一位主要聯絡人來協助客戶的需求。
隱私性	取決於受僱者的經驗和能力。	客戶隱私是MFO的優先考量，但因共用資源，所以專屬性較低。
專業資格	通常尋找家族更願意接受的解決方案，而非創新的解決方案。	各領域專家能找到客製化且高效的解決方案來滿足家族的各別需求。
專業執照	通常僅有一至兩位持有美國或亞洲合格執照之人員。	擁有美國及亞洲專業執照且曾處理廣泛類型案件的會計師及律師。
專業領域及經驗	通常局限於家族所面臨的案件類型；多由缺乏相關承辦經驗的人員處理。	具有廣泛挑戰（尤其是來自法律及稅務機構）經驗的專業人士，擅長運用標準化解決流程，再為不同家族進行調整及客製化。
組織架構	約三分之二的SFO僱用10名或更少的員工。	通常為100多名員工組成的公司（其中約有三分作為對接客戶的窗口）。
專業服務費用	固定員工薪資、獎金及外包顧問的費用多超過每年40萬美元（每名員工10萬美元）；行政費用通常每年增長5%~10%。	年度諮詢費通常為固定數，2.5~10萬美元不等；但就特定投資及一次性項目的法律及會計費用等，則需另行支付。
付款頻率及性質	持續支付費用，客戶需積極管理。家族通常至少每年進行一次員工績效評估。	費用在委任時及完成預定目標時支付。
管理費級距（依總資產百分比計算，不包括外部投資管理費用）	• 總資產少於1億美元者，管理費約為總資產的0.75%~1.5%。 • 總資產在1億至3億美元之間者，管理費約為總資產的0.5%~1%。 • 總資產在3億至5億美元之間者，管理費約為總資產的0.35%~0.65%。	僅收取家族所需的項目費用： • 通常總資產少於1億美元者，管理費每年最多為5萬美元。 • 總資產超過1億美元者，管理費每年最多10萬美元。

Item	Single-Family Office (SFO)	Multi-Family Office (MFO)
Total Maintenance Expenses (as % of Total Assets, excluding external investment management fees)	0.75% ~ 1.50% for Families with Total Assets of <US$100 million; 0.50% ~ 1.00% for Families with Total Assets of US$100 million ~ US$300 million; 0.35% ~ 0.65% for Families with Total Assets of US$300 million ~ US$500 million.	Limited to the number of items that are required by the family, typically capping out at US$50,000 per annum for Families with Total Assets of <US$100 million and US$100,000 per annum for Families with Total Assets of >US$100 million.

In essence, the primary difference lies in the number of families served, the level of personalization, the proficiency of entity employees, and the total annual operating expenses. A Single-Family Office is highly bespoke, while a Multi-Family Office leverages economies of scale to provide cost-effective yet comprehensive services to multiple families.

What are the most important criteria when selecting a Multi-Family Office?

Selecting a Multi-Family Office (MFO) is a critical decision for high-net-worth families. Here are the most important criteria to consider:

1. Reputation and Track Record:
   - Reputation: Research the MFO's reputation within the industry. Look for reviews, testimonials, and any potential red flags.
   - Track Record: Evaluate the MFO's history of performance. This includes their success in managing wealth, client satisfaction, and the stability of their client relationships over time.

2. Services Offered:
   - Comprehensive Services: Ensure the MFO offers a wide range of services, including investment management, tax planning, estate planning, risk management.
   - Customization: Assess their ability to tailor services to meet the specific needs of your family.

3. Expertise and Experience:
   - Professional Team: Evaluate the qualifications and experi-

綜上所述，單一家族辦公室（SFO）及聯合家族辦公室（MFO）主要區別在於服務的家族數量、客製化程度、實體員工的專業程度及年度營運總費用等面向。單一家族辦公室（SFO）提供高度客製化但相對昂貴的服務，而聯合家族辦公室（MFO）則利用規模經濟為多個家族提供高經濟效益且全面的服務。

選擇聯合家族辦公室（MFO）時最重要的標準是甚麼？

對於高淨值家族來說，選擇聯合家族辦公室（MFO）是一個關鍵的決定。以下是需要考慮的最重要標準：

1. 名聲及業績紀錄：
   - 名聲：查詢 MFO 在業界的聲譽，搜尋該 MFO 相關的評論、口碑和任何潛在的危險訊息。
   - 業績紀錄：評估 MFO 的業績歷史，包括在財富管理、客戶滿意度以及長期客戶關係穩定性方面的成功。
2. 提供的服務：
   - 全面性的服務：確保 MFO 提供廣泛的服務，包括投資管理、稅務規劃、遺產規劃、風險管理。
   - 客製化：評估 MFO 客製化其服務的能力是否能滿足家族的特定需求。
3. 專業與經驗：
   - 專業團隊：評估 MFO 團隊的資格和經驗，包括財務顧問、稅務專家、法律顧問及其他專業人士。
   - 專業度：考量 MFO 是否有與和家族具有相似財務狀況及需求的家族合作的經驗。
   - 國際經驗：跨境家族應特別關注 MFO 過去在跨境稅務

ence of the MFO's team. This includes financial advisors, tax experts, legal advisors, and other professionals.
- Specialization: Consider whether the MFO has experience working with families with similar financial profiles and needs.
- International Exposure: Cross-border families should pay special attention to the firm's past experience with cross-border tax and estate planning.

4. Philosophy and Strategy:
   - Alignment: Ensure the MFO's philosophy align with your family's goals, risk tolerance, and values.
   - Asset Class: Evaluate whether the MFO has experience working with your family's preferred investments, especially if your family has a large position in a particular asset class.

5. Transparency and Communication:
   - Reporting: Check the frequency and clarity of financial reporting. Transparent, regular reports are crucial for tracking performance and making informed decisions.
   - Communication: Evaluate the MFO's communication practices. They should be accessible, responsive, and proactive in keeping you informed.

6. Fees and Cost Structure:
   - Fee Structure: Understand the fee structure and ensure it is transparent. These often include annual consulting fees and itemized service charges. Certain MFOs may also charge a fee as a percentage of total assets or assets under management.
   - Value for Money: Assess whether the services provided justify the costs. Compare the fee structures of different MFOs.

7. Client-to-Advisor Ratio:
   - Attention: A lower client-to-advisor ratio generally means more personalized attention and better service.
   - Accessibility: Ensure your family will have sufficient access to advisors and their support.

及遺產規劃方面的經驗。
4. 理念與策略：
   - 一致性：確保 MFO 的理念符合家族的目標、風險承受能力及價值觀。
   - 資產類別：評估 MFO 是否有處理家族首選投資的經驗，特別是如果家族在特定資產類別中擁有大量持分。
5. 透明度及溝通：
   - 財務報告：檢視 MFO 財務報告的頻率及透明度，因為透明、定期的報告對於追蹤績效及做出明智的決策至關重要。
   - 溝通：家族也可透過評估 MFO 顧問及相關人士的溝通作業方式來判斷其服務是否合宜，專業 MFO 應便於溝通、反應迅速並主動向家族通報進度。
6. 收費及成本結構：
   - 費用結構：瞭解費用結構並確保其透明度，費用通常包括年度諮詢費及逐項服務費，某些 MFO 可能會另以總資產或管理資產的一定百分比收取費用。
   - 服務與收費：評估所提供的服務與收費是否得當，列舉不同 MFO 的服務及收費較能客觀比較優劣。
7. 客戶與顧問的比例：
   - 關注度：較低的客戶與顧問比率通常表示客戶將獲得較高的關注度及較快速精緻的服務。
   - 洽詢充分性及便利性：確保家族能享有充分機會洽詢顧問並獲得協助。

8. Cultural Fit and Trust:
   – Cultural Fit: Ensure the MFO's culture and values align with your family's. This includes their approach to wealth management and client relations.
   – Trust: Building a trusting relationship is crucial. You should feel confident in their ability to manage your resources and act in your best interests.

9. Technology and Innovation:
   – Technology: Evaluate the MFO's use of technology in managing investments, reporting, and client communication.
   – Innovation: Consider whether they are innovative and adaptable to changing financial landscapes and client needs.

10. Regulatory Compliance and Risk Management:
    – Compliance: Ensure the MFO adheres to regulatory standards and has strong governance practices.
    – Risk Management: Evaluate their risk management practices and how they protect clients' assets.

11. Client References:
    – References: Ask for and check client references. Speaking with current or former clients can provide valuable insights into the MFO's performance and client satisfaction.

Selecting the right Multi-Family Office involves thorough research and careful consideration of these criteria to ensure they meet your family's specific needs and can effectively manage and grow your wealth.

8. 文化契合度與信任度：
   - 文化契合度：確保 MFO 的文化及價值觀與家族相符，包含其資產管理及客戶關係的管理方式，高度契合的 MFO 可增加合作的順暢度。
   - 信任度：客戶與 MFO 建立信任關係至關重要。為了最佳利益，應信任所選任的 MFO 之財富管理能力。
9. 科技應用與創新方案：
   - 科技應用：評估 MFO 在管理投資、報告及客戶溝通方面使用的科技是否與時俱進。
   - 創新性：考量 MFO 提供的策略方案是否具創新性，以因應不斷變化的金融環境及客戶需求。
10. 法令遵循與風險管理：
    - 法令遵循：確保 MFO 遵守主管機關的監管標準並採行有效的治理措施。
    - 風險管理：評估 MFO 的風險管理的機制以及保護客戶資產的實務操作。
11. 客戶推薦：
    - 推薦：要求 MFO 提供並查詢其客戶推薦；與 MFO 目前或以前的客戶訪談，獲取有關該 MFO 的績效及客戶滿意度的寶貴見解。

　　選擇適合的 MFO 時，需對上述標準進行全面研究及仔細考量，以確保其滿足家族的特定需求，並能夠有效地管理及增長財富。

What is bookkeeping? How can it help Wealth Creators?

Bookkeeping is a foundational aspect of financial management, crucial for both U.S. irrevocable trusts and U.S. companies. It involves maintaining accurate and detailed records of all financial transactions, supporting informed decision-making, regulatory compliance, and overall financial health. Here's an in-depth look at its role in these two contexts:

Key Roles and Responsibilities

1. Recording Financial Transactions
   - Income: Documenting all sources of income, including interest, dividends, rental income for trusts, and sales, services, and other revenue streams for companies.
   - Expenses: Tracking all expenses, such as administrative costs, management fees, payroll, rent, utilities, and other operational costs.
   - Assets and Liabilities: Maintaining detailed records of assets and liabilities, including acquisitions, sales, valuations, and depreciation.

2. Maintaining the General Ledger
   - Double-Entry System: Using a double-entry accounting system where each transaction affects at least two accounts, ensuring accuracy and balance in the books.
   - Account Reconciliation: Regularly reconciling bank statements, credit card statements, and other financial accounts to ensure accuracy and consistency.
   - Chart of Accounts: Customizing their chart of accounts to fit the specific needs of their business, making it easier to organize and track financial transactions.

3. Producing Financial Statements
   - Balance Sheet: Summarizing the financial position at a specific point in time, showing assets, liabilities, and equity for companies, or net worth for trusts.
   - Income Statement: Detailing financial performance over a period, including revenue, expenses, and profits or losses.
   - Cash Flow Statement: Tracking cash inflows and outflows, pro-

第五章 全球家族辦公室的崛起與家族信託

甚麼是記帳？它如何幫助創富者？

記帳是財務管理的一個基本方面，對美國不可撤銷信託和美國公司都至關重要。記帳關乎維護所有金融交易的準確和詳細的記錄，記帳同時幫助公司做出明智決策、建立稅務合規性並維持公司財務體質的穩健。在此便對記帳的功能進行深入解析：

記帳所扮演的角色和職責

1. 記錄財務交易
   - 收入：記錄所有收入來源，包括利息、股息、信託的租金收入，以及公司的銷售、服務和其他收入來源。
   - 費用：追蹤所有費用，例如行政成本、管理費、工資、租金、水電費和其他運營成本。
   - 資產和負債：維護資產和負債的詳細記錄，包括收購、出售、估值和折舊。
2. 維護總帳
   - 複式記帳系統：使用複式記帳系統，每筆交易至少讓兩個科目產生變動，確保帳簿的準確性和平衡性。
   - 帳戶核對：定期對銀行對帳單、信用卡對帳單和其他財務帳戶進行對帳，以確保準確性和一致性。
   - 會計科目表：訂製他們的會計科目表以滿足其業務的特定需求，從而更容易組織及追蹤財務交易。
3. 編製財務報表
   - 資產負債表：總結特定時間點的財務狀況，顯示公司的資產、負債和權益，或信託的淨資產。
   - 損益表：詳細說明特定期間內的財務績效，包括收入、

viding insights into liquidity and cash management.

4. Supporting Tax Compliance
    - Tax Documentation: Keeping accurate records to support tax filings, including income, deductions, credits, and other relevant data.
    - Tax Filings: Assisting in the preparation and timely filing of federal, state, and local tax returns for both trusts and companies.

Importance of Professional Bookkeeping

1. Accuracy and Reliability
    - Error Reduction: Professional bookkeepers reduce the risk of errors that can lead to financial misstatements or regulatory issues.
    - Timely Reporting: Ensuring financial data is recorded promptly, allowing for up-to-date financial reporting and decision-making.

2. Regulatory Compliance
    - Legal Compliance: Staying current with changes in tax laws, labor laws, and other regulations affecting financial reporting.

3. Operational Efficiency
    - Streamlined Processes: Implementing efficient bookkeeping processes and leveraging accounting software to automate routine tasks.

支出和損益。
- 現金流量表：追蹤現金流入和流出，提供流動性和現金管理的相關資訊。
4. 支持稅務合規性
- 稅務資料建檔：保留準確的記錄以支援稅務申報，包括收入、扣除額、抵免額和其他相關數據。
- 報稅：協助準備和及時提交信託和公司的聯邦、州和地方稅的申報書。

專業記帳的重要性

1. 準確性和可靠性
   - 減少錯誤：專業記帳員可降低可能導致財務錯誤或監管問題的錯誤風險。
   - 即時報告：確保即時記錄財務數據，從而實現最即時的財務報告和決策。
2. 監管合規
   - 法律合規：及時瞭解稅法、勞動法和其他影響財務報告的法規的變化。
3. 運營效率
   - 簡化流程：實施高效的記帳流程並利用會計軟體自動執行日常任務。

Illustrative Accounting Treatment (Trusts and Single-Member LLCs)

Since single-member LLCs are passthrough entities for income tax purposes, their transactions are typically combined with the trust's transactions. The end result is typically consolidated financial statements for the trust.

When establishing a trust or making a cash gift to the trust, the transaction is typically recorded as such:
    Cash..XX
        Capital..................................XX

Expenses incurred by the trust (or a wholly owned LLC) are typically recorded as such:
    Expenses...................................XX
        Cash.....................................XX

When a distribution is made from a trust, the transaction is typically recorded as such:
    Distribution................................XX
        Cash.....................................XX

When a trust (or a wholly owned LLC) purchases stock (or bonds), the transaction is recorded as such:
    Investments in Stock (or Bonds) XX
        Cash.....................................XX

When the stocks pay dividends and bonds pay interest, the transaction is recorded as such:
    Cash.......................................XX
        Dividend Income......................XX
        Interest Income.......................XX

Upon the disposition of these investments, the transaction is typically recorded as such:
    Cash.......................................XX
        Investments in Stock (or Bonds)...XX

會計處理示範（信託和單一成員有限責任公司）

由於單一成員有限責任公司（single-member LLC）在所得稅上屬於穿透實體，因此他們的交易通常與信託的交易相結合，而最終結果通常是信託與 LLC 的財務報表結合變成合併財務報表。

在設立信託或向信託進行現金注資時，交易通常按以下方式記錄：

{ 現金 XX
　　資本 XX

信託（或單一股東有限責任公司）產生的費用通常記錄為：

{ 費用 XX
　　現金 XX

當從信託進行分配時，交易通常記錄為：

{ 分配 XX
　　現金 XX

當信託（或單一股東有限責任公司）投資金融商品時，交易記錄如下：

{ 金融商品投資 XX
　　現金 XX

當收到股息及利息時，交易記錄如下：

{ 現金 XX
　　股利收入 XX
　　利息收入 XX

在出售（或贖回）金融商品時，交易通常記錄為：

{ 現金 XX
　　金融商品投資－股票或債券 XX

When a trust (or a wholly owned LLC) purchases real estate, the transaction is recorded as such:

    { Property·····································XX
         Cash·····································XX

The property is subsequently depreciated:

    { Depreciation Expense·····················XX
         Accumulated Depreciation·················XX

If the property yields rent, the transaction is recorded as such:

    { Cash·····································XX
         Rental Income····························XX

If improvements are made to the property, the transaction is recorded as such:

    { Property·····································XX
         Cash·····································XX

Upon the sale of the property, the transaction is recorded as such:

    { Cash·····································XX
      Accumulated Depreciation·················XX
         Capital Gain·····························XX
         Property·································XX

Investments in corporations or multi-member LLCs are recorded (by the trust) as such:

    { Investment·································XX
         Cash·····································XX

Illustrative Accounting Treatment (Corporations and Multi-Member LLCs)

Corporations (including LLCs that have filed an entity classification election to be taxed as a corporation) in the U.S. are subject to corporate tax rates. LLCs may also be taxed as a partnership for U.S. income tax purposes. As such, unlike single-member LLCs, investments in corporations and multi-member LLCs are generally treated separately from the trust.

當信託（或單一股東有限責任公司）購買房地產時，交易記錄如下：

{ 建築物 XX
{ 　　現金 XX

購入之建築物按年折舊：

{ 折舊費用 XX
{ 　　累計折舊 XX

若該建築物進行出租進而產生租金，則交易記錄為：

{ 現金 XX
{ 　　租金收入 XX

如果對建築物進行改良，則交易記錄如下：

{ 建築物 XX
{ 　　現金 XX

當出售房產時，交易記錄如下：

{ 現金 XX
{ 累計折舊 XX
{ 　　資本利得 XX
{ 　　建築物 XX

對公司或多成員有限責任公司的投資（由信託）記錄為：

{ 投資 XX
{ 　　現金 XX

會計處理示範（公司和多成員有限責任公司）

在美國，公司（包括已提交實體分類選擇以公司身分進行課稅的有限責任公司）需按公司稅率納稅。在所得稅法上，有限責

When establishing a corporation or making an investment in the corporation, the transaction is typically recorded as such:

```
 Cash ·······································································XX
    Capital ································································XX
```

A corporation's capital is typically also further divided into par value and additional paid-in capital.

Investments in stocks, bonds and real estate and expenses are typically recorded as a trust would (described in the previous section).

When the books of the corporation are closed by the end of a specific accounting period, the following journal entries are typically made:

```
 Cash ·······································································XX
    Revenue ·······························································XX

 Expenses ·······························································XX
    Cash ···································································XX

 Income Summary ·················································XX
    Retained Earnings ·············································XX
```

If the corporation elects to pay a dividend, it is typically recorded as such:

```
 Retained Earnings ················································XX
    Dividends Payable ···········································XX

 Dividends Payable ················································XX
    Cash ···································································XX
```

When closing a corporation, the journal entries can be recorded in two primary ways:

1. Transferring assets and liabilities to a newly established corporation or LLC, including any mark-to-market adjustments to the assets.
2. Liquidating the existing corporation.

任公司也可以選擇以合夥企業的身分進行課稅。因此，與單一成員有限責任公司不同，公司和多成員有限責任公司的帳務處理通常與信託分開處理。

在成立公司或對公司進行投資時，交易通常記錄如下：

$$\begin{cases} 現金 \quad\cdots\cdots\cdots\cdots XX \\ \quad 資本 \quad\cdots\cdots\cdots\cdots XX \end{cases}$$

公司的資本通常還進一步分為按面值計價的資本和額外實收資本。

對股票、債券和房地產的投資以及費用的帳務處理通常會比照信託（已在上一節中描述）。

公司的帳簿在特定會計期間結束關帳前，通常會作以下日記帳分錄：

$$\begin{cases} 現金 \quad\cdots\cdots\cdots\cdots XX \\ \quad 收入 \quad\cdots\cdots\cdots\cdots XX \end{cases}$$

$$\begin{cases} 費用 \quad\cdots\cdots\cdots\cdots XX \\ \quad 現金 \quad\cdots\cdots\cdots\cdots XX \end{cases}$$

$$\begin{cases} 本期損益 \quad\cdots\cdots\cdots\cdots XX \\ \quad 保留盈餘 \quad\cdots\cdots\cdots\cdots XX \end{cases}$$

如果公司決定支付股息，該交易通常記錄為：

$$\begin{cases} 保留盈餘 \quad\cdots\cdots\cdots\cdots XX \\ \quad 應付股利 \quad\cdots\cdots\cdots\cdots XX \end{cases}$$

$$\begin{cases} 應付股利 \quad\cdots\cdots\cdots\cdots XX \\ \quad 現金 \quad\cdots\cdots\cdots\cdots XX \end{cases}$$

如果要關閉一家公司，日記帳分錄通常會按以下方式記錄：

1. 將資產和負債轉移給新成立的公司或有限責任公司，包括對資產進行任何按市值計價的調整。

Below are the relevant ledgers for each scenario:

Scenario 1: Transferring assets and liabilities to a newly established corporation or LLC, including any mark-to-market adjustments to the assets

If the shareholder decides to close the old corporation and transfer the assets and liabilities to the new corporation, the ledger for the old corporation would be recorded as follows:

    Debt XX
        Equity XX
        Property XX

The ledger for the new corporation would be recorded as follows:

    Property XX
        Debt XX
        Equity XX

Scenario 2: Liquidation

If the shareholders decide to end the operation of the corporation, the first step in the accounting treatment will usually involve selling the assets as follows:

    Cash XX
    Accumulated Depreciation XX
        Gain or Loss XX
        Property XX

After selling the assets, the corporation is obligated to pay off the remaining debt.

    Long-Term Obligation XX
    Short-Term Obligation XX
        Cash XX

2. 對現有公司進行清算。

以下是每個方案的相關分類帳：

情況一：將資產和負債轉移給新成立的公司或有限責任公司，包括對資產進行的任何按市值計價的調整

如果股東決定關閉舊公司並將資產和負債轉移給新公司，則舊公司的分類帳將按以下方式記錄：

$$\begin{cases} 負債 \cdots\cdots\cdots\cdots\cdots\cdots\cdots\cdots\cdots\cdots XX \\ \quad 權益 \cdots\cdots\cdots\cdots\cdots\cdots\cdots\cdots\cdots\cdots XX \\ \quad 資產 \cdots\cdots\cdots\cdots\cdots\cdots\cdots\cdots\cdots\cdots XX \end{cases}$$

新公司的分類帳將按以下方式記錄：

$$\begin{cases} 資產 \cdots\cdots\cdots\cdots\cdots\cdots\cdots\cdots\cdots\cdots XX \\ \quad 負債 \cdots\cdots\cdots\cdots\cdots\cdots\cdots\cdots\cdots\cdots XX \\ \quad 權益 \cdots\cdots\cdots\cdots\cdots\cdots\cdots\cdots\cdots\cdots XX \end{cases}$$

情況二：清算

如果股東決定結束公司的運營，會計處理的第一步通常涉及出售資產，如下所示：

$$\begin{cases} 現金 \cdots\cdots\cdots\cdots\cdots\cdots\cdots\cdots\cdots\cdots XX \\ 累計折舊 \cdots\cdots\cdots\cdots\cdots\cdots\cdots\cdots XX \\ \quad 處分利益／損失 \cdots\cdots\cdots\cdots\cdots XX \\ \quad 資產 \cdots\cdots\cdots\cdots\cdots\cdots\cdots\cdots\cdots\cdots XX \end{cases}$$

出售資產後，公司有義務償還剩餘債務。

$$\begin{cases} 長期負債 \cdots\cdots\cdots\cdots\cdots\cdots\cdots\cdots XX \\ 短期負債 \cdots\cdots\cdots\cdots\cdots\cdots\cdots\cdots XX \\ \quad 現金 \cdots\cdots\cdots\cdots\cdots\cdots\cdots\cdots\cdots\cdots XX \end{cases}$$

After paying off all the remaining debt, if the corporation still has remaining assets (e.g. cash), it shall return the capital to its shareholders.

    { Capital XX
          Cash XX

Illustrative Accounting Treatment (BVI Corporation)

The bookkeeping for a corporation registered in the British Virgin Islands (BVI) is quite similar to that of a US corporation. The most significant discrepancy occurs when the BVI corporation is under the control of a trust. We begin our illustration with a common scenario where a corporation is the shareholder of the BVI corporation. Then we will illustrate the different bookkeeping for the BVI corporation under the trust.

Scenario1: Trust is not the shareholder of the BVI corporation

When a BVI corporation invests in another corporation, the ledger for the BVI corporation is recorded as follows:

    { Investment XX
          Cash XX

When the invested corporation books the earnings but before distributing the dividends, the ledger for the BVI corporation is recorded as follows:

    { Investment XX
          Investment gain XX

When the BVI corporation receives the dividend, the ledger for the BVI corporation is recorded as follows:

    { Cash XX
          Investment XX

Scenario2: Trust is the shareholder of the BVI corporation

When a BVI corporation under a trust invests in another corporation, the ledger for the BVI corporation's investment is recorded in the same way as in Scenario 1.

在清償全部剩餘債務後,如果公司仍有剩餘資產(例如:現金),則應當將資產視作資本返還給股東。

　　｛資本 ……………………………………… XX
　　　　現金 …………………………………… XX

會計處理示範(信託和單一成員有限責任公司)

英屬維京群島(BVI)公司的記帳與美國公司的記帳分錄非常相似,然而,當 BVI 公司是信託下的被投資公司時,分錄會有顯著不同。以下我們將從常見的情況,也就是公司投資 BVI 公司開始示範,然後我們將說明不同情況下的記帳方式。

情況一:信託不是 BVI 公司的股東。

當 BVI 公司投資於另一家公司時,BVI 公司的分類帳記錄如下:

　　｛投資 ……………………………………… XX
　　　　現金 …………………………………… XX

當被投資公司記入收益但在分配股息之前,BVI 公司的分類帳記錄如下:

　　｛投資 ……………………………………… XX
　　　　投資收益 ……………………………… XX

當 BVI 公司實際收到股息時,BVI 公司的分類帳記錄如下:

　　｛現金 ……………………………………… XX
　　　　投資 …………………………………… XX

情況二:信託是 BVI 公司的股東。

當信託下的 BVI 公司投資於另一家公司時,BVI 公司的投資分類帳紀錄方式會與情況一相同。

```
⎧ Investment······································XX
⎨
⎩   Cash····················································XX
```

However, in Scenario 2, since the BVI corporation adopts the cost method rather than the equity method for booking investment income, it records the investment income only when it receives the cash dividend. Assuming a BVI company receives dividends from a Taiwanese company, Taiwan will withhold 21% tax on dividends paid to foreign shareholders.

```
⎧ Foreign Tax (21%)······················XX
⎨   Cash················································XX
⎩   Dividend Income······················XX
```

Conclusion

Bookkeeping is a vital function in both U.S. irrevocable trusts and companies, underpinning financial health, regulatory compliance, and strategic decision-making. By maintaining accurate and detailed financial records, bookkeepers provide the data necessary for efficient management, regulatory adherence, and business growth. Professional bookkeeping services and advanced accounting software can enhance the accuracy, efficiency, and effectiveness of this critical function.

```
⎧ 投資 ································· XX
⎨
⎩    現金 ······························· XX
```

　　然而，在情況二中，由於 BVI 公司採用成本法而非權益法記錄投資收益，因此只有在收到現金股利時才記錄投資收益。假定 BVI 從台灣公司收到股利，台灣對支付予境外股東的股利會扣繳 21%。

```
⎧ 外國稅款（21%）··············· XX
⎨    現金 ······························· XX
⎩    股利收入 ·························· XX
```

結語

　　記帳在美國不可撤銷信託和公司中都是一項至關重要的功能，是財務健康、監管合規和戰略決策的基礎。通過維護準確和詳細的財務記錄，記帳員提供了有效管理、遵守監管和業務增長所需的數據。專業的記帳服務和先進的會計軟體可以提高這一關鍵功能的準確性、效率和有效性。

How do Wealth Creators pass on their relationships with their advisors to their next generation?

Passing on relationships with advisors to the next generation is an important aspect of ensuring continuity and stability in wealth management. Here's how Wealth Creators can effectively pass on these relationships:

1. Early Introduction and Involvement:
   – Introduce Early: Introduce the next generation to advisors early on. This helps build familiarity and trust.
   – - Involve in Meetings: Involve the next generation in regular meetings with advisors to understand the financial strategies and decisions being made.

2. Education and Training:
   – Financial Education: Provide financial education to the next generation to ensure they understand the basics of wealth management.
   – Advisor's Role: Educate them about the role of each advisor and the value they bring to the table.

3. Joint Decision-Making:
   – Collaborative Decisions: Include the next generation in decision-making processes. This can help them feel more engaged and responsible for the family's wealth.
   – Gradual Transition: Gradually transition responsibilities to the next generation with the guidance of advisors.

4. Building Trust:
   – Shared Goals: Ensure the next generation understands and aligns with the family's financial goals and values.
   – Trust-Building Activities: Facilitate activities that help build trust between the next generation and the advisors.

5. Open Communication:
   – Transparent Discussions: Have open and transparent discussions about the family's wealth, goals, and the role of

創富者如何將他們與顧問的關係傳遞給下一代？

將創富者與顧問的關係傳承給下一代是確保財富管理連續性及穩定性的一個重要面向。以下是創富者如何有效地傳遞其顧問關係的方式：

1. 及早介紹與參與：
   - 及早介紹：儘早將下一代介紹給顧問，有助於建立熟悉度與信任度。
   - 參與會議：讓下一代一同參加與顧問的定期會議，以熟悉財務策略及所採行的決定。
2. 教育訓練：
   - 財務教育：為下一代提供財務教育，以確保他們瞭解財富管理的基礎知識。
   - 顧問的角色：讓下一代瞭解每位顧問的角色及其貢獻的價值。
3. 聯合決策：
   - 協同決策：讓下一代參與決策過程，以助其對家族財富管理更有參與感及責任感。
   - 逐步傳承：在顧問的指導下逐步將責任傳承給下一代。
4. 建立信任：
   - 共同目標：確保下一代理解並符合家族的財務目標及價值觀。
   - 建立信任活動：推動有助於下一代與顧問之間建立信任的活動。
5. 開放式溝通：
   - 透明化的討論：就家族的財富、目標及顧問的角色進行

advisors.
- Feedback Loop: Create a feedback loop where the next generation can voice their opinions and concerns regarding the advisors and their strategies.

6. Formalizing Relationships:
   - Formal Agreements: Consider formalizing the relationship through agreements that outline the roles and responsibilities of advisors and the next generation.
   - Succession Planning: Develop a clear succession plan that includes the role of advisors in the transition process.

Should Wealth Creators Pass on Their Relationships with Advisors?

Benefits of passing on advisor relationships to the next generation may include:

1. Continuity and Stability
   - Seamless Transition: Continuity of advisor relationships can provide stability and ensure a seamless transition of wealth management practices.
   - Preserved Knowledge: Advisors who have a long history with the family possess valuable knowledge about the family's financial history, goals, and values.

2. Established Trust
   - Trusted Relationships: Existing advisors have already established trust with the family, which can be difficult to replicate with new advisors.
   - Proven Performance: These advisors have a track record of managing the family's wealth effectively.

3. Consistent Strategy
   - Strategic Alignment: Maintaining the same advisors ensures that the financial strategies remain consistent and aligned with the family's long-term goals.
   - Avoiding Disruption: Changing advisors can disrupt financial plans and strategies, leading to potential losses or mis-

公開及透明的討論。
- 回饋循環：建立讓下一代能表達對顧問及其策略的意見及擔憂的回饋機制。
6. 正式化關係：
- 正式協議：透過載明顧問及下一代的角色及責任的協議來正式化關係。
- 傳承計劃：制定明確的傳承計劃，其中包括顧問在交棒過程中的角色。

創富者應該將其與顧問的關係傳承下去嗎？

將顧問關係傳承給下一代的好處包括：

1. 持續性及穩定性
   - 無縫接軌：保持與顧問的關係可提供穩定性，確保財富管理執行的無縫接軌。
   - 家族知識的積累：與家族長期合作的顧問對家族的財務歷史、目標及價值觀擁有寶貴的知識。
2. 已建立信任感
   - 信任關係：現有顧問已與家族建立信任關係，而新顧問很難複製此關係。
   - 實證的績效：現有顧問已具備有效管理家族財富的成功紀錄。
3. 貫徹性的策略
   - 策略一致：維持相同的顧問能確保財務策略保持一致，符合家族的長遠性目標。
   - 避免計劃中斷：更換顧問可能會中斷原先的財務計劃及

management.

While passing on advisor relationships to the next generation can provide continuity, stability, and preserved knowledge, it's also important to consider the next generation's preferences and the evolving financial landscape.

Wealth Creators should balance maintaining trusted relationships with the potential benefits of new perspectives and expertise. Ensuring that the next generation is involved, educated, and comfortable with the professional advisors is key to a successful transition.

How can Wealth Creators use Offshore (BVI) Companies to their advantage?

Wealth Creators often use British Virgin Islands (BVI) companies to distribute their wealth due to the jurisdiction's favorable legal, tax, and regulatory environment. Here's how they typically leverage BVI companies for wealth distribution:

1. Establishing a BVI Company
   - Incorporation:
     Wealth Creators can incorporate a BVI company quickly and with relative ease. The process is efficient, and the costs are generally lower compared to other jurisdictions.
   - Anonymity and Confidentiality:
     BVI companies offer a high level of privacy. Shareholder information is not publicly accessible, which helps protect the privacy of the Wealth Creator.

2. Holding and Managing Assets
   - Asset Holding:
     BVI companies are often used to hold various types of assets, including real estate, investments, intellectual property, and business interests. This centralizes asset management and provides a clear structure for wealth distribution.
   - Investment Vehicles:
     Wealth Creators can use BVI companies to invest in global markets. The company can hold and manage a diverse port-

策略，導致潛在損失或管理不善。

雖然將顧問關係傳承給下一代可提供持續性、穩定性及知識的積累，但考量下一代的偏好及不斷變化的財務環境也不容忽視。

創富者應在保持信任關係與尋求新視角及專業知識的潛在利益之間取得平衡。確保下一代的參與、傳授以及與專業顧問的融洽相處是成功交棒的關鍵。

創富者如何運用離岸公司（英屬維京群島（BVI）公司）獲取優勢？

創富者通常運用英屬維京群島（BVI）公司來分配他們的財富，因為該司法管轄區具有良好的法律、稅收及監管環境。以下是創富者通常運用 BVI 公司進行財富分配的方式：

1. 建立 BVI 公司
   - 公司註冊：
     創富者得迅速且相對容易地註冊一家 BVI 公司。此過程高效，成本通常比其他司法管轄區低。
   - 匿名性及保密性：
     BVI 公司提供高度的隱私保護。股東的信息不對外公開，有助於保護創富者的隱私。
2. 持有及管理資產
   - 資產持有：
     BVI 公司通常用於持有各種類型的資產，包括房地產、投資、知識產權及業務利益。藉此得集中管理資產，並為財富分配提供清晰的架構。
   - 投資工具：

folio of investments, providing flexibility and efficiency in wealth management.

3. Tax Efficiency
   – Tax Benefits:
   BVI companies benefit from zero corporate tax, no capital gains tax, and no inheritance tax in the jurisdiction. This makes them an attractive vehicle for wealth preservation and growth.
   – International Tax Planning:
   Wealth Creators use BVI companies as part of a broader international tax planning strategy. This can help in minimizing tax liabilities and optimizing the tax efficiency of their wealth distribution plans.

4. Succession Planning
   – Transfer of Ownership:
   Shares in a BVI company can be transferred easily to heirs, ensuring a smooth succession process. This can be done during the Wealth Creator's lifetime or through provisions in their estate plan.
   – Avoiding Probate:
   By holding assets through a BVI company, Wealth Creators can avoid the lengthy and often costly probate process in other jurisdictions. The company's shares can be transferred directly to beneficiaries.

5. Legal Protection and Risk Management
   – Asset Protection:
   BVI companies provide strong legal protection for assets. They can safeguard wealth from political instability, economic uncertainties, and legal disputes in other jurisdictions.
   – Limited Liability:
   As with other corporate structures, BVI companies offer limited liability, protecting the personal assets of the Wealth Creator from business liabilities.

6. Flexibility and Control
   – Control over Assets:

創富者得透過 BVI 公司投資全球市場。BVI 公司得持有及管理多樣化的投資組合，為財富管理提供靈活性及效率性。
3. 稅務效率
   – 稅務優惠：
   BVI 公司在該司法管轄區享有零企業稅、零資本利得稅及零遺產稅的優惠，使它們成為具吸引力的財富保全及增長媒介。
   – 國際稅務規劃：
   創富者將 BVI 公司作為更廣泛的國際稅務規劃策略的一環，以助於最小化稅務負擔，並優化其財富分配計劃的稅收效率。
4. 繼承規劃
   – 所有權轉移：
   BVI 公司的股份可以容易地轉讓給繼承人，確保繼承過程順利進行。移轉可以在創富者在世時完成，也可以透過其遺產計劃中的規定完成。
   – 避免遺囑認證程序：
   透過 BVI 公司持有資產，創富者得避免其他司法管轄區冗長且通常昂貴的遺囑認證程序。BVI 公司的股份可以直接轉讓給受益人。
5. 法律保護與風險管理
   – 資產保護：
   BVI 公司為資產提供強大的法律保護，使其不受其他司法管轄區的政治不穩定性、經濟不確定性及法律紛爭的

Wealth Creators can retain control over the assets held by the BVI company while setting up mechanisms for their distribution. This includes establishing directorships and management structures that align with their wealth distribution goals.
- Flexible Corporate Structures:
BVI companies offer flexible corporate structures that can be tailored to the specific needs of the Wealth Creator. This includes creating multiple classes of shares, implementing shareholders' agreements, and customizing governance rules.

7. Geographic Diversification
   - Global Reach:
   Using BVI companies allows Wealth Creators to diversify their asset holdings geographically. They can invest in different regions, such as Asia, North America, and Europe, ensuring that their wealth is not concentrated in a single jurisdiction.

8. Estate Planning and Legal Compliance
   - Estate Planning:
   BVI companies can be integrated into comprehensive estate plans that consider the Wealth Creator's global assets and heirs. This ensures that the distribution of wealth is orderly and aligned with the family's long-term goals.
   - Regulatory Compliance:
   BVI companies are subject to certain regulatory standards, which helps in maintaining compliance with international laws and reduces the risk of legal challenges.

By utilizing BVI companies, Wealth Creators can effectively manage and distribute their wealth in a tax-efficient, legally protected, and geographically diversified manner. This strategy supports their objectives of wealth preservation, privacy, and smooth succession across generations.

影響。
- 有限責任：
  與其他公司結構一樣，BVI 公司提供有限責任，保護創富者的個人資產免受業務責任的影響。
6. 靈活性與控制權
  - 資產控制權：
    創富者得在保有對 BVI 公司持有資產的控制權同時，建立其分配機制，包括建立與其財富分配目標一致的董事會及管理結構。
  - 靈活的公司結構：
    BVI 公司提供靈活的公司結構，得根據創富者的特定需求進行定制，包括建立多種類股份、實施股東協議及定制治理規則。
7. 地域多元化
  - 跨及全球：
    使用 BVI 公司得讓創富者在其持有資產的地域性多元化。創富者得在不同的地區進行投資，例如亞洲、北美洲及歐洲，確保其財富不集中在單一司法管轄區。
8. 遺產規劃與法律合規
  - 遺產規劃：
    BVI 公司得納入涵蓋創富者全球資產及繼承人的整體遺產計劃中，以確保財富的分配有序且與家族的長期目標一致。
  - 法律合規：
    BVI 公司受到一定的監管標準約束，有助於其保持符合

What role does Europe play for Cross-Border Wealth Creators?

Europe, particularly the European Union (EU), plays a crucial role for cross-border Wealth Creators due to its unique combination of benefits that support global investment, asset protection, and family security. Strategic Advantages include:

1. Freedom of Movement
    – Visa-Free Travel: EU citizenship or permanent residency allows for unrestricted travel across all 27 EU member states, facilitating business trips and family holidays without visa hassles.
    – Residence Flexibility: Wealth Creators can live, work, and study in any EU country, providing numerous options for relocation and business expansion.

2. Business Opportunities
    – Single Market Access: The EU single market enables seamless business operations across member states, reducing regulatory barriers and tariffs, thus enhancing trade efficiency.
    – Diversification: Holding EU citizenship or residency is part of a broader strategy to diversify assets, investments, and residency options.
    – Diverse Economic Landscapes: From tech hubs in Germany to financial centers in Luxembourg, the EU offers varied environments for different business ventures.
    – Asset Protection: Ensuring wealth is protected in stable jurisdictions with robust legal frameworks.

3. Education and Healthcare
    – Top-Tier Education: Access to high-quality education systems across the EU, often at reduced costs, ensures that families can secure excellent educational opportunities for their children.
    – Comprehensive Healthcare: EU countries offer some of the best healthcare services globally, ensuring peace of mind regarding medical needs.

國際法律,並降低法律挑戰的風險。

通過 BVI 公司的運用,創富者得以稅負高效、受法律保障且地域性分散的方式有效地管理及分配其財富。此策略有助於創富者實現世代間財富保全、隱私保護及順利傳承的目標。

歐洲對跨境創富者得扮演甚麼角色?

歐洲,特別是歐洲聯盟,對跨境創富者至關重要,因為它具有支持全球投資、資產保護及家族安全的獨特優勢組合。其優勢包括:

1. 遷徙自由
   - 免簽旅行:歐盟公民身分或永久居留權得在 27 個歐盟成員國之間自由旅行無需簽證,有利於商務出差及家族度假。
   - 居住彈性:創富者得在歐盟任何國家生活、工作及學習,為移居及業務擴展提供眾多選項。
2. 商業機會
   - 單一市場准入:歐盟單一市場使業務得以在成員國間無縫運作,減少監管壁壘及關稅,從而提升貿易效率。
   - 多元化:擁有歐盟公民身分或居留權是更廣泛策略的一環,以多元化資產、投資及居住選擇。
   - 多樣化的經濟環境:從德國的科技樞紐到盧森堡的金融中心,歐盟為不同的商業企業提供多樣化的環境。
   - 資產保護:確保財富在穩定司法管轄區內受到健全法律框架的保護。
3. 教育及醫療保健

4. Tax Optimization
   - Favorable Tax Regimes: Several EU countries offer tax incentives for new residents, including exemptions on foreign income or reduced tax rates.
   - Double Taxation Treaties: Extensive treaties help in minimizing tax liabilities, making financial planning more efficient.

5. Quality of Life
   - High Living Standards: EU countries frequently rank high in global living standards, offering safe, clean, and culturally rich environments.
   - Cultural and Social Benefits: Rich cultural heritage and stable political systems enhance the overall living experience.

6. Legal and Political Stability
   - Robust Legal Frameworks: The EU's strong legal protections ensure the safety of assets and investments.
   - Stable Political Environment: The predictable political landscape of the EU provides a secure environment for wealth preservation and growth.
   - Contingency Planning: Providing a stable alternative residence option in case of instability in the home country.

7. Generational Benefits
   - Inheritance and Succession: EU citizenship can be passed down, ensuring that the benefits extend to future generations.
   - Educational Opportunities for Descendants: Long-term access to top educational institutions for children and grandchildren.

- 頂尖教育：在歐盟各地得進入高質量的教育系統，通常成本較低，確保家族能夠為子女提供優質的教育機會。
- 全面醫療保健：歐盟國家提供全球一流的醫療服務，確保滿足醫療需求。

4. 稅務優化
- 有利的稅收制度：許多歐盟國家為新居民提供稅收優惠，包括對外國收入的免稅或降低稅率。
- 雙重課稅條約：廣泛的條約有助於最小化稅務負擔，使財務規劃更有效率。

5. 生活質量
- 高生活水平：歐盟國家在全球生活水平排名中經常位居前列，提供安全、清潔及文化豐富的環境。
- 文化及社會利益：豐富的文化遺產及穩定的政治體制提升整體生活體驗。

6. 法律及政治穩定
- 健全的法律框架：歐盟強大法律的保護確保資產及投資的安全。
- 穩定的政治環境：歐盟可預測的政局為財富保全及增長提供安全的環境。
- 應急計劃：在原居住地國政局不穩定時，提供穩定的替代居住選擇。

7. 世代利益
- 繼承及傳承：歐盟公民身分可以傳承，確保福利延續到未來世代。

Advantages of EU Member State Status in Cross-Border Wealth Transfer Planning

Over the past 30 years, numerous wealth-creating families have built substantial businesses and accumulated significant wealth. As the first generation of wealth creators now faces the crucial task of planning for inheritance, they often hope that their descendants will inherit their wisdom and good fortune, ensuring the longevity of their wealth. As the Chinese proverb says, "Starting a business is difficult, but maintaining it is even harder." Given the increasing geopolitical tensions, stricter tax regulations, and heightened information disclosure requirements, along with the fact that family members often relocate to different countries to meet their personal living needs, family wealth will inevitably extend globally across multiple generations.

To effectively manage investments spread across the globe, high-net-worth family members must be able to move freely between countries. However, increasingly stringent international technology controls and travel restrictions have become significant obstacles for these families. In this context, having EU member state status offers the following advantages:

1. Harmonized Legal Framework: The EU provides a unified legal structure for inheritance and estate planning across member states, simplifying asset management and cross-border transfers.

2. European Certificate of Succession: EU citizens benefit from a recognized certificate that facilitates proving heir status or executorship throughout EU nations, streamlining estate administration.

3. Tax Benefits: Bilateral agreements among EU states prevent double taxation on inheritances and estate transfers, ensuring financial savings for beneficiaries.

4. Access to Financial Services: EU residency grants access to diverse financial services and products across member states, enhancing flexibility in managing inherited wealth.

5. Freedom of Movement: EU residents can freely relocate within member states, enabling strategic moves to jurisdictions with favorable tax laws or inheritance regulations.

6. Property Rights Protection: Robust EU regulations safeguard property rights, ensuring efficient management and transfer of inherited assets.

- 後代的教育機會：為子女及孫子女提供長期進入頂尖教育機構的機會。

歐盟成員國身分在跨境財富傳承規劃中的優勢

為數不少的創富者家族在過去 30 多年間成就了一番事業，累積了可觀的財富。第一代創富者當前正處於規劃傳承的重要時刻，他們往往會希望自己的後代能承襲前人的智慧以及幸運，將財富長長久久傳承下去。如同中國古諺「創業維艱，守成不易」所云，鑑於近期大國間的對立日益加劇，稅務法規及資訊揭露日趨嚴格，再加上創富者家族開枝散葉，家庭成員基於各自生活需要，前往不同國家定居生活，家族的財富觸角勢必會在多個世代間往世界各地延伸。

為了能順利的管理散布世界的投資項目，高資產家庭成員勢必要能夠在各個國家之間自由移動，然而，國際間日益嚴格的技術管制以及人員移動限制，對於這些高資產的家庭來說，儼然已成為管理上的嚴重的阻礙，在這種背景下，擁有歐盟成員國身分提供了以下幾個優勢：

1. 統一的法律框架：歐盟為成員國之間的繼承和遺產規劃提供了統一的法律結構，簡化了資產管理和跨境轉移。

2. 歐洲繼承證書：歐盟公民可以受益於歐洲繼承證書，以證明自己是繼承人或遺囑執行人，該證書可大幅簡化遺產管理程序。

3. 稅收優勢：歐盟成員國間的避免雙重徵稅協議，可以防止遺產和遺產轉移的雙重徵稅，顯著降低了繼承人和受益人的稅務負擔。

4. 獲得歐盟金融服務：歐盟成員國的居民可以使用歐盟範圍

7. Simplified Legal Procedures: Enhanced cooperation among EU states reduces bureaucratic hurdles in legal matters related to inheritance and estate planning, promoting streamlined processes.

Should Wealth Creators apply for Permanent Residency (PR) in the EU? As an example, would applying for a Bulgaria PR be appropriate for them?

Bulgaria offers a particularly attractive program for Cross-Border Wealth Creators. It's investment requirement, ~€500,000 in an Alternative Investment Fund (AIF), is particularly low compared to other countries in the EU.

In addition, Wealth Creators typically receive their EU Permanent Residency (PR) card within 6 – 8 months and can apply for full Bulgarian Citizenship within 5 years from the initial PR application. Bulgarian citizens enjoy visa-free travel to 142 countries around the world.

Furthermore, Bulgaria's flat 10% income tax rate only applies to income derived from within the country and the country does not tax its residents on any income derived from outside Bulgaria.

In summary, Europe provides a comprehensive suite of benefits for Cross-Border Wealth Creators, from business and tax advantages to high quality of life and robust legal protections.

Acquiring EU citizenship or permanent residency can significantly enhance personal and family security, business opportunities, and overall wealth management strategies.

內的各種金融服務和產品,為管理和投資繼承財富方面提供更大的靈活性。

5. 自由移動和居住:歐盟居民可以在任何歐盟成員國自由移動和居住,這種靈活性允許居民遷移到稅法或繼承法上更為有利的國家,提升財富轉移的效率和保護。

6. 財產權保護:歐盟提倡基本人權保障,歐盟法規長期以來致力於保護個人財產權,並確保資產能順利、高效地轉移給受益人。

7. 簡化的法律程序:歐盟長期以來鼓勵成員國進行法律事務上的合作,包括遺產和遺產規劃中的各種法律議題,這種合作簡化了遺產繼承的法律程序並減少了跨境財富轉移中的官僚障礙。

創富者是否該申請歐盟國家的永久居留權?以申請保加利亞的永久居留權為例,是合適的選項嗎?

保加利亞為跨境創富者提供了一個別具吸引力的計劃,約 50 萬歐元投資於另類投資基金(AIF)的投資門檻,遠較其他歐盟國家低。

創富者通常在申請送件後 6 至 8 個月內即可取得歐盟永久居留權(PR)卡,並且可在最初 PR 申請後起算 5 年內申請保加利亞公民身分。保加利亞公民享有前往全球 142 個國家的免簽證旅行權利。

此外,保加利亞 10% 均一所得稅稅率僅適用於來自該國境內的收入,該國不對居民來自保加利亞境外的任何收入課稅。

總體而言,從商業及稅負優勢到高品質的生活及強大的法律保護,歐洲為跨境創富者提供了全面性的福利。

Advantages of Obtaining Bulgarian Citizenship

In the past, Asian wealth creators typically chose countries like Portugal, Spain, Greece, and Cyprus for investment immigration to Europe, seldom considering Bulgaria. However, since Bulgaria became a Schengen member state on March 31, 2024, Bulgarian citizens no longer need a passport to travel to most EU countries, Norway, and Switzerland. This enhanced mobility allows Bulgarian citizens to freely move, work, and invest across European countries, gradually making Bulgarian citizenship an option for wealth creators seeking investment immigration. The advantages of investment immigration to Bulgaria are summarized as follows:

1. Fast Track to Residency and Citizenship: Bulgaria offers a rapid pathway to residency and citizenship, particularly through investment immigration programs. This allows foreign nationals to obtain permanent residency in a short period and apply for citizenship within a relatively short time frame.

2. Low Cost of Living: Compared to living in the United States, the cost of living in Bulgaria is relatively low, including expenses for housing, food, transportation, and other daily necessities, making it an ideal choice for economic immigration to Europe.

3. Favorable Tax System: Bulgaria has one of the lowest tax rates in Europe, with the lowest personal and corporate income tax rates in the EU. This provides an attractive tax environment for entrepreneurs and high-income individuals. Bulgaria's personal income tax rate is only 10%, the lowest in the EU. Additionally, those who reside in Bulgaria for less than 183 days are considered non-tax residents and are exempt from personal income tax. For dividend income, Bulgaria imposes a 5% tax, but for EU citizens, the dividend tax rate is 0%. Bulgaria has also signed numerous tax treaties with other countries (e.g., China-Bulgaria Double Taxation Avoidance Agreement) to prevent double taxation and promote foreign investment.

取得歐盟公民身分或永久居留權得顯著強化個人及家族的安全、商業機會以及整體財富管理策略。

取得保加利亞國籍身分的優勢有哪些？

過去亞洲的創富者在選擇投資移民入籍歐洲時，通常會將葡萄牙、西班牙、希臘、賽普勒斯等國作為首選，甚少考慮到保加利亞，然而，隨著保加利亞自 2024 年 3 月 31 日起成為申根國，保加利亞公民前往大部分歐盟國家、挪威、瑞士將不再需要護照，保加利亞公民的移動能力增強，可在歐洲各國自由移動、工作、投資，讓保加利亞身分漸漸成為創富者進行投資移民的選項之一。投資移民保加利亞的優勢簡述如下：

1. 快速的居留和公民身分獲取途徑：保加利亞提供快速的居留和公民身分獲取途徑，尤其是對投資移民計劃，允許外籍人士在短時間內獲得永久居留權，並在相對較短的時間內申請公民身分。

2. 低生活成本：與居住於美國相比，保加利亞的生活成本相對較低，包括住房、食品、交通等日常開支，使其成為歐洲經濟移民的理想選擇。

3. 有利的稅收制度：保加利亞在歐洲國家中屬於低稅率國，擁有歐洲最低的個人和公司所得稅稅率，為企業家和高所得人士提供了極具吸引力的稅收環境，保加利亞的個人稅率僅 10%，為歐盟最低標準，另外，只要在保加利亞居住少於 183 天，則為非當地稅務居民，即可免納個人所得稅；股利所得稅方面，保加利亞對非租稅協定成員國的股利所得扣繳 5% 的所得稅，但如果是歐盟成員國公司收取的保加利亞股息，其扣繳稅率為 0%；保加

EU Member States Personal Income Tax Rates	
Country	Highest Personal Income Tax Rate
Slovenia	50%
Germany	45%
France	45%
Italy	43%
Turkey	40%
Croatia	34.5%
Poland	32%
Slovakia	25%
Serbia	20%
Czech Republic	15%
Romania	10%
Bulgaria	**10%**

EU Member States Corporate Income Tax Rates:	
Country	Corporate Income Tax Rate
France	31%
UK	25%
Turkey	25%
Italy	24%
Czech Republic	21%
Slovakia	21%
Poland	19%
Slovenia	19%
Croatia	18%
Romania	16%
Germany	15.825%
Serbia	15%
Bulgaria	**10%**

4. EU Member State Status: As an EU member state, Bulgarian citizens enjoy the right to freely travel, work, study, and receive local health insurance benefits (e.g., can apply for the European Health Insurance Card, EHIC) in other EU countries. This provides immigrants with the flexibility and opportunities to live across the EU in the future. Furthermore, Bulgarian nationality law supports the acquisition of Bulgarian nationality for family members of its citizens without age restrictions, allowing wealth creators to consider family-based immigration.

利亞目前已與其他國家簽訂了多項租稅協定（例如中國 – 保加利亞避免雙重徵稅協定），避免投資移民被雙重徵稅以促進外國投資。

歐盟國家個人稅稅率表	
國家	個人最高稅率
斯洛維尼亞	50%
德國	45%
法國	45%
義大利	43%
土耳其	40%
克羅埃西亞	34.5%
波蘭	32%
斯洛伐克	25%
塞爾維亞	20%
捷克	15%
羅馬尼亞	10%
保加利亞	**10%**

歐盟國家個人稅稅率表	
國家	公司最高稅率
法國	31%
英國	25%
土耳其	25%
義大利	24%
捷克	21%
斯洛伐克	21%
波蘭	19%
斯洛維尼亞	19%
克羅埃西亞	18%
羅馬尼亞	16%
德國	15.825%
塞爾維亞	15%
保加利亞	**10%**

4. 歐盟成員國身分：作為歐盟成員國，保加利亞公民享有在其他歐盟國家自由旅行、工作、學習並取得當地醫療保險給付（例如可申請歐洲健康保險卡 EHIC）的權利，這為移民者提供了未來在歐盟各地生活的靈活性及機會，且保加利亞國籍法支持其公民之家人無年齡限制獲得保加利亞國籍，創富者可考慮進行家

5. Visa-Free Access to Multiple Countries: Holding a Bulgarian passport allows visa-free travel not only within Schengen countries without passport checks but also to up to 142 countries, including the UK and Canada.

6. Pleasant Natural Environment and Climate: Bulgaria boasts beautiful natural scenery, such as magnificent mountains and the Black Sea coast, along with a pleasant climate, making it an ideal place to live and enjoy life.

These advantages make Bulgarian citizenship a compelling choice for those considering investment immigration, offering economic benefits, increased mobility, and a favorable living environment.

An Overview of Bulgaria

Bulgaria is located in southeastern Europe on the Balkan Peninsula, bordered by Romania, Serbia, North Macedonia, Greece, and Turkey, with the eastern coastline along the Black Sea. The capital city, Sofia, serves as the country's political, economic, and cultural hub. Known as the last piece of untouched land in Europe, Bulgaria boasts rich historical landmarks, natural landscapes, unique artistic treasures, and a warm, hospitable culture.

1. Religion: Bulgaria is predominantly Eastern Orthodox (82.6%), with a significant Muslim minority (12.2%). The country upholds religious freedom, allowing its citizens to practice their faith freely.
2. Language: The official language is Bulgarian, with English widely spoken as a common second language.
3. Climate: Bulgaria experiences a temperate continental climate. The eastern regions are influenced by the Black Sea, and the southern regions by the Mediterranean, resulting in a Mediterranean-type climate. The average annual temperature is about 10.5°C, with January being the coldest month (average temperatures between -1°C and 2°C) and July the warmest (average temperatures between 20°C and 25°C). The annual average precipitation is around 450 millimeters.

族式移民。

5. 多國免簽待遇：持有保加利亞護照不僅可以在申根國家內免簽證旅行，無需護照檢查，還可以免簽證前往英國和加拿大等多達 142 個國家。

6. 宜人的自然環境和氣候：保加利亞擁有美麗的自然風光，如壯麗的山脈和黑海海岸，以及宜人的氣候，使其成為適合居住和享受生活的理想地點。

上述優勢使得保加利亞成為考慮移民歐洲時的一個具有吸引力的選擇。

保加利亞是一個甚麼樣的國家？

保加利亞位於東歐巴爾幹半島東南部，與羅馬尼亞、塞爾維亞、馬其頓、希臘、土耳其接壤，東部瀕臨黑海。保加利亞首都為索菲亞（Sofia），是該國政治、經濟、文化中心。保加利亞被譽為歐洲最後一塊未受破壞的土地，擁有豐富的歷史地標、自然景觀、獨特的藝術珍品和熱情好客的文化。

1. 宗教信仰：保加利亞主要是東正教（82.6%），還有大量的穆斯林少數民族（12.2%）。該國維護宗教自由，允許其公民自由實踐他們的信仰。

2. 語言：保加利亞官方語言為保加利亞語，英語作為通用的第二語言被廣泛使用。

3. 氣候：保加利亞屬溫帶大陸性氣候。東部地區受黑海影響，南部地區受地中海影響，形成地中海型氣候。年平均氣溫約為 10.5°C，其中 1 月是最冷的月份（平均氣溫在 -1°C 至 2°C 之間），7 月是最熱的月份（平均氣溫在 20°C 至 25°C 之間）。年

4. Population and Ethnicity: Bulgaria has a total population of approximately 6.9 million people. The ethnic composition is primarily Bulgarian (84%), with a significant Turkish minority (8.8%), and the remaining population consisting of various other ethnic groups.

5. Economy: Bulgaria's economy is primarily based on agriculture, with roses, yogurt, and wine being internationally renowned products. The national currency is the Lev (BGN), which has maintained a stable exchange rate, currently pegged at approximately 1 Euro = 1.95583 Lev. Following the pandemic, Bulgaria has sustained a stable economic growth rate, with a 3.4% growth in 2022 and an impressive 7.6% growth in 2021, indicating recovery from the impact of COVID-19. Additionally, Bulgaria's stable political and investment environment continues to attract numerous foreign investors and entrepreneurs.

How to Obtain Bulgarian Citizenship & Investment Planning After Obtaining Bulgarian Citizenship

Obtaining a Bulgarian residence permit is the first step towards acquiring EU citizenship. With a Bulgarian residence permit, you can immediately open a personal bank account in Bulgaria, establish a local company, and open corporate bank and investment accounts, laying a solid foundation for future family wealth transfer, tax planning, and legal risk management.

Typically, acquiring Bulgarian residency through investment immigration involves the following steps:

1. Invest in the Bulgarian Immigration Fund: Invest 500,000 euros to obtain a permanent residence permit in Bulgaria.
2. Get a Local Mobile Phone: Apply for a Bulgarian mobile phone, which serves as a basic tool for opening personal or company bank accounts and activating banking apps.
3. Establish a Local Company: Set up a local Bulgarian company, whether it be an investment company, operational company, or holding company.
4. Open a Local Personal Bank Account: Open a personal bank account in Bulgaria.
5. Acquire Real Estate: As a permanent resident, you can hold

平均降水量約為 450 毫米。

4. 人口民族：保加利亞的總人口目前達 690 萬，其中保加利亞族佔 84%，土耳其族佔 8.8%，剩餘為其他民族人口。

5. 經濟：保加利亞境內主要產業以農業為主，玫瑰、優格和葡萄酒在國際市場上享有盛名。保加利亞的法定貨幣為列弗（BGN），長期保持匯率穩定，目前兌換比例約為 1 歐元 =1.95583 列弗。保加利亞在疫情過後維持相當穩健的經濟成長率，2022 年經濟成長率為 3.4%；2021 年增長率為 7.6%，顯示該國已逐漸走出新冠疫情影響，此外保加利亞穩定的政治及投資環境，也持續吸引許多外國投資者與企業家投資。

如何取得保加利亞身分及取得之後的投資規劃

取得保加利亞居留證是取得歐盟身分的第一步。取得保加利亞居留證可立即於歐盟境內的保加利亞開立個人銀行帳戶，成立保加利亞本地公司，並立即開立公司銀行與理財帳戶，未來家族財富傳承、稅負與法務風險奠定良好基礎。

通常，藉由投資移民取得保加利亞居留權需要經歷以下過程：

1. 投資保加利亞移民基金 50 萬歐元，取得保加利亞永久居留證。

2. 申辦保加利亞本地手機，作為開立個人或公司銀行帳戶及開通銀行 APP 之基本連結工具。

3. 成立保加利亞本地公司（投資公司、營運公司或控股公司）。

4. 開立保加利亞本地個人銀行帳戶。

5. 以保加利亞永久居留證身分持有保加利亞本地土地所有權或房地產。

local land ownership or real estate in Bulgaria.

6. Hold Offshore Holding Company: Hold overseas holding companies under Bulgarian investment company name.

7. Open Investment Accounts in the US: Open investment accounts in the US investment banks in the name of the offshore holding company.

8. Internationalize Asian Equity Holdings: Transfer personal equity holdings in Asia to the offshore holding company.

9. Transfer Bulgarian Holding Company Equity to a US Family Trust: Transfer the equity of the Bulgarian holding company to a US family trust to achieve cross-border inheritance, asset protection, and tax planning purposes.

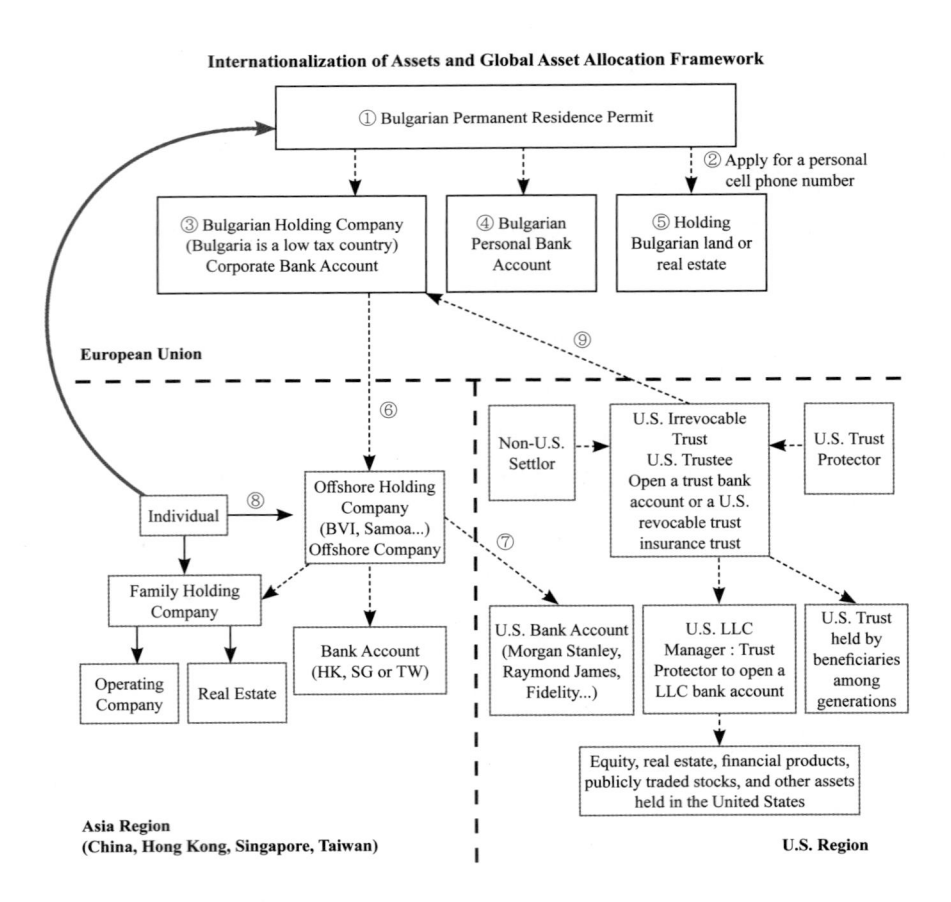

Internationalization of Assets and Global Asset Allocation Framework

① Bulgarian Permanent Residence Permit

② Apply for a personal cell phone number

③ Bulgarian Holding Company (Bulgaria is a low tax country) Corporate Bank Account

④ Bulgarian Personal Bank Account

⑤ Holding Bulgarian land or real estate

European Union

⑥

Individual ⑧

Family Holding Company

Operating Company | Real Estate

Offshore Holding Company (BVI, Samoa...) Offshore Company

Bank Account (HK, SG or TW)

⑦

Non-U.S. Settlor

U.S. Irrevocable Trust
U.S. Trustee
Open a trust bank account or a U.S. revocable trust insurance trust

U.S. Trust Protector

U.S. Bank Account (Morgan Stanley, Raymond James, Fidelity...)

U.S. LLC Manager : Trust Protector to open a LLC bank account

U.S. Trust held by beneficiaries among generations

Equity, real estate, financial products, publicly traded stocks, and other assets held in the United States

Asia Region
(China, Hong Kong, Singapore, Taiwan)

U.S. Region

第五章 全球家族辦公室的崛起與家族信託

6. 以保加利亞投資公司名義持有境外控股公司。
7. 以境外控股公司名義至美國投資銀行開立投資理財帳戶。
8. 將個人持有亞洲地區股權國際化並移入境外控股公司。
9. 將保加利亞控股公司股權移入美國家族信託，達成跨境傳承、財產保護、稅務籌劃之目的。

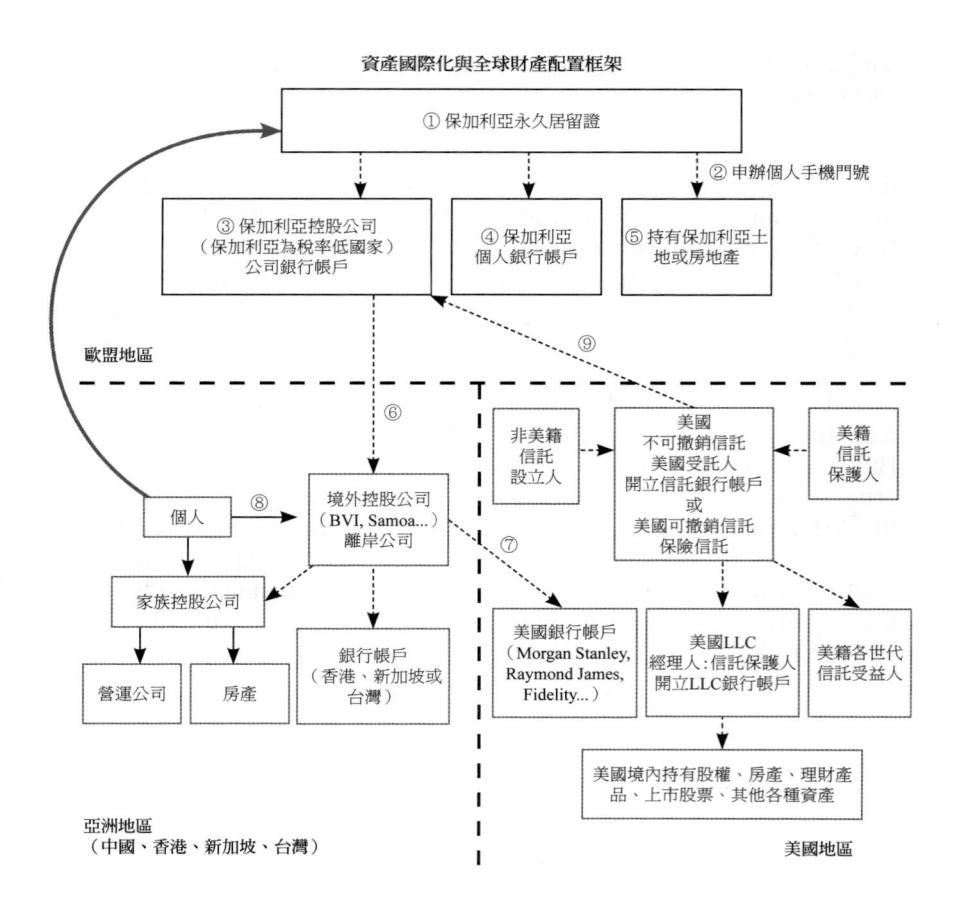

資產國際化與全球財產配置框架

```
                    ① 保加利亞永久居留證
                                              ② 申辦個人手機門號
   ③ 保加利亞控股公司        ④ 保加利亞           ⑤ 持有保加利亞土
   （保加利亞為稅率低國家）    個人銀行帳戶          地或房地產
   公司銀行帳戶

歐盟地區
─────────────────────────────────────────────
                                    美國
                        非美籍      不可撤銷信託        美籍
                        信託        美國受託人          信託
                        設立人      開立信託銀行帳戶    保護人
                                    或
                                    美國可撤銷信託
         ⑥                          保險信託
              境外控股公司
   個人  ⑧   （BVI, Samoa...）  ⑦
              離岸公司
                                美國銀行帳戶   美國LLC         美籍各世代
   家族控股公司                  （Morgan Stanley, 經理人:信託保護人 信託受益人
                                Raymond James,  開立LLC銀行帳戶
              銀行帳戶          Fidelity...）
   營運公司 房產 （香港、新加坡或
              台灣）
                                美國境內持有股權、房產、理財產
                                品、上市股票、其他各種資產
亞洲地區
（中國、香港、新加坡、台灣）                          美國地區
```

After obtaining Bulgarian citizenship, wealth creators can consider transferring the equity of a Bulgarian holding company into a U.S. irrevocable dynasty trust to further enhance the potential for multigenerational family asset transfer. By combining a U.S. dynasty trust with a Bulgarian holding company, wealth creators can achieve EU citizenship while ensuring that their wealth is protected under U.S. law.

Bulgaria Investment Immigration Program & AIF Investment Immigration Fund

To assist wealth-creating families with investment immigration, Ginkgo Investment Company directly engages local Bulgarian immigration lawyers and introduces the innovative AIF (Alternative Investment Fund) investment immigration service. This service aids clients interested in immigrating to Bulgaria by investing in AIF, facilitating the acquisition of permanent residency and subsequent Bulgarian citizenship.

The operation and investments of AIF must strictly comply with Bulgarian laws. The Bulgarian AIF project primarily invests in Bulgarian company stocks and bonds, aligning with the immigration criteria under Bulgarian citizenship law. Investors participating in the AIF program are required to invest 500,000 euros (approximately 1 million levs). After investing for 6-8 months, they can obtain permanent residency. After 60 months of holding permanent residency, they qualify for Bulgarian citizenship, thereby gaining full EU citizenship rights.

取得保加利亞身分後，創富者可以考慮將保加利亞控股公司股權移入美國不可撤銷朝代信託，進一步強化家族資產世代傳承的可能性。藉由結合美國朝代信託以及保加利亞控股公司，創富者可同時取得歐盟身分並確保財富能獲得美國法律的保護。

保加利亞投資移民方案 & AIF 投資移民基金

為協助創富者家庭進行投資移民，銀杏投資公司（Ginkgo Investment Company）直接聘任保加利亞當地移民律師，獨創 AIF 投資移民服務，協助有意移民保加利亞的客戶透過投資 AIF（Alternative Investment Fund）投資移民基金取得永久居民身分，並於未來進一步取得保加利亞公民。

AIF 的運營及投資須嚴格遵守保加利亞法律，此項保加利亞 AIF 項目，主要投資標的為保加利亞公司股票及債券，以符合保加利亞公民法有關移民條件之相關規定。參與 AIF 方案的投資人，需要投資 500,000 歐元（約 100 萬列弗），在投資 6～8 個月後即可獲批成為永久居民，獲得永久居民資格後 60 個月，即取得保加利亞公民，正式擁有歐盟身分。

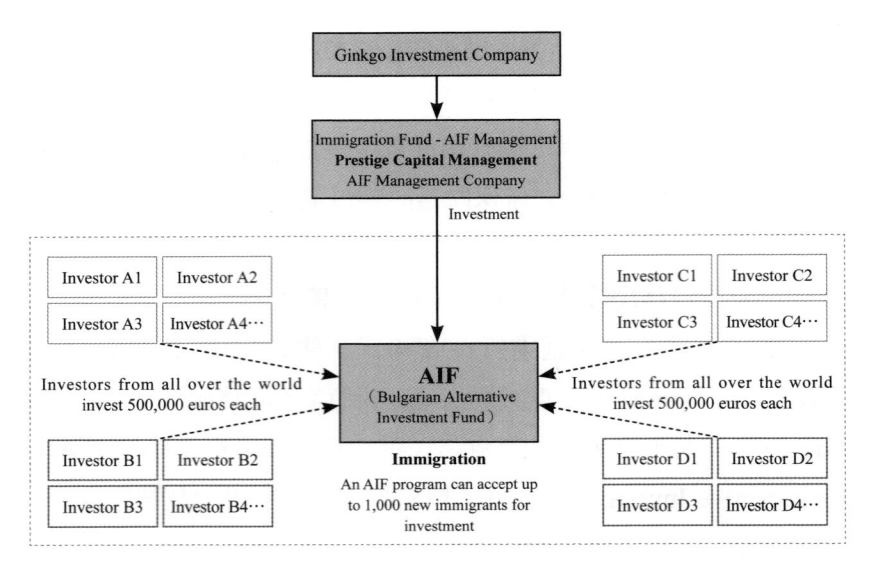

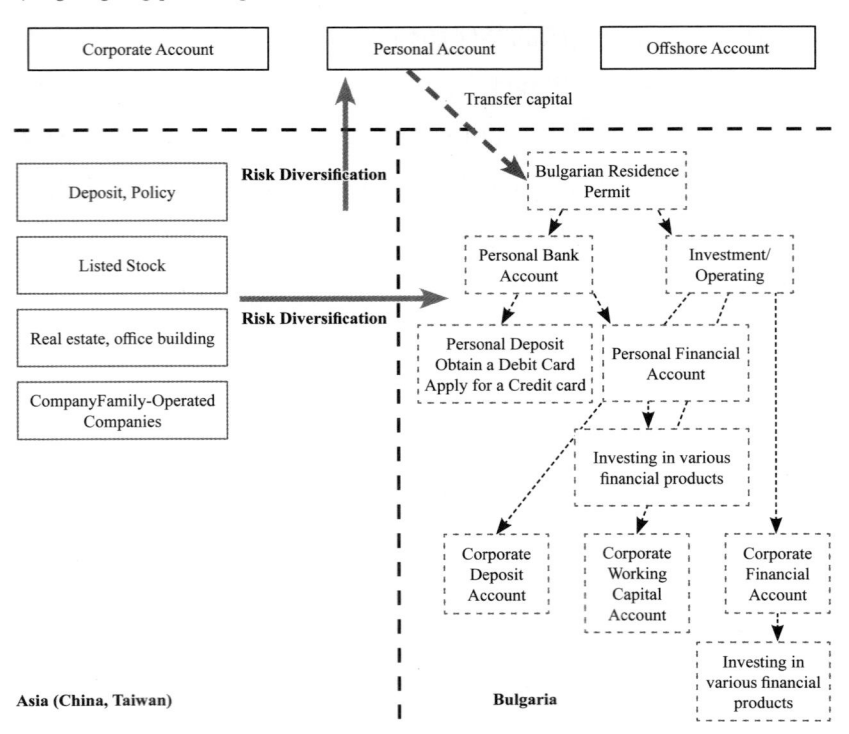

U.S. Trust and Estate Planning ◆ Chapter 5

```
Ginkgo Investment Company
            ↓
Immigration Fund - AIF Management
    Prestige Capital Management
      AIF Management Company
            ↓ Investment
```

Investor A1, Investor A2, Investor A3, Investor A4···
Investor B1, Investor B2, Investor B3, Investor B4···
Investor C1, Investor C2, Investor C3, Investor C4···
Investor D1, Investor D2, Investor D3, Investor D4···

Investors from all over the world invest 500,000 euros each

AIF
（Bulgarian Alternative Investment Fund）

Immigration
An AIF program can accept up to 1,000 new immigrants for investment

Offshore Region
(Hong Kong, Singapore, Shanghai OBU accounts)

Corporate Account | Personal Account | Offshore Account

Transfer capital

Risk Diversification

- Deposit, Policy
- Listed Stock
- Real estate, office building
- Company Family-Operated Companies

Bulgarian Residence Permit
→ Personal Bank Account
→ Investment/Operating

Personal Deposit, Obtain a Debit Card, Apply for a Credit card
Personal Financial Account
Investing in various financial products

Corporate Deposit Account | Corporate Working Capital Account | Corporate Financial Account

Investing in various financial products

Asia (China, Taiwan)　　　　Bulgaria

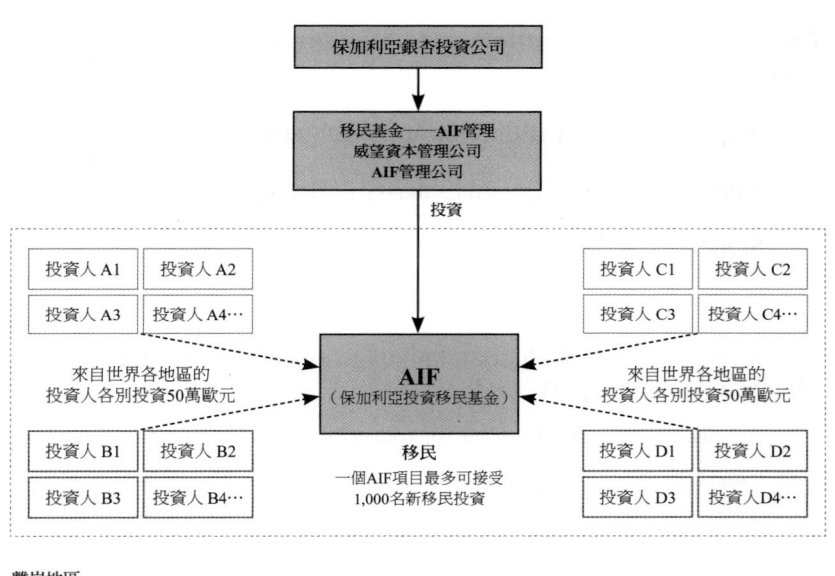

第五章 全球家族辦公室的崛起與家族信託　　295

```
                    ┌──────────────────────┐
                    │   保加利亞銀杏投資公司   │
                    └──────────┬───────────┘
                               ↓
                    ┌──────────────────────┐
                    │ 移民基金——AIF管理       │
                    │   威望資本管理公司      │
                    │     AIF管理公司         │
                    └──────────┬───────────┘
                              投資
```

┌─────────────┬─────────────┐   ┌─────────────┬─────────────┐
│ 投資人 A1   │ 投資人 A2   │   │ 投資人 C1   │ 投資人 C2   │
├─────────────┼─────────────┤   ├─────────────┼─────────────┤
│ 投資人 A3   │ 投資人 A4… │   │ 投資人 C3   │ 投資人 C4… │
└─────────────┴─────────────┘   └─────────────┴─────────────┘

來自世界各地區的　　　　　　　　　　　　　　　　　來自世界各地區的
投資人各別投資50萬歐元　　　　　　　　　　　　　投資人各別投資50萬歐元

                    ┌──────────────────────┐
                    │   AIF   │
                    │ （保加利亞投資移民基金）│
                    └──────────────────────┘

                            移民
                    一個AIF項目最多可接受
                      1,000名新移民投資

┌─────────────┬─────────────┐   ┌─────────────┬─────────────┐
│ 投資人 B1   │ 投資人 B2   │   │ 投資人 D1   │ 投資人 D2   │
├─────────────┼─────────────┤   ├─────────────┼─────────────┤
│ 投資人 B3   │ 投資人 B4… │   │ 投資人 D3   │ 投資人 D4… │
└─────────────┴─────────────┘   └─────────────┴─────────────┘

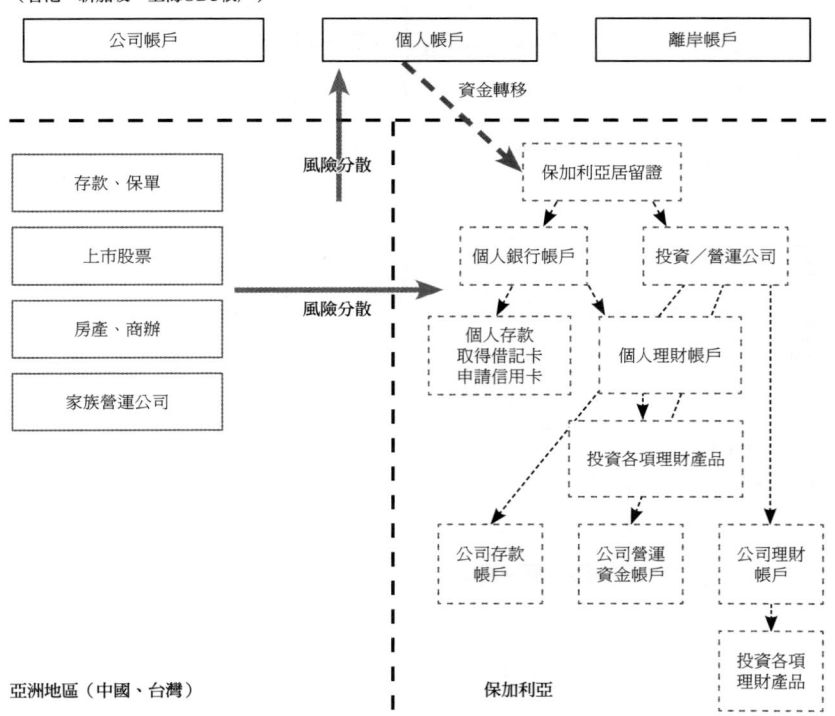

離岸地區
（香港、新加坡、上海OBU帳戶）

| 公司帳戶 | 個人帳戶 | 離岸帳戶 |

資金轉移

亞洲地區（中國、台灣）

- 存款、保單
- 上市股票
- 房產、商辦
- 家族營運公司

風險分散

保加利亞

- 保加利亞居留證
- 個人銀行帳戶
- 投資／營運公司
- 個人存款　取得借記卡　申請信用卡
- 個人理財帳戶
- 投資各項理財產品
- 公司存款帳戶
- 公司營運資金帳戶
- 公司理財帳戶
- 投資各項理財產品

The process of immigration and obtaining Permanent Residency (PR)

Step 1 : Apply for Immigration to Bulgaria in person

Step 2 : Visit the Bulgarian Embassy in Beijing / Shanghai in person

Step 3 : Visit Bulgaria again to appy for PR

Step 4 : Obtain PR (Permanent Residence Permit)

Step 5: Pass the Bulgarian language exam and obtain Bulgarian citizenship and passport

Bulgarian Immigration Program Application Process and Required Documents

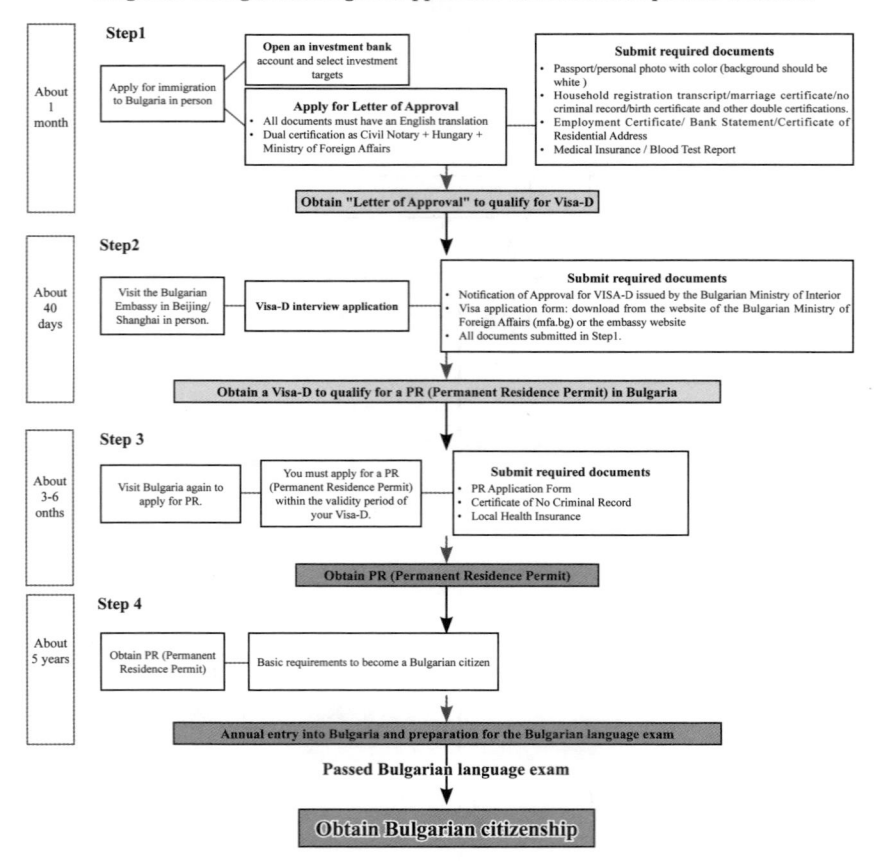

Step 1 (About 1 month)
- Apply for immigration to Bulgaria in person
- Open an investment bank account and select investment targets
- Apply for Letter of Approval
  - All documents must have an English translation
  - Dual certification as Civil Notary + Hungary + Ministry of Foreign Affairs
- Submit required documents
  - Passport/personal photo with color (background should be white)
  - Household registration transcript/marriage certificate/no criminal record/birth certificate and other double certifications.
  - Employment Certificate/ Bank Statement/Certificate of Residential Address
  - Medical Insurance / Blood Test Report

Obtain "Letter of Approval" to qualify for Visa-D

Step 2 (About 40 days)
- Visit the Bulgarian Embassy in Beijing/Shanghai in person.
- Visa-D interview application
- Submit required documents
  - Notification of Approval for VISA-D issued by the Bulgarian Ministry of Interior
  - Visa application form: download from the website of the Bulgarian Ministry of Foreign Affairs (mfa.bg) or the embassy website
  - All documents submitted in Step1.

Obtain a Visa-D to qualify for a PR (Permanent Residence Permit) in Bulgaria

Step 3 (About 3-6 months)
- Visit Bulgaria again to apply for PR.
- You must apply for a PR (Permanent Residence Permit) within the validity period of your Visa-D.
- Submit required documents
  - PR Application Form
  - Certificate of No Criminal Record
  - Local Health Insurance

Obtain PR (Permanent Residence Permit)

Step 4 (About 5 years)
- Obtain PR (Permanent Residence Permit)
- Basic requirements to become a Bulgarian citizen

Annual entry into Bulgaria and preparation for the Bulgarian language exam

Passed Bulgarian language exam

Obtain Bulgarian citizenship

移民程序與永久居留權（Permanent Residency，簡稱 PR）取得流程

步驟1：本人親至保加利亞申請移民
步驟2：本人前往駐保加利亞北京／上海大使館
步驟3：本人再度前往保加利亞申請永久居留證
步驟4：本人取得永久居留證
步驟5：保加利亞語文考試通過，取得保加利亞公民身分與護照

保加利亞移民方案申請程序與所需文件

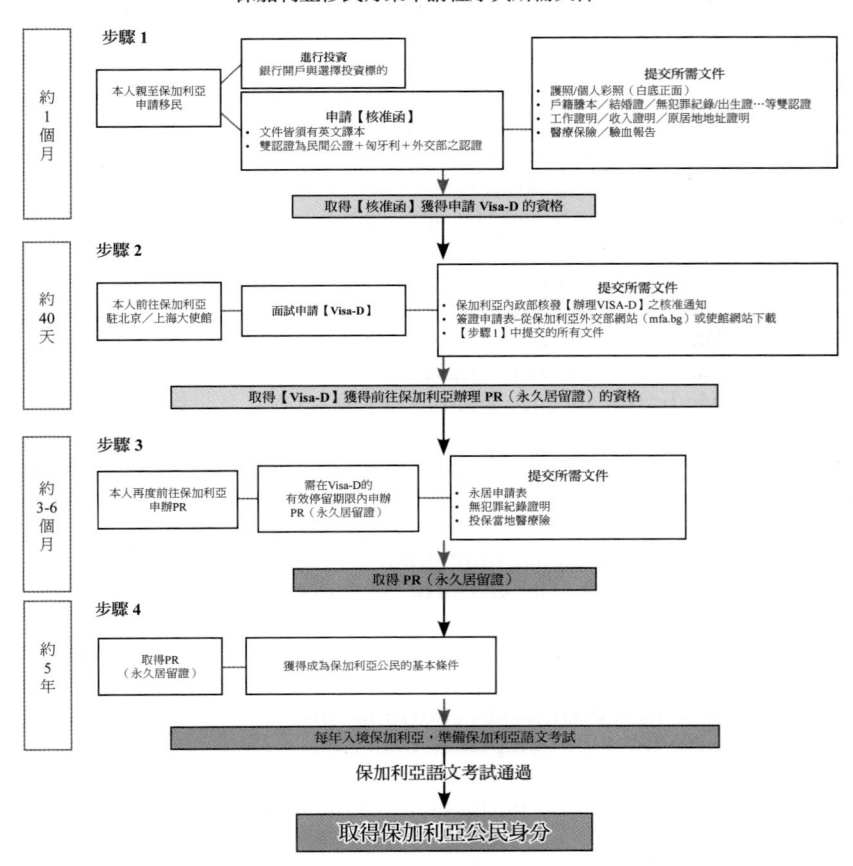

步驟1（約1個月）
- 本人親至保加利亞申請移民
- 進行投資：銀行開戶與選擇投資標的
- 申請【核准函】
  - 文件皆須有英文譯本
  - 雙認證為民間公證＋匈牙利＋外交部之認證
- 提交所需文件：
  - 護照／個人彩照（白底正面）
  - 戶籍謄本／結婚證／無犯罪紀錄／出生證…等雙認證
  - 工作證明／收入證明／原居地地址證明
  - 醫療保險／驗血報告

→ 取得【核准函】獲得申請 Visa-D 的資格

步驟2（約40天）
- 本人前往保加利亞駐北京／上海大使館
- 面試申請【Visa-D】
- 提交所需文件：
  - 保加利亞內政部核發【辦理VISA-D】之核准通知
  - 簽證申請表–從保加利亞外交部網站（mfa.bg）或使館網站下載
  - 【步驟1】中提交的所有文件

→ 取得【Visa-D】獲得前往保加利亞辦理 PR（永久居留證）的資格

步驟3（約3-6個月）
- 本人再度前往保加利亞申辦PR
- 需在Visa-D的有效停留期限內申辦PR（永久居留證）
- 提交所需文件：
  - 永居申請表
  - 無犯罪紀錄證明
  - 投保當地醫療險

→ 取得 PR（永久居留證）

步驟4（約5年）
- 取得PR（永久居留證）
- 獲得成為保加利亞公民的基本條件
- 每年入境保加利亞，準備保加利亞語文考試
- 保加利亞語文考試通過

→ 取得保加利亞公民身分

How do I apply for Permanent Residency in Bulgaria through investment?

1. Research Bulgaria
   – Due Diligence: Conduct thorough due diligence on the program, investment opportunities, and the agents or firms assisting with the process.
   – Legal Advice: Seek comprehensive legal and financial advice to understand all implications, including tax obligations and compliance requirements.
   – Reputable Agents: Use reputable and certified advisors who have a proven track record in managing citizenship by investment applications.
   – Stay Informed: Keep abreast of any changes in the political and regulatory landscape of the chosen country and the EU as a whole.

2. Prepare relevant documents, including:
   – Passport and personal photos with a white background.
   – Household registration transcript.
   – Marriage certificate (if applicable).
   – No criminal record certificate.
   – Birth certificates.
   – Employment certificate.
   – Bank statements.
   – Certificate of residential address.
   – Medical insurance and blood test report.

3. Translate relevant documents, including those listed above, to English.

4. Hire a professional immigration consulting law firm to prepare applicable forms. The law firm typically provides the following services:
   (1) Advises on and prepares supporting documentation for the client's pre-approval process.
   (2) Obtains a certificate confirming the client's eligible investment from the competent authority.
   (3) Advises on and prepares supporting documentation for the client's visa and permanent residence applications, guiding

如何通過投資在保加利亞申請永久居留權？

1. 研究保加利亞
   - 盡職調查：對計劃、投資機會以及協助申請過程的代理人或公司進行全面性的盡職調查。
   - 法律建議：尋求全面性的法律及財務建議，以瞭解所有可能的影響，包括稅務義務及合規要求。
   - 信譽良好的代理人：委任信譽良好、經過認證且在處理投資移民申請有良好紀錄的顧問。
   - 隨時瞭解狀況：及時瞭解所選國家及整體歐盟在政治及監管環境的任何變化。
2. 準備相關文件，包括：
   - 護照及帶白色背景的個人照片
   - 戶籍登記證明
   - 結婚證書（如適用）
   - 無犯罪紀錄證明
   - 出生證明
   - 工作證明
   - 銀行對帳單
   - 居住地址證明
   - 醫療保險及血液檢驗報告
3. 將相關文件（包括上述文件）翻譯成英文。
4. 委任專業移民諮詢律師事務所準備相關表格。律師事務所通常提供以下服務：

（1）對客戶的預先批准程序提供建議並準備支持文件。

（2）從相關當局取得確認客戶符合資格投資的證書。

the client through these processes.
(4) Liaises with Bulgarian authorities following the issuance of permanent residence approval and assists with local population register compliance.
(5) Organizes and accompanies the client to their Permanent Residence Permit issuance appointment, assisting with the issuance and collection of the Permanent Residence Permit.
(6) Advises on and prepares supporting documentation for the spouse's and children's visa and permanent residence applications, guiding them through these processes.

5. Prepare funds including the investment of €500,000 and applicable fees required of advisors and local attorneys.

6. Invest €500,000 into a government-approved Alternative Investment Fund by transferring funds from the investor's personal account (typically in the U.S., Hong Kong or Singapore).

7. Apply for Pre-Approval and Visa-D from the Bulgaria Ministry of Foreign Affairs:
   – Visit a Bulgarian Consulate in Los Angeles or Washington D.C. in the U.S. or Shanghai or Beijing in China.
   – Submit applicable documents and forms, including the Visa-D Application.
   – Receive Preliminary Letter of Approval and Visa-D.

8. Apply for Permanent Residence:
   – Visit Bulgaria: Travel to Bulgaria to apply for the permanent residence permit within the validity period of the Visa-D.
   – Submit required documents including:
     • PR application form.
     • Certificate of no criminal record.
     • Local health insurance.
   – Obtain Permanent Residence Permit: Complete the application process.

9. After receiving Permanent Residency, Wealth Creators should:
   – Maintain Bulgarian Residency: Ensure annual entry into Bulgaria and maintain a Bulgarian residential address.

（3）對客戶的簽證及永久居留申請提供建議並準備支持文件，指導客戶完成相關程序。

（4）在永久居留批准後與保加利亞當局聯繫，協助客戶遵循當地人口登記的合規要求。

（5）安排並陪同客戶前往永久居留證發放的會面預約，協助完成永久居留證的發放及領取。

（6）對客戶配偶及子女的簽證及永久居留申請提供建議並準備相關證明文件，指導其完成相關程序。

5. 準備資金，包括 50 萬歐元的投資及顧問與當地律師所需的費用。

6. 從投資者的個人帳戶（通常位於美國、香港或新加坡）轉移資金，將 50 萬歐元投資於政府批准的另類投資基金。

7. 向保加利亞外交部申請預先批准及 D 類簽證：
   - 前往美國洛杉磯或華盛頓特區、或中國上海或北京的保加利亞領事館。
   - 提交相關文件及表格，包括 D 類簽證申請。
   - 取得初步批准信及 D 類簽證。

8. 申請永久居留權：
   - 前往保加利亞：在 D 類簽證有效期內前往保加利亞申請永久居留許可證。
   - 提交所需文件，包括：
     - 永久居留申請表。
     - 無犯罪證明。
     - 地方健康保險。
   - 領取永久居留證：完成申請流程。

- Apply for Citizenship: After keeping Permanent Residence status for five years, Wealth Creators can apply for Bulgarian citizenship.
- Obtain a Local Cell Phone Number: Necessary for communicating and opening bank accounts.
- Open a Personal Bank Account: Required for financial transactions in Bulgaria and in the EU.
- Establish an operating or investment company in Bulgaria.
- Open corporate bank or investment account(s).

The above summarizes the comprehensive process of obtaining Bulgarian permanent residency.

9. 取得永久居留權後，創富者應：
   - 維持保加利亞住所：確保每年進入保加利亞並保持保加利亞的住所地址。
   - 申請公民身分：保持永久居留身分滿 5 年後，創富者得申請保加利亞公民身分。
   - 申辦當地手機號碼：用於溝通及開立銀行帳戶所需。
   - 開立個人銀行帳戶：在保加利亞及歐盟進行財務交易所需。
   - 在保加利亞成立營運或投資公司。
   - 開立企業銀行帳戶或投資帳戶。

以上總括取得保加利亞永久居留權的完整過程。

NOTE :

KEDP Global
全球業務簡介
Contacts and Services

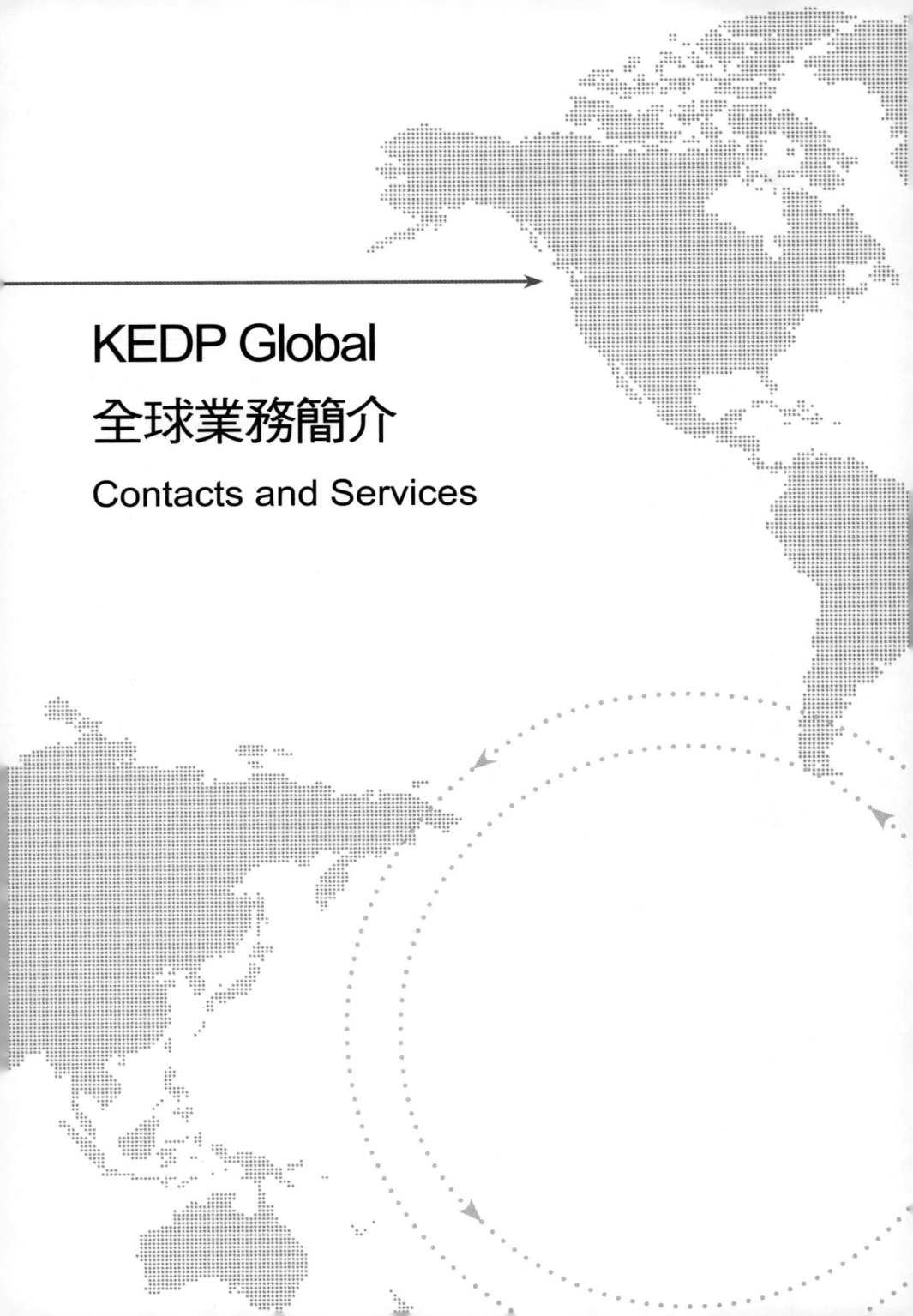

■ 安致勤資會計師集團　KEDP CPAs Group

「安致勤資會計師集團」(KEDP CPAs Group)創立旨在提供美國、台灣及中國兩岸三地華人與跨境經商人士專業、即時、價格合理之服務，目前已分別於美國洛杉磯、舊金山、台灣台北及中國北京、上海、廣州、成立會計師事務所或專業稅務及投資諮詢之服務據點，期望搭建涵蓋美、中、台三地的服務網絡，進而提供跨境稅務諮詢、跨境投資控股規劃、跨境稅務申報、家族財富傳承、保全以及移民前後美國稅務服務。

KEDP CPAs Group 鑒於美、中、台三地企業家族對於財富傳承與保全的殷切需求，結合美國稅務律師、信託律師與美國註冊會計師之完整服務資源，依據美、中、台華人客戶之需求，從初始接觸的家族財富瞭解、到服務項目確認、工作時程規劃、近而到後續追蹤管理……均以專業服務管理系統掌控案件；本諸跨境專業、保密、獨立與客觀之精神；期以提供華人朋友面對跨國性稅務規劃時，最優質而全面的稅務諮詢服務。

目前跨境業務項目可分為下：

一、經常性業務：美國年度所得稅申報(1040表)、美國各州州稅申報、美國各項揭露申報(FinCEN 114、5471、3520、8854等表)、跨境個人稅務規劃、審計及企業諮詢、移轉定價報告、企業上市前之整帳、會計代理及諮詢服務，美國信託設立及記帳報稅等。

二、非經常性業務：境外公司(Anguilla、Seychelles、SAMOA、BVI、Hong Kong、Singapore 等)設立及維持、中國、美國及台灣公司登記設立、移民前後稅務諮詢與籌劃、企業融資及投資服務、人力資源及培訓服務等。

除了上述兩大項業務，安致勤資聯合會計師事務所近年來更因應美籍華人之稅務問題，協助客戶審慎評估移民前、移民中、移民後之相關稅務規劃，在享有美籍身分所帶來好處的同時，也能評估必要的租稅負擔。

■ 安致勤資 KEDP CPAs 服務據點及諮詢窗口

洛杉磯
地址：888 S. Brea Canyon Road Suite 225, Diamond Bar, CA 91789
電話：+1 (310) 343 2568
聯絡人：潘裕人／Roy Pan (Wechat: roypan_uscpa)

拉斯維加斯
地址：1129 S Maryland Pkwy, Las Vegas, NV 89104
電話：+1 (617) 388 9422
聯絡人：呂嘉昕／Max Lu (Wechat: clfcmax)

舊金山
地址：2960 Privet Drive, Hillsborough, CA 94010
電話：+1 (617) 388 9422
聯絡人：呂嘉昕／Max Lu (Wechat: clfcmax)

臺灣臺北

地址：11051 臺北市信義區基隆路一段420號11樓
電話：＋886 2 8780 7766／傳真：＋886 2 8780 7711
聯絡人：

- 跨境稅務諮詢：馮俏玲／Alice Feng (Wechat: kedpalice)
- 臺灣境內稅務諮詢：林明輝／Tim Lin (Wechat: wxid_jnczhfmhnxi412)
- 內控制度輔導、帳務處理、會計制度諮詢：陳遠東／YT Chen (Wechat: yuantungchen)
- 跨境傳承執行：陳怡如／Megan Chen (Wechat: luluchen8802)

臺灣高雄

地址：80654 高雄市前鎮區民權二路380號20樓之一
電話：＋886 7 3316 726／傳真：＋886 7 3316 326
聯絡人：張清富律師／Paul Chang (Wechat: wxid_1bbyqnivsckd22)

大陸北京、華北地區

地址：北京市東城區建國門內大街18號恆基中心1座辦公樓18層1803室（郵編：100005）
電話：＋86 10 6517 4711／傳真：＋86 10 6517 7331
聯絡人：張國禮／Tom Zhang ＋86 152 0116 6003
　　　　(Wechat: wxid_wu3bau59gomv22)

大陸上海、華東地區

地址：上海市浦東新區陸家嘴東路161號招商局大廈1403室
　　　（郵編：200120）
電話：＋86 21 5878 0519 ／ ＋86 21 5878 1833
　　　（傳真同電話，接通後請加撥 807）
聯絡人：周建琳／Cathy Zhou ＋86 189 1719 6369
　　　　(Wechat: KEDP_SH_US_TAX)

大陸廣州、香港、華南地區

地址：廣東省廣州市天河區林和西路9號耀中廣場B座909房
（郵編：510610）
電話：+86 20 3730 7512／+86 20 3730 7513
聯絡人：蕭益新／Leon Xiao +86 139 2618 0789（香港）／
+86 189 2275 1789（廣州）
(Wechat: Leonxiao3／Leon18922751789)

新加坡

地址：新加坡直落亞逸街137號03-04室（郵編：068602）
電話：+65 9369 0432
聯絡人：田凌溪／Isabella Tian (WhatsApp: +65 9369 0432)

馬來西亞新山

地址：#05-05,Blok 1, No 5, Pangsapuri Molek Pine 4, Jalan Molek 1/27, Taman Molek, 81100 Johor Bahru
電話：+60 19 770 9121
聯絡人：張再茂／William Teo (Wechat: wxid_ncilmmseaokj12)

■ KEDP叢書簡介

　　安致勤資會計師集團（**KEDP CPAs**）為解決中國、台灣及美國三地之華人常見之稅務問題，邀集了三地專業的會計師及律師，將多年執業過程中最常見、最棘手的案件，整理為清晰易懂的問答集。KEDP 叢書從中國和台灣在地，一直到跨國間的個人及企業之相關稅務問題，均搜羅了全面且詳盡的問答，期望華人朋友在一問一答間尋找到最便捷的答案。以下為KEDP叢書簡介：

《呂旭明會計師教您如何節稅致富與跨境傳承》
台灣報稅必備稅務問題集！

　　作者藉由多年的稅務經驗，感受到稅負最重的人，往往不是最富有的人或最會賺錢的人，而是「無知的人」。因為不瞭解稅法，這群無知的人常道聽塗說，甚而跌入租稅陷阱成為「稅奴」。本書係針對一般大眾有關的「個人租稅」加以介紹，並以個別案例深入淺出地闡明如何減少不必要的租稅負擔與風險，使您辛苦賺進來的每一分錢都能如潺潺細水匯成江海，享受富裕人生。

《最新美國報稅與海外財產揭露》2023最新版本
華人圈內最實用的報稅指南

　　本書最初版為《美中台跨國稅務Q&A》，2009年出版後即收到美中台三地讀者的熱烈迴響，讓作者群及全體參與同仁體認到跨境人士在面對申報美國稅務及海外財產的確常面臨困難。本書出版至今已歷經多此校訂改版，此次 2023 年最新校訂版本，除將全書焦點聚焦在具有美國稅務身分的華人，也隨著美國國稅局每年更新的稅務申報要求，以及對於雙重國籍、具有海外收入及海外帳戶的重大查緝政策，逐年跟進，為的就是要提供讀者對於美國國稅局近年政策實施近況有全盤的理解，不再因為片面不全的資訊而不知所措。

在歷經多次的改版，作者群更發現在許多華人申報的案件中，不乏高資產人士除了有申報美國稅的需求，更對資產規劃有相當程度的需求。因此此次修訂版特地針對如何妥善運用財富規劃工具（例如信託設立），做了許多說明，期望對於此類讀者群有所幫助，畢竟報稅是最基本的，讓財富長長久久地傳承下去才是最終目的。

《美國信託與跨境傳承》
高資產家族家族傳承必備寶典

在財富跨境轉移的時代潮流下，傳承籌劃不再是紙上理論；不再是統一模版，而是講求操作步驟與細節，以因應躲藏於規劃細節中的各種風險。在規劃財富跨境傳承的同時，更應謹慎依照各家族之特殊文化背景及傳承需求，提出具體可行的實際操作方案。

本書作者參與各家族之跨境傳承籌劃，其中各種籌劃工具皆透過自身家族先行進行操作，以美國信託成立為例，作者在過去十年當中尋求與拜訪美國信託律師、稅務律師、會計師、受託公司等專業人士多達數百位，多方參酌美國本地專業人士的經驗和意見，以確認所有操作執行細節及稅務和法律風險，務求籌劃工具能收到一定成效，也更能符合高資產家族之傳承需求！

KEDP叢書 14

U.S. Trust and Estate Planning
美國信託規劃實務

作　　　者	呂旭明（Peter Lu）・呂嘉昕（Max Lu）
出　版　者	哈佛人出版有限公司（H. I. Publishers, Inc.）
負　責　人	呂旭明
責任編輯	哈佛人出版社編輯團隊
地　　　址	110 台北市信義區基隆路一段380號6樓
電　　　話	02-2725-1823
傳　　　真	02-2725-5962
會計稅務顧問	呂旭明會計師
法律顧問	張清富律師
出版日期	西元2024年8月
版　　　次	初版
定　　　價	新台幣1,000元

國家圖書館出版品預行編目資料

美國信託規劃實務 = U.S. trusts and estate planning／
呂旭明(Peter Lu), 呂嘉昕(Max Lu)作.
-- 初版. -- 臺北市：哈佛人出版有限公司, 2024. 08
面　；　公分. --（KEDP叢書；14）
中英對照
ISBN 978-986-5807-14-6（平裝）

1.CST: 信託財產 2.CST: 美國

563.3952　　　　　　　　　　　113011368

This publication is designed to provide competent and reliable information regarding the subject matters covered. However, it is sold with the understanding that the author and publisher are not engaged in rendering legal, financial or other professional advice in any country. Laws and practices often vary from state to state and country to country and if legal, accounting or other expert assistance is required, the services of a professional should be sought. **The author and publisher specifically disclaim any liability that is incurred from the use or application of the contents of this book.**

本書內容解釋係依照一般性的會計與法律準則，因個案之發生地與特殊性而有差異。此出版品旨在提供所列案例之正確與可資信賴之參考訊息，出版社不需負擔提供法律與會計相關之專業服務。若需要進一步之專業服務，請向專業人士洽詢，以保障自身權益。（此宣言由一美國律師協會及一出版商協會共同發表。）

本書作者於撰寫本著作時參考許多專業研究和報告，並盡力於書中載明參考及引用出處，惟難免仍有錯誤或疏漏，敬請各位專家先進見諒，若有錯誤或疏漏事宜，當於再版中更正。

本書版權由安致勤資管理顧問有限公司授權哈佛人出版有限公司出版繁體中文版
版權所有・翻印必究